C. 2013 AFP
99.00

MW01278206

A Conflict of Interest

A Conflict of Interest

MJ Greene

iUniverse LLC
Bloomington

A Conflict of Interest

iUniverse books may be ordered through booksellers or by contacting:

iUniverse LLC
1663 Liberty Drive
Bloomington, IN 47403
www.iuniverse.com
1-800-Authors (1-800-288-4677)

Photo image on front cover taken by author.

ISBN: 978-1-4917-0929-0 (sc)
ISBN: 978-1-4917-0930-6 (hc)
ISBN: 978-1-4917-0931-3 (e)

Library of Congress Control Number: 2013917649

Printed in the United States of America.

iUniverse rev. date: 10/29/2013

To my father, who taught me the true
meaning of the word *courage*.

In war, truth is the first casualty.

—Aeschylus

CONTENTS

Preface

A Conflict of Interest is my firsthand account of living and working in Afghanistan. Primarily, it chronicles the day-to-day goings-on of multinational organizations in the region, but it does so from my personal perspective as an Australian woman. My introduction to the Afghan world was quite a culture shock, to say the least. In writing this book, I sought to capture all that and more. I wanted to provide a candid, unvarnished view of my experiences, not just as a Westerner working as the general manager for a NATO subcontractor but also as a woman. Perhaps my most significant intent in writing this book was, is, and always will be to empower all women everywhere to stand up for themselves, to trust their intuition, and to fight for the truth.

When I left for Afghanistan, I knew I was going to a war zone. But I had no idea as to all that *war zone* implied. I was about to find out. Join me on the journey of discovering what it means to live and work in a conflict zone—and what it means to fight corruption, unearth the truth, speak out against human rights abuses, and realize the depths of our own courage and resilience.

This is my story.

—*MJG*

MJ Greene lived in Afghanistan while she worked as the general manager of a NATO subcontractor. Drawing upon her inner resilience and courage, she bravely exposed the corruption and human rights violations that she encountered in her organization. She wrote this book in order to share her experiences and empower other women to muster the courage to reveal the truth whenever it is hidden and to stand up for what is right regardless of the potential personal costs.

Acknowledgments

Writing this book was an incredibly cathartic experience. I hope this serves as the perfect medium for offering solace to those who have suffered at the hands of others and to those whose voices were never heard. I hope this book proves that every voice can be heard, even if we never see the face that belongs to it.

To all those who have helped me along the way, this book is a tribute to each of you, and I thank you.

To my dear friends and family, without your ongoing support, I would not have undertaken such an arduous project. My core band of sisters and brothers—you know who you are—thank you for spurring me on to complete this.

My special thanks to my mentor, PP, my very own Obi Wan, protecting us against the dark side of the force.

To LD, "whose blood is definitely worth bottling!" (as we put it in Aussie speak), thank you for assisting me enormously with the *deets* and in weaving the pieces together.

And finally, to iUniverse, thank you for making this happen!

INTRODUCTION

As described in the preface, this book is a personal account of how I, MJ Greene, an Aussie female with no prior experience of living or working in the Middle East or Central Asia, took on the role of general manager for one of the largest multinational organizations in Afghanistan, TerraTota Suppliers,* a subcontractor to NATO-led International Security Assistance Force (ISAF). It is a story of the daily challenges of being in that war-torn region and the toll it takes on body, mind, and spirit.

But all that is self-evident by living and working in a war zone, especially for a Western woman like me, as yet unaccustomed to such an environment. Other aspects of conflict zones are not that self-evident. This book is about those too. The dark and shadowy corners of the human soul, the personal grit needed to survive in a place where death is always palpable. No one ever knows the moment when death might strike, but in a war zone that moment is constantly at hand for everyone. This book shows how that

* TerraTota Suppliers is a fictitious entity, like all the names of persons and organizations used throughout this book (other than public figures and organizations known to the general public [i.e., NATO, ISAF, etc.]). However, all accounts and events are true and are related accurately and truthfully to the best of the author's ability.

reality changes a person, blurring the lines of which actions are acceptable because of the environment. But this book also shows what it takes to find within us the core of strength necessary to buck the system and stand up for what is right regardless of where we are.

Entering a zone of conflict has many inherent risks, and only those with innate courage and resilience will survive. There are always conflicts of interest in such circumstances, and that means trouble is never far away. The very term *conflict of interest* is layered with many nuances. Only by peeling away the layers one at a time can the truth be revealed. And the truth is the key to surviving—with our self-respect intact. The labyrinth of corruption is circuitous indeed, and frequently a conscience and moral compass are the only defenses against utter personal destruction.

This book is about all this and more. It is a story of personal discovery, including finding the valor and fortitude necessary to uncover the truth, challenge the status quo of corruption, fight the all-too-frequent abuses of human rights, and help put an end to discernible wrongdoing.

Consider a few comments about reading this book: The experiences and events I relate happened far earlier than the wisdom and deductions that arose from them, so my descriptions of what I learned or deduced—and subsequently came to understand and appreciate—are not concurrent with the sequence of events. I also emphasize and reemphasize certain things throughout the book in order to show their importance; these are not inadvertent repetitions but intentional underscoring. Please indulge me in all this, as it is the best way I know to relate things accurately while also describing my feelings and the wisdom I gained through hindsight. Similarly, as I progressed through my journey of uncovering the truth and standing up for what I felt was right, the prevailing circumstances became increasingly complex. As a result, the earlier chapters in this book are much shorter than the later chapters, especially where I detail reaching the turning point and taking action. Finally, in order to effectively capture the local atmosphere, regional terminology and supply-chain jargon appear throughout this book, but I did not want to clutter the narrative with parenthetical definitions. Please refer to the glossary for explanations and descriptions of any terms, abbreviations, acronyms, etc., that are unfamiliar.

Author's Note: *The ISAF provides every subcontractor with a Military Technical Agreement (MTA) for Afghanistan. This document, which details the agreement in place between the ISAF (including any military support personnel, such as subcontractors like TerraTota) and the Interim Administration of Afghanistan stipulates what is deemed appropriate in terms of supply of provisions into and out of Afghanistan, and alcohol is not included as appropriate because of local Afghan laws.* Technically *alcohol can be supplied if a bonded warehouse exists on a compound (i.e., an embassy, which is therefore exempt from taxes because it is on diplomatic/neutral soil). No such bonded warehouse existed during my tenure. Nor was I provided with any such agreement prior to assuming my role as general manager. Interestingly, the Afghan Senate has sought to terminate the MTAs.**

* GHANIZADA, "Afghan Senate Urges to Cancel NATO-Afghan MTA Agreement," September 5, 2011, http://www.khaama.com/afghan-senate-urges-to-cancel-nato-afghan-mta-agreement.

1

WELCOME TO AFGHANISTAN

Fateful Encounters

My life in Australia was inadequate preparation for my work as general manager of TerraTota Suppliers, a huge multinational organization and NATO subcontractor in Afghanistan. Let me qualify that by saying that I'm not convinced *anything* could have sufficiently prepared a Western woman to live and work in Afghanistan. I'm quite certain *nothing* had prepared me.

The first order of business was learning how to manage fear—not ordinary anxiety or neurosis but true, visceral fear, the kind that paralyzes us and turns our blood cold. I can't really explain how I learned to manage it. I can only say that I did. Somehow.

In the early days of my tenure in Afghanistan, I struggled to overcome my fear of not knowing whether the car next to me held a suicide bomber. Eventually, as I said, I learned how to do this. But it was a struggle in the beginning. Every day. I had to be constantly aware of who was traveling next to me. Were the number plates original, or were they from Pakistan? It was unnerving to have to be so vigilant, hyperalert at every single moment.

Sometimes the tenseness in the air was palpable. I could just feel it… literally. Energy, perhaps, or just some power in the air that made it seem ready to pop and snap, like the moment before a monstrous summer thunderstorm. Other times it was not really palpable but more like knowledge derived from a deeper sense—intuition warning that a suicide bomber was close by. This uncanny knowing develops quickly. It is a survival skill, natural instincts taking over as a means of self-preservation. I learned to trust my intuition because if I didn't, I could be dead the next minute. The next second.

This is just the way it is in Afghanistan. Others there also had to learn to trust their instincts and intuition just as I had to. There were also specific things I had to learn about. Convoys were among the first of these. They were always the prime target of the suicide bombers. I quickly learned to keep my distance from the convoys. Not all lessons were quite so handily learned.

Driving along the road, something that is simple and ordinary in Australia, is a complex excursion fraught with danger in Afghanistan. I often found my body bathed in cold sweat as I struggled to breathe; I was that overcome with fear. The raw visceral fear I described. Sheer terror.

Even now, I can still recall isolated moments with vivid clarity. The fear etched them into my memory.

I remember one time when it was so dangerous that I traveled lying on the floor of my vehicle. My driver, Hasib, placed black plastic over the rear passenger windows. We had been warned of several imminent attacks—suicide attacks. Al-Qaeda was looking for soft targets, easy prey traveling in soft skin (that is, unarmored vehicles). That was us. It had become almost a predictable occurrence for a suicide bomber to carry out their attacks between the hours of 6:00 a.m. and 1:30 p.m. We often believed that this was the time when they were most driven, most zealous, and also the time when their targets were most vulnerable.

As I lay on the floor of the vehicle, I felt the sweat pouring out of my body, pooling beneath me where I pressed myself against the rough carpet. It was dark inside the vehicle because of the black plastic on the rear windows. My heart hammered in my chest, and I couldn't catch my breath, even though I knew a few deep breaths would help calm me. The blood rushed through my veins, throbbing at the base of my jaw and making my head ache.

At last, Hasib said, "We're okay, Boss."

After a few seconds, I was able to breathe again, but it felt like I'd lived through eternity—and not in the serene setting we imagine eternity will be. Sheer relief flooded me, and my body began to return to normal; however, I was shaking like a leaf and was cold and clammy all over.

And that wasn't even my closest call with a suicide bomber. No, believe it or not, that wasn't the worst of it. Not by a long shot.

Actually, my closest call with a suicide bomber happened six weeks after I first arrived in Afghanistan. We had been in the process of moving warehouses, and it was also the start of Eid al-Fitr celebrations. It was a tradition as part of the Muslim culture to celebrate with three days of feasting after thirty days of Ramadan, fasting dawn till dusk. Eid was a time of celebration, when extremists would often sacrifice their lives in return for the keys to the gateway of heaven. Eid and just afterward was renowned for being one of the most dangerous periods.

My assistant, Nicholas, who had already been based in Afghanistan for two years, had decided to drive because Hasib had been given this time off to celebrate. First, here's a brief description of Nicholas. A native of the Baltics, he was middle-aged, balding, and paunchy. Married twice and the father of five children, he had chosen to work in Afghanistan long-term in order to avoid his responsibilities back home—at least that's the most diplomatic way I can describe it. He was a first-rate assistant, though, I will say that.

As a result of his prior driving experience in the military, he handled our four-wheel-drive vehicle extremely well. Four-wheel-drive vehicles were mostly driven by internationals and wealthy Afghans. The three most common vehicles driven were Prados, Surfs, and Front Runners. Since it was at the time of public holiday, our choices were limited, which left us with a red Surf vehicle to drive. Suffice it to say this was like driving with a target marked on our backs!

Being in a country where the environment was hostile and vulnerable to change at any moment, we had to ensure that our vehicle had excellent tires and solid brakes and that it could go from zero to sixty in a split second.

Our new warehouse was about a ten-minute drive from the existing one, and the only way we could get from one site to the other was to travel along our favorite road—good old Jalalabad Road (J'bad Road for short). This road was once referred to as the second most dangerous road in the world after Baghdad. Why? It was notorious for suicide attacks.

We had already traveled along this road twice before on this particular day, and as our accommodation was located near the city, we would travel at least twice along J'bad Road daily.

The day had been busy. We were determined to move locations as quickly as possible despite having limited manpower and resources. Nicholas and I had decided to make one last run, which meant traveling once again along J'bad Road.

The road itself was deserted. Usually on a Friday, which was a day of rest, children would be playing outside their houses or alongside the road, and people wearing their Sunday best would be walking about as well. But that day was altogether different. It was as if we were the only car on the road. It was an incredibly eerie feeling. Something was wrong. *Very* wrong. That peculiar tension in the air was absent. This was intuitive—raw gut instinct heralding danger ahead. It would take a few fateful moments for me to realize that, though.

We had just passed a block of containerized local shops when, on my right-hand side, I noticed out of the corner of my eye that a young man had suddenly appeared out of a side street. He was like any other Afghan man in appearance. He had slightly dark skin and a bedraggled beard, and he wore the local *salwar kameez* attire. I estimated him to be about three or four car lengths away, and he quickly moved in the direction of our car.

The events that transpired during the few seconds that followed would change the dynamics completely, showing me without equivocation that I would have to trust my intuition in order to survive.

It was so surreal and happened so quickly that I almost felt as if everything had freeze-framed and was now in slow motion. But I will never forget his eyes. They seemed the size of pickled onions, marked with the defiance of unbridled rage.

As he moved closer, I couldn't help but notice that there was something under his clothing, something that was protruding. I kept staring at him, almost in disbelief, my eyes moving quickly, darting from him to the group of shops to see if perhaps I had been mistaken.

But I had not been mistaken. I felt my stomach churn, and my legs started to shake—all involuntary reactions as my subconscious began to process what was happening. The subliminal message had finally kicked in.

That was the actual moment when I realized that I had no choice but to trust my instincts and intuition. Doing so would likely mean the difference between life and death, between survival and destruction.

These terrifying moments of staring at the man chiseled themselves into my mind, a psychological scar that time will never erase. As I said earlier, these things are etched into my memory, where they will remain for the rest of my life.

Nicholas, who was no stranger to this environment, had thankfully seen this man move toward us a lot sooner than I had. Keeping a cool head, he immediately swerved and then accelerated without hesitation. Though utterly necessary, these actions were so quick that I could not prevent my body from jerking about, and I slammed my elbow into the panel of the door while I was trying to regain my composure. Nicholas continued to accelerate, and we sped off.

It took a good thirty seconds at least before I was able to turn to face Nicholas so I could ask him what had just happened. I stared at him, and he stared at me. The look on his face said it all. His eyes were wide, and he was as white as a sheet! Even so, my mind was still in shock. I could not believe what had just happened.

My mouth and throat were as dry as dust. "Was that a …?" I rasped, struggling to form the rest of the question and then pausing for a moment.

He looked away, trying to downplay the incident, and said, "I think so, Boss."

We both knew what we had just seen, but even more importantly, we knew how lucky we were to have escaped the potential fateful death of a suicide bomber. We weren't exactly sure why or how, but somehow we had been miraculously blessed and able to intercept his intention before he had a chance to hit our vehicle and detonate on impact.

I didn't put it down to just astonishingly good luck but rather to the simple fact that it was just not our time to go. Once instinctive intuition kicks in, such philosophies quickly follow suit. Besides, I'd already learned this—the philosophy part, I mean—growing up. Both my parents subscribed to the wisdom that all things happen for a reason, and I'd long since embraced the idea myself.

* * *

That night, after we safely returned to our accommodation, we sat in shock. We simply could not believe what had just transpired. We kept asking ourselves what had really happened, and we had quite a few stiff drinks to settle our nerves. That same night, as we sat drinking and watching the news, we saw how a suicide bomber had exploded that day in the city of Kandahar. Another martyr had struck, sacrificing many innocent lives.

Several days later, I asked Hasib, "Why were we spared?"

He said, "Boss, the day of our death is already written."

I agreed completely. Those events proved to me that not only would I *not* survive unless I trusted my instincts and intuition but also that it would be pointless to fight fate or try to change it—equally important lessons for living in a war zone. The lens of Afghanistan can provide crystal clarity. Very often frighteningly so.

An Ominous Beginning

Those fateful encounters changed me, fortifying me with resilience and courage, and it's important to understand their significance. But I should begin at the beginning, not just my arrival in Afghanistan but what brought me there in the first place.

Born and raised in relative privilege in Australia, I was a member of the world's minority, as opposed to the majority who live in poverty and without freedom and other basic human rights. I always knew how lucky I was, and I also always sensed that somehow I would put my talents and life benefits to better use. I just never knew exactly how or when.

The moment came when I was thirty-seven, and I reached a crossroad in my career. I wanted to do something new and challenging, exciting and meaningful. And then the opportunity to work as general manager for TerraTota arose. I couldn't pass it up. It seemed like an answered prayer and unimaginable adventure all rolled into one. I threw myself into preparing for my new position body and soul, but as I've said, nothing could have prepared me for what I would encounter.

* * *

The journey from Australia to Afghanistan had been long, and it was now twenty-four hours since I had last seen my bed. When we landed on the runway, everything seemed surreal. I knew that there was to be no turning back—at least not for the first twelve months, or I would be liable for a percentage of my contract. Fortunately, I did see a certain beauty in the Afghan landscape, in its people, and in its culture. Just as well. It would be my home indefinitely, for there was no telling how long this job might last.

The plane traveled along the runway, and I was glad that we had flown commercial, unlike the first time I visited Afghanistan. That had been the last hurdle of the interview process, and as a trial run, my future boss, Kurtis, had flown me on the company's own airplane, an old illusion about fifty years old. I mused about that first trip now, letting my mind wander as I settled into the reality that I was in the Afghan theater for the duration.

She was flown by the Russians, who knew every inch of their planes and insisted on doing their own maintenance. As we approached the plane, we saw a man on the wing. He wielded a wrench and appeared to be servicing the aircraft. He was casually dressed, much like men dress on weekends: T-shirt, shorts, and flip-flops. Despite his casual appearance, he appeared to know exactly what he was doing, and he soon hopped down from the wing where he had been doing mechanical work. About twenty minutes later, we saw him sitting in the cockpit. He was one of our pilots.

As with all old aircraft, the entrance was underneath, with a steep staircase leading into the plane. We climbed up the stairs and into the plane, soon meeting several pilots, all of them Russian and ready to help us. Three of us boarded the flight: Kurtis, an English guy with a wicked sense of humor, and me. It was a cargo plane, so we had to sit at the front, just after the cockpit, in an area that had a makeshift table and two long bench seats on either side. Opposite us was an old Russian pilot still wearing his army overalls. He instantly reminded me of my own father, an ex-military man who never really left the army. The old Russian sat on an old milk crate. He appeared to be trying to untangle some kind of tape that looked a bit like the old cassette tapes but thicker and larger. We were all watching him, wondering what all that tape was. There was a box beside him, and it appeared to be the source of this tangled mass of tape. We all continued to watch him until one by one we fell asleep. I watched Kurtis and the English guy both nod off, and then I also fell asleep. The trip had been a fairly long ordeal—a flight direct from Sydney to Dubai followed by several hours of mad shopping, a three-and-a-half-hour interview that was more like a severe interrogation, and then dinner with

Kurtis. The next day we had an early morning flight to Kabul. I was understandably exhausted.

After I slept for at least forty minutes, I woke up and glanced over to see what the old Russian was doing. It was uncanny, but the English guy had awoken at the same time, so we appeared to look at the Russian together. We both realized what he was doing, looked at each other, and laughed in amazement. He had lost his patience with the tangled tape, used scissors to cut it, and then affixed sticky tape to join it back together once it unraveled. The box that was beside him, although it was orange, was indeed the famous black box flight recorder, and the purpose of the tape was to record data.

The English guy kind of shrugged, still looking at me.

I gave him a half smile and said, "Oh, well. I guess if we crash now, no one will ever know exactly what happened!"

It was too crazy to forget a moment like that. Besides, once the plane landed safely, we were the only ones who would care to remember!

As we drew closer to landing, I decided to read the little piece of information I had been given on what to do and what not to do upon arriving in Kabul. Don't stray from the car, don't drink the water, make sure you have your passport with you at all times, and when you land, don't stray from the plane, particularly from the runway, as not all areas had been de-mined. Not too much to remember, and all of it rather essential. I took a breath, inwardly reminding myself of what a fantastic opportunity this general manager position with TerraTota was.

We landed, and after we taxied along for a bit, we stopped just short of the end of the Kabul Afghanistan International Airport (KAIA) runway. Clearly, the three Russians had done this many times before, and after several cups of tea they wasted no time in exiting the plane. The three of them stood together at the edge of the runway, taking a leak. This was rather comical, given our clear instructions not to stray from the plane or the runway because of mines.

I chuckled to myself while I thought of that first visit to Afghanistan. It had all felt so thrilling and rather unreal.

It was still thrilling, but this time it *was* for real. I was now on a new journey—a journey that I knew would be nothing short of challenging yet extremely eventful. It was a journey I had decided to commit to knowing full well that at times my life might be in grave danger but also full of excitement. The sense of adventure had motivated me, as had the complexity of my role as general manager. Danger, excitement, challenge, and complexity were all things I was guaranteed to experience while I was working and living in Afghanistan. Getting off the plane, however, I had no idea what all the implications of those guarantees would actually be.

I arrived with hand luggage containing two bottles of duty-free alcohol that I had quite innocently purchased. I didn't know that I couldn't bring it with me. As soon as I realized my dilemma, I immediately told Kurtis.

He found it rather amusing. "No problem," he said. "I'll get it in for you. Just give it to me."

I felt quite stupid and guilty for not knowing, but it was genuinely an innocent mistake. I knew TerraTota supplied and sold alcohol in Afghanistan, so I didn't think there was any issue with bringing it in. I felt rather nervous that now I had put Kurtis at risk with customs, but it didn't seem to bother him in the slightest. In fact, he exuded confidence, which led me to believe that perhaps he had done this before.

Things were about to get a lot more complicated. I soon discovered that the commercial airline had somehow misplaced my luggage. So now my total possessions consisted of two bottles of alcohol, the contents of my handbag, and the clothes on my back. To make matters worse, my clothing was not suited to the local weather. It was very hot, around 90 degrees Fahrenheit (30 degrees Celsius), and I was dressed more appropriately for winter, wearing jeans, boots, and a knitted top. I hadn't expected the weather to be so warm, and we had been told to cover up with a scarf and to wear long-sleeve tops. I was now praying that I was just tired and the suitcase had already been placed on the floor. Perhaps I had just missed it. No such luck. The case was quite easy to spot, and my father, the ex-army man he was, had decided to put a large blue cross on each side using gaffer tape. The problem was that perhaps it had been mistaken for medical supplies, which someone had likely perceived as valuable and so decided to steal. My entire identity in belongings had disappeared in one flight. Everything that was important to me was inside that suitcase. So now I had a problem. How was I to survive without all my packed possessions? Every day thereafter for several consecutive weeks, we checked with the airlines, visited Kabul Airport, and checked their lost luggage cargo containers in the hope of finding my luggage. I did this relentlessly throughout those weeks, not once losing faith. But I never did find my luggage.

Before I knew for sure that my luggage was gone forever, I was aware that I was now living in a male-dominated country where most females I could see walking along the street wore a *burqa*. As general manager, I would have to liaise on a regular basis with the military, so wearing the traditional female Afghan dress was not an option. I knew I had to present a more corporate, tailored image, one fitting the profile of my role, reflected in the apparel I had carefully prepared in my suitcase. I would have to start from scratch to re-create my wardrobe—at least until my luggage arrived, as I then still hoped it would.

But I'm getting ahead of myself. Before I could spend my first week in Afghanistan, I had to get through my first night there.

* * *

The first night I spent in Afghanistan was an experience. A very interesting experience, to say the least. Kurtis had been good enough to give me a black T-shirt he found in one of the cupboards in my new office—no doubt this T-shirt had belonged to the previous general manager. At least I now had something to sleep in. All I needed was to find out what I could use as a bath towel, and being new, I didn't want to make a fuss, so I opted to use some paper towels that had been left in the bathroom. The bathroom itself was quite old and dilapidated. The paint on the ceiling was peeling and covered in mold. It didn't really matter. I was looking forward to having a long warm shower after my many hours of travel. As I turned on the shower and stood underneath it, I soon discovered that the long-awaited shower was nothing more than a trickle, and the water temperature quickly moved from extremely hot to icy cold. So my first experience of taking a shower in Afghanistan was to be very brief.

My accommodation was in a rather large three-story mansion, which over here they referred to as a guesthouse. We had guards posted at the gate and were located not far from the British embassy accommodation. The rooms were unbelievably spacious. My room on the top floor was big enough for five people. I had no doubt I would be comfortable, except for the one thing that really mattered to me. All I had were the clothes on my back!

As my head hit the pillow, it suddenly dawned on me that I had also lost something of great sentimental value—the rosary bead necklace my mother had given me as a keepsake. I was worried that without this her health might be at risk. Plus, if anything happened to her, it was the last thing she had given me. And now it was gone. The thought brought tears to my eyes. I squeezed my eyes shut to fight the tears. Soon the exhaustion took hold, and I fell fast asleep.

* * *

I rose fairly early the next day. This was to be my first full day in the Afghan theater, September 11, 2007, the sixth anniversary of the attacks on the World Trade Center and the Pentagon in the United States. I woke to the sound of someone praying. There was a mosque just behind our guesthouse, and the sound filled my room. It was like a scene out of a movie, and it took a few moments for my awareness to kick in. This was no movie. It was for real.

Well, it was a brand-new day, and it was time to get started with it. I prepared to take another shower, which I hoped would be better than the last one. I needed to be alert and raring to go, as Kurtis had many things to show me. He planned to stay in Afghanistan for only a week and then go back to Dubai. After I took yet another brief shower that was no better than the one the night before, I picked up the one possession I was grateful to still have with me—my hairbrush. With two strokes of the brush, it broke. I stopped, staring at the broken thing and thinking that perhaps I was in a place of hell where everything did go wrong!

So now I had no choice but to find a place where I could go shopping. The problem was that we were scheduled to fly to a remote location down south the very next day, so I would have no time for shopping until we returned. Consequently, I still had only the clothes on my back to wear. Thankfully, I could wash my underwear daily, and the heat would ensure that it dried overnight.

The next day we flew out to a place called Tarin Kowt (better known as TK), which was made up of Dutch and Australian forces. We flew once again on one of our own planes, known as the "Fruit-and-Veg" flight, with the Russians.

It was about an hour-long flight, and our destination was south of Kabul. We sat on a bench seat alongside the windows of the plane, surrounded by large cardboard tri-walls full of fresh food. A lot different compared to traveling on a commercial flight.

No sooner had we taken in the scenery and made several attempts at trying to have a conversation over the noise of the engine than we commenced our sharp descent. We landed on a runway made of dirt and gravel, as expected in such a remote location as this. We were surrounded by mountains and what appeared to be an Afghan village situated in a valley not too far away.

The visit was to be only two days, and it had to also coincide with flights going back to Kabul, which of course depended on when the next Fruit-and-Veg flight was due to arrive. We had a scheduled meeting with Commander Van Koenraad, the camp commander, and his assistant, Deputy Groesbeck, in order to go over some issues they were having with our service and as a way to introduce me as the new GM. The meeting itself went quite smoothly, as it appeared they hadn't had the pleasure of entertaining a female civilian for several months. They completely ignored Kurtis during our conversation, resulting in his having to move his chair twice to get their attention.

While we spoke, a loud noise resounded. *Boom!* The whole space shook. It was the Dutch howitzer, which was constantly firing outgoing shells on the insurgents. Kurtis almost jumped out of his skin. I was mid-conversation and just kept talking. Having a father in the military, I'd grown up attending parades and visiting rifle ranges, so the sound of the howitzer caused me no consternation whatsoever. In fact, it was very familiar.

* * *

We flew back two days later from TK, and there was no sign of my lost luggage, so Kurtis finally agreed for me to go shopping. This was a day to remember. The company had given me the generous amount of US$1,000 as my clothing allowance, so I was all ready to go shopping. My head of security, Molvik, a Romanian and ex-military man, was to accompany me to downtown Kabul along with our local Afghan driver, Hasib, and our interpreter, Kareem. I could hardly wait.

I'll never forget my first time walking around the city of Kabul. The streets themselves were busy with the hustle and bustle of daily trade as expected. There was a pungent smell in the air coming from the sewage that spilled out onto the streets, and I could almost taste the oil burning out of the exhausts from the oncoming traffic. It was a far cry from the most recent shopping trip I had experienced in Dubai.

I soon realized that it was probably one of the first times a fair-skinned, blue-eyed, blonde Australian had walked along one of their streets to do a bit of local shopping. And it was one of their most notorious streets, known as "Chicken Street." I had been instructed by my security that I only had two hours because of the security risk, so I had no time to waste. What I didn't realize at first, but which soon became clearly obvious, was that most of the shops I walked into were for men. How was I to find something suitable? Everything I tried on was either too big or looked masculine! I must have walked into at least twenty shops only to have the same thing happen each time. Finally, I decided to enter a shop that appeared to be in a basement. There was only one minor problem. The generator used to power the shop's electricity was not working, and the shop was therefore in total darkness! I was determined to succeed in my mission, so a little darkness was not going to stop me. It just meant that I had to rely on my escort's good judgment in terms of what looked best on me. With very little time left, I still had to buy some more underwear. After all, I couldn't keep washing the one pair, hoping that it would dry overnight and be ready to wear the next morning. The shop I was taken to was a grocery store on one level. On the next level, practically everything else available in Afghanistan was for sale. Suffice it to say that Afghan women's fashion definitely required a little updating. The underwear I had to choose from resembled the underwear I remembered my grandmother wearing. I had no choice but to buy it or go without.

Well, that was it, my first shopping experience in Afghanistan! I am sure my former head of security will never forget it. The man hated shopping, and it was also the first time he had ventured into the city even after he had worked in Afghanistan for thirteen months.

* * *

The next few days were long and tiresome. Kurtis had planned to spend about a week with me in a handover of TerraTota's day-to-day operations as a turnkey global supply source and then slowly drip-feed me over the next six months with all the behind-the-scenes operations. This environment made operations a lot tougher, quite understandably. Nothing ever runs smoothly or according to plan in a theater of war. There is no daily routine, and things can change in a second. There can be a rocket attack in a location or a suicide threat, and then the entire operation is in lockdown. Again, all this was perfectly understandable, and I thought it was the usual operational protocol. The six months that followed would begin to paint an entirely different picture.

Prior to my offer and acceptance of the role of GM and in the days following our arrival in Kabul, I had learned the story of how my predecessor had fallen into the hands of Afghan corruption and been terminated for bribery. It wasn't until a few months later that it became apparent that this story had not ended with my predecessor. Rather, it was going to continue on its course as a conflict of interest, a severe miscarriage of justice, and an eighteen-month nightmare.

Perhaps I should have paid closer attention to my premonition of doom that first night in Kabul when I realized I'd lost my mother's rosary beads. But then again, it might not have made any difference. That early on during my stay in the Afghan theater, I felt confident and enthused. My rallying to persevere despite my lost luggage buoyed my spirits, and I felt the seeds of resilience begin to grow. As yet, though, I had no idea just how much I would need all the resilience and courage I could muster… or why.

2

STEPPING INTO THE ROLE OF GENERAL MANAGER

As I've indicated, nothing in my background had really prepared me for my position as general manager with TerraTota Suppliers, as working for a multinational organization in the middle of a war zone is not something that Western life can adequately equip any of us to handle. For a Western woman living in Afghanistan, this is an even greater challenge than it would be for a man. Before describing the deeper details of my story, I need to outline TerraTota's role in the region, as well as the scope of its influence as a multinational corporation.

Like most multinationals, TerraTota offers full-service supply-chain solutions worldwide. These solutions are usually described as "end to end" and/or "turnkey," and they range the gamut: fuel/food supply, procurement, transportation, storage, technology, site services, and so on. Among TerraTota's clients are defense organizations, national governments, and an array of companies/organizations in the private sector.

That description was not intended to appear as a corporate mission/vision statement, but it truly is the best objective summary I can provide. Even more important, upon arriving in Afghanistan,

I sincerely believed the company provided what it set out to—and did so with honor and integrity. I was not so naive as to be unaware of the existence of intrigue and corruption in a corporate setting, much less deny that existence, but it was also not in my nature to be pejorative or judgmental. For this reason, I listened to the statements made about my predecessor, but I took them with a grain of salt, desiring to uncover the truth behind them and form my own opinions based on that truth... whatever it proved to be.

I'm getting ahead of myself again. During those first few days in Afghanistan, I sought to acclimate myself to the region, both its climate and culture, while I simultaneously absorbed all the information Kurtis continually bombarded me with. I understood that I needed to hit the ground running, so to speak, but it was an awful lot to take in during such a short span of time, especially in light of the culture shock I needed to overcome. Nevertheless, I steeled my resolve, summoned my reserves of energy, and threw myself into the role full-bore. My positive attitude and enthusiasm had not waned, and these assisted me tremendously ongoing.

Over the course of several days of long and grueling hours, Kurtis managed to convey what he considered to be the essentials—everything I needed to know in order to carry out my daily duties as GM. The multinational organizations that provide the entire supply chain to a theater of war bear an enormous burden. The work is hard, the hours are long, and the responsibility is great. Certainly I did not wonder about how I would fill my days! If anything, my curiosity about my predecessor deepened. How would anyone have time for extracurricular activities when fulfilling all the demands of the legitimate business?

At the beginning, I simply sought to dig in my heels, figure out the best way to do my job effectively and efficiently, and accustom myself to life in Afghanistan. I let all the big-picture concepts of corporate responsibility remain on the periphery. I didn't really have a choice. More often than not, unless an abuse appears right in front of our face, we're not aware of the gray areas behind the scenes. Most of what I became aware of later on lay hidden at the start, and I simply didn't know enough about the situation and prevailing dangers to realize just how much there was to uncover. My initial reaction to learning that my predecessor had succumbed to corruption was that he had probably been overwhelmed by the work and the environment. I didn't really give more thought to it than that, not other than, as I've said, to determine that I wouldn't judge him until I knew exactly what had transpired. As with the suicide bomber encountered early on, I had to allow my instincts and intuition to take the lead, and then I had to learn how to recognize and trust them. While clearly understanding how critical all this was, it still took a bit of time and considerable effort for me to adjust to my new way of being in this foreign landscape.

Early on, TerraTota seemed like any other multinational in the Afghan theater—a company profiting from controlling the supply chain just as corporations and all sorts of power brokers since time immemorial have done during wartime. The deeper I delved into the prevailing arrangements between the NATO/ISAF suppliers and the local Afghan government, the more adept I became at discerning the hypocrisy, the special rules and circumstances, and eventually the conflict of interest that led me to an exposé of corruption and things far worse than that. But while Kurtis was still in the process of handing over responsibilities to me, my awareness of these ills amounted to little more than infinitesimal whiffs and whispers, and my senses and instincts had yet to be honed.

Deepening Intrigue about My Predecessor

After several days, the handover was well underway. One evening, Kurtis announced that he did not have much left to show me that was crucial in terms of day-to-day operations, and he planned to leave Afghanistan in a week or so. Of course, he would be able to answer questions as needed from his office in Dubai, but he urged me to use the following week to learn as much as I could from him face-to-face.

That seemed fair enough. I wanted to learn all I could from him while he was still in Afghanistan, but truth to tell, I was eager to be on my own. I've never much cared for micromanaging. Nor have I ever needed my superiors to hold my hand. I took his statements and demeanor at face value, not fully considering the enormous responsibility entailed by being a multinational supply-chain GM in Afghanistan. To qualify that, I understood how much responsibility I would have to shoulder, but I couldn't possibly fathom all that would actually be involved on a daily basis until I was in the position. Flying solo. Only then would I see all the details—and all the dangers.

I'll never forget the morning that followed Kurtis's announcement of his imminent departure. He deposited a pile of paperwork on my desk, explained the contents brusquely, and walked out of my office. "I'll be back, MJ," he said over his shoulder.

I didn't think much of this behavior, as he was always a little distant toward me, and I had come to realize that this was just his manner. He was quite shy in many ways and somewhat reserved by nature. I later discerned that perhaps he had specific reasons for displaying this demeanor, but those reasons would not become clear for some time.

While I was waiting for Kurtis to return, I concentrated on the latest items of business he had handed over to me.

After spending some time with our admin team, Kurtis came back into my office. "We've decided to take export off your hands, MJ," he said without any preamble. "We'll handle it from here on."

"All right," I said evenly. "Whatever you think best." The term *export* was more or less a euphemism for selling alcohol not legally housed in Afghanistan. I knew that much, but the wider implications and ramifications I had yet to understand.

He went on to explain that the next part of the handover would occur that afternoon, when he and I would visit the company warehouse together.

I nodded, conveying my enthusiasm for my ongoing training and orientation. My primary goal was to appear cooperative, flexible, and team-oriented. I had more than enough to acclimate myself to, and I wanted to succeed in my new role as GM. Plus, although I knew very little about the export area of the business that soon after arriving, I had already heard enough snippets about the fate of my predecessor to know that it was just as well for me to not have to be involved in the same activities as he had been, and export had been among his main priorities. I had been concerned about this and was quietly relieved to know that I would not have to worry about it. I certainly did not want to suffer the same fate as my predecessor, and I took Kurtis's statement at face value just as I'd taken all his statements up to that point, believing that I would be kept out of all the issues that export entailed.

Still ignorant of the grim details, I had yet to learn the truth and unearth all the facts behind what had really happened. His vague "we'll handle it from here on" was something I didn't really focus on at the time. It seemed to merely indicate that he would handle whatever pending issues remained following my predecessor's departure—certainly nothing more than that. Looking back with the wisdom and clarity of hindsight, I of course see all the signs. Just starting out in a brand-new job in an environment and culture utterly alien to me, however, none of this left more than a vague impression. I suppose this is true for most of us in new jobs, even when not in a different culture. There is so much new information, so many new people to get to know that we cannot possibly realize early on what may subsequently become critical. The most accurate way I can describe my reactions at the time would be to say that the stories I'd heard about my predecessor since my arrival in Afghanistan were entirely believable, and yet something deep inside me kept telling me to keep an open mind. Something was not quite right about the whole thing. I just couldn't put my finger on precisely what that something was. I believed that perhaps things would make more sense as time went by, that I just didn't have sufficient data to develop an informed opinion. I therefore decided to continue to gather more information, piece by piece, convinced that one day I would learn the whole truth.

All this was not in the forefront of my day-to-day thoughts, though. It was more of an undercurrent, actually subconscious more often than not. That whiff and whisper of instinctive, intuitive awareness that I described earlier. Yes, I recognized that something was not quite right, and I did trust my intuition on that score; however, I had no idea how deep and pervasive it was, how potentially dangerous it would prove to be. I was about to find out.

Between a Rock and a Hard Place

That afternoon, as promised, Kurtis took me to visit TerraTota's warehouse as the next part of the handover prior to his return to Dubai the following week. It was at this time that things began to become clearer. At least a little bit.

"You remember that I explained you're to be removed from the business of export, right, MJ?" Kurtis asked.

"Yes, of course," I replied, biting my tongue to keep from adding that he'd only told me that hours before. Nothing gained from appearing sarcastic or disagreeable.

"Well, that is so," he said, measuring his words. "But as GM, you'll still have to sign the documents."

"I see," I said, using the same even tone I'd employed earlier. Inwardly, however, my mind raced at all the implications of what he was saying. This meant that, in essence, I would be accountable for the alcohol leaving our warehouse as export, while the exchange of money and other related dealings would remain a separate process handled by others. The situation I was in was potentially dangerous, and I felt my stomach flip for an instant as I wondered just what had happened with my predecessor after all. Forcing myself to breathe normally, I maintained my composure and listened to the rest of what he had to say, realizing that I had to keep my wits sharp and my eyes and ears open. Clearly, there was far more to this entire situation than met the eye, but I still had to figure out exactly what that "more" comprised.

The story Kurtis presented was that the green light to carry out export had come from the top, with the intention of supplying one of the leading local operatives in Afghanistan who would then on-sell alcohol to the local market. Furthermore, this had been organized after TerraTota's business came close to financial catastrophe the day that the Afghan government woke up and decided to prohibit the sale of alcohol out of one of our main outlets, which was located at the time outside the wire. It was a huge supermarket that pumped alcohol day and night. Everyone from subcontractors to embassies to local businesses frequented this venue. It was a huge moneymaking enterprise for TerraTota—a real cash cow, as the expression goes. The problem was that as a company we were technically breaking the law of the land and jeopardizing the rest of our business, as the Afghan government had decided that we were liable for taxes on our business operations outside the wire. This of course was not going to happen because it would have opened up a whole can of worms for the rest of our business, which operated behind the wire. It also would have meant having separate cargo, which would have also been a logistical nightmare. Along with the prohibition of selling alcohol outside the wire came the expired stock. Hundreds of containers of beer, wine, and spirits sat in the warehouse, and we couldn't sell it without a viable solution. Expired stock was taking a huge financial toll on our business, namely beer. So out of desperation and for the sake of saving the business, my predecessor had come up with a rescue plan now referred to as export. In a nutshell, export was the quickest and easiest solution both financially and logistically.

This was how Kurtis finished his relating of the origins of export, but I somehow sensed it was only the tip of the iceberg. *What is export really?* I wondered to myself. *What do its sales consist of precisely? Exactly who are our customers?* I had enough business experience to recognize that my predecessor's financial/logistic solution might offer a good quick fix, but it was also potentially dangerous. In fact, it might be the most potentially damaging and dangerous risk that a global company could undertake, especially in a theater of war.

"So you see, MJ, you're out of it all, really," I heard Kurtis say. "Just sign all the documents so we have the proper paper trail, and that's it."

It seemed fair enough. After all, I was the GM, not a minion. My education in export was just beginning.

The Slippery Slope of Multinational Presence in Afghanistan

Let me reemphasize that at this point I had no knowledge of the Military Technical Agreement (MTA) in place between the ISAF (including any military support personnel, such as subcontractors like TerraTota) and the Interim Administration of Afghanistan.

No one had told me of such an agreement, much less shown the document to me, so I had no objective source of local legalities against which to assess the veracity of Kurtis's claims about export. All I had were my instincts, intuition, and common sense. I briefly recalled the instance with the alcohol in my carry-on bag upon arriving in Afghanistan—and Kurtis's reaction and response—and my sense that things were not quite right, and the story about my predecessor not quite accurate (or at least incomplete), continued to intensify.

My primary goal at this point was still to do a great job in my new position; however, I couldn't shake the sense that the wool was being pulled over my eyes, and I didn't like the feeling. I did trust my intuition and my moral compass (and that trust would only expand and deepen over time), and I wasn't about to shy away from standing up to wrongdoing if it came down to it; however, I also told myself not to read more into it than was actually there. After all, this wasn't just a traditional for-profit enterprise in the West; it was a multinational organization operating in the middle of a war zone. There were bound to be gray areas, and I would have to learn how to effectively navigate them. I was no shrinking violet. I'd long ago squared my shoulders and stepped up to the plate. That was why I was here in the first place. I had the guts and the brains to find my way and to succeed. Now was the time to do it.

I was about to discover how true resilience, courage, and fortitude help us protect ourselves while simultaneously doing the right thing. It was a grand discovery, but the journey was far bumpier than I ever could have imagined.

Corporate Bending of Local Laws

I never did unearth all the records of the very beginning of export. Nor did I ever learn all the details concerning it, but those individuals who became my trusted sources have told me that it was just a handful of select customers at first. They sometimes purchased whole containers of alcohol at a time from TerraTota, and then it was their business to on-sell it. The customers either paid for the containers in advance (just prior to delivery) or paid in cash at the time of delivery. This process continued after I started, but as Kurtis had indicated, I was not involved in export other than to sign the documents connected to the alcohol leaving the warehouse. Again, I was quite relieved to be outside the process. The risk the company was taking from the perspective of both business and security surprised me. It seemed rife with corruption and collusion, as potentially dangerous and damaging as dealing with organized crime or any underworld entity. I was glad to be kept out of it.

Remember that at the beginning Kurtis had led me to believe that I *would* be kept out of it, and although the signing of the documents did cause me concern, I didn't have any hard evidence or solid reason to doubt his word or not trust him. I just had the vague sense that something wasn't right, and that kind of sense didn't seem sufficient to warrant panic or hasty action. At the time, having no awareness of the MTAs, I also still had yet to fathom the full magnitude of the danger and wrongdoing entailed by export vis-à-vis local Afghan laws. I cannot overemphasize how much this lack of knowledge impacted me, especially during my subsequent tenure as GM.

Semantics versus Legalities

Of course, as time went on, I learned and discovered more and more about the situation, both what had befallen my predecessor and what lay in store for me. I realized that I had been earmarked as the scapegoat just as the ill-fated GM before me had been. In other words, I was now the one in the hot seat because it was my signature on all the documents! This was very dangerous, of course, but I knew that if I resigned my position as GM and left TerraTota before I found out the truth, I could still be blamed for whatever happened.

Kurtis's words echoed through my brain. "So you see, MJ, you're out of it all, really. Just sign all the documents so we have the proper paper trail, and that's it."

That's it, indeed! I began to see the dilemma of shared responsibility in a corporate situation. Technically, we shared the responsibility, but the only signature on the documents would be mine. I imagined that this was exactly what had happened to my predecessor, and I vowed inwardly to learn from his mistakes. It was bad enough that he had suffered misfortune. My following in his footsteps would benefit no one, least of all me.

I then began to think about all the complexities and nuances of the situation, and this begged a series of extremely complicated and uncomfortable questions. If the responsibility was shared, were we all equally accountable? And if all those supposedly sharing responsibility refused to accept accountability, where would the responsibility and accountability actually reside? To put this colloquially, if it all hit the fan, whose head would roll? It would inevitably all hit the fan, of course. It was just a question of when and how. And the head that would roll would be mine just as it had been my predecessor's.

It was essential for me to gather accurate information now, to fill in the details Kurtis seemed to have deliberately glossed over, lest I be the next casualty. I had no intention of allowing that to happen, regardless of what the powers that be within TerraTota had planned for me.

I knew I had my work cut out for me, and I struggled to remain calm and clearheaded. This predicament I found myself in by no fault of my own would prove to be one of the most burdensome and stressful experiences I had ever endured. I grew increasingly angry and worried, but I would not let myself give in to fear or despair. The key to surviving this with my self-respect intact and my reputation unimpeachable was to stay sharp. Only resilience would get me through this, and I realized that resilience would come from the combination of strength, flexibility, intuition, and courage.

That determined, I decided that the first order of business was to get solid reliable answers, and the only way to do that was by asking the right questions. Who was the person actually responsible for this whole export situation? Was it a decision made at the top and trickled down, as Kurtis had originally informed me, or was it the work of my immediate superiors? How much if any of it had my predecessor designed, and how much had simply been foisted on him just as signing the documents had been foisted on me?

Many thoughts and difficult questions would filter through my mind during the months that followed, and I would continually sift through them, searching for answers. I didn't know what to believe, and I didn't know who I could trust. The one thing I did know was that whoever was involved, whoever had masterminded this elaborate scheme had done so blatantly as a conflict of interest—and I would find out who... and why.

But I've gotten ahead of myself again. Before these more pressing questions and concerns really perturbed me, I was still in the process of handover and then of seeing to the day-to-day business at hand. So business as usual—whatever that can actually be in a theater of war—was the next step in the process before I could recognize, much less address and tackle, the graver and more sinister issues beneath the surface.

3

BUSINESS AS USUAL

Taking Inventory

As I began to gain competence in my role, my confidence grew, and my courage strengthened. And then I worked on formulating a plan to investigate the history of export and my status as would-be scapegoat. As much as I wanted and needed to get to the truth, I knew that I would only prevail if I did my job excellently. There would have to be nothing to call my character or abilities into question. If anything like that were to happen, whatever plan I developed would be to no purpose. It would all fall apart. I would still be the one blamed, and then whoever had set me up as scapegoat would win. I couldn't, and wouldn't, let that happen.

Thus, I just went about my day-to-day activities as GM, fulfilling my duties and responsibilities to the best of my ability. In the course of doing so, I learned much about TerraTota's role as a NATO/ISAF subcontractor. It would not be fair to say that I was certain of illegal and/or corrupt activities, but my intuitive feeling that something was just not right continued to intensify. The longer I lived in Afghanistan, the more I honed my instincts. Interacting with the local Afghans and the expats contributed to this significantly.

Suffice it to say that legitimate business and corruption were not separate from one another. There was no black and white in Afghanistan. Everything fell into a murky and amorphous gray area, and it took time and experience to differentiate the shadings and shadows thereof. Business as usual in a war zone is difficult and stressful at best; combating corruption and illegal activities in the midst of it makes the challenges and stress almost unbearable. I was on a tenuous path, little better than a thread, and only my resilient tenacity enabled me to persevere—both in uncovering the truth and in surviving.

A Cast of Thousands, Each with a Hidden Agenda

The best way to describe how I learned to navigate these murky and amorphous gray areas of war-zone "business as usual" is to relate some typical encounters I had with local Afghans and expats in the region. Although such encounters were in no way unusual, some of them were quite unforgettable in the uncanny way that seemingly ordinary events so often are, especially when we are in unfamiliar surroundings or new situations. Perhaps that phenomenon more so than anything else made me recognize that this was just the way things would be in Afghanistan. It was my new normal.

Two of these early encounters actually occurred before Kurtis departed for Dubai and, therefore, before I was flying solo as GM. I distinctly remember returning from a camp visit one morning and encountering a Russian lady. She appeared to be in her fifties, but she looked rather haggard. Her complexion was dark, and the heat and harsh environment had dried her skin. Anyone might easily have mistaken her for a Pakistani refugee. I almost did until Kurtis's sotto voce comment that she was Russian. She was dressed like a gypsy, complete with a sequined drawstring purse and a colorful scarf. Everything about her enabled her to blend in well. I surmised, without asking Kurtis, that she was an immigrant, and I couldn't imagine what sort of dealings she might have with TerraTota.

I soon learned that she had come to see Kurtis, and as it turned out, she was no immigrant. At least she was not a newly arrived immigrant. In fact, she was a very successful businesswoman and restaurateur who had been in Afghanistan for some time. The purpose of her visit was to purchase liquor in large quantities—to be precise, by the container load.

I couldn't help but wonder if she was what Kurtis and the staff referred to as an export customer. It was far too early for me to jump to any conclusions or to even understand exactly what was going on; however, my instincts and intuition were running full-throttle, and nothing about the encounter seemed ordinary. That early on I had yet to be aware of the new normal or the constant gray areas of business as usual. It just seemed odd and not quite right. So I just kept my mouth shut and my senses keen.

The Russian woman did not beat around the bush. She was up front as to why she had come to see Kurtis.

Clutching the sequined purse and raising it into our line of vision, she said, "I have $30,000 to give you on deposit." She further confirmed that this was US dollars. Even with as little as I knew of the situation, which was actually barely more than nothing, it was obvious that the woman was desperate to purchase the alcohol. (A moment or two later she indicated that the on-selling of alcohol was part of her livelihood, and so it was clear to me that my observation of her desperation was accurate.)

Kurtis appeared a little apprehensive, and after he listened to what she had to say, he told her, "I'll have to evaluate the situation further, and I'll be in touch." He said it all very matter-of-factly, and then he showed her out.

Kurtis came back into the office and resumed our routine operations discussions, as if the entire interlude with the woman had never occurred. That was the first and last time I saw that Russian woman, but I'll never forget the encounter.

That day was rather a busy one actually. Later on we had two other visitors on a more official matter. One was a representative for customs from the Ministry of Interior (MoI). He wore a business suit and appeared to be well educated. The other was the man's assistant, also clad in a Western suit. They had come to discuss customs duty TerraTota owed on goods previously sold in one of our largest outlets, which had since ceased operations.

"TerraTota Suppliers owes the Afghan government duty tax because your outlet was trading outside the wire," the customs official from the MoI declared, arguing that it didn't matter that this outlet was no longer viable—TerraTota was still responsible, and we would be held liable.

The entire exchange was tense and unpleasant, both the body language and the exchange of words, on both sides of the conversation. I could feel that Kurtis and the Afghan official were on the verge of a serious argument.

Allowing my instincts and intuition to guide me, I decided it was time to ease the strained atmosphere, the tension of which you could cut with a knife. Addressing the higher-level official, I remarked, "Your country is very beautiful. I'm sure you know that."

My observation distracted him somewhat, and my soft tone of voice caught his attention.

His assistant nodded, and the higher-level official smiled at me, seeming to realize that I did not necessarily share my boss's views and opinions. “Thank you,” he said. “Yes, I agree. Our country is beautiful.”

I had managed to defuse the tension and cool the atmosphere, even if only for a few moments. It was obvious to me that the aggressive tone Kurtis had taken did nothing to ameliorate the situation or appease the Afghan officials. If anything, it had simply added more fuel to the fire, and I sensed that this was a fire that rarely died down to embers. More likely than not, it needed little to stoke it into raging flames.

Kurtis and the customs official continued their discussion, and although their tone had slightly softened, it was obvious that the two men had an extreme dislike for each other.

The customs official made the MoI’s final points of demand, and then he and his assistant left. The entire exchange took a bit longer than five minutes.

Kurtis didn’t say a word to me, and I observed him silently, wondering if he knew why I had spoken when I did and in the way that I did. Although he never indicated it specifically, he did seem to understand. Thankfully, he did not perceive it as my speaking out of turn.

This exchange, too, will always stand out in my memory. The new normal would be anything but easy or ordinary, and intuition would clearly provide better means for navigating these gray areas of business as usual than mere vision or even the most cutting-edge corrective lenses possibly could. Not even binoculars or a telescope could possibly provide keener sight than intuition, the unerring inner compass that guides us all.

Tuning the Moral Compass

I came to rely on that compass more than I could possibly have imagined at that time. It provided me with more than just an uncanny sense of what to do and how and when to do it. It was a bellwether of right and wrong. It was my survival compass and my moral compass all rolled into one. And I learned to tune it quickly indeed. "Baptism by fire," I believe, would be a most appropriate description!

The events described above with the Russian woman and the MoI customs officials occurred several years ago when I was a lot younger and far less wise. In fact, it seems now that I was far younger than the mere chronological number of years that have passed since then. It's amazing how an environment like Afghanistan can age us so quickly that the months and years pass by without our even realizing that we have undergone a complete metamorphosis, a total inner transformation. Living in a war zone grounds us in one way, making us appreciate how precious life is. And yet in another way it opens us to aspects of life and thought that are anything but grounded. It's not that we necessarily embrace principles that are so lofty as to elevate us beyond the earthly plane. No, living in such an environment keeps us quite earthbound and necessarily so. It's more that we learn how to extend the parameters of our thinking, opening our minds and broadening our horizons. To put this another way, we begin to think on a different level because we develop a *third knowledge*—what I've referred to as instinct and intuition up to now. Eastern philosophies often call the seat of this knowing the third eye, and they locate it in the part of the brain that is just above and in between the eyes, roughly in the center of the forehead.

I didn't think about all this in these terms at the time, of course. In fact, I didn't have the luxury for such deep pondering even later on in my tenure in Afghanistan. It's only lately that I've begun to think along these lines. My intuition—my third knowledge—was a survival tool. My moral compass, powered by my intuition, would soon become one as well. But I'm getting ahead of myself again. It's important to understand how I felt during my early days in Afghanistan.

Being so new to the environment, I was completely naive and trusting. My excitement and enthusiasm overpowered everything else. I was fascinated by everything I did and everything I saw. I truly believed that I was the luckiest and happiest person alive. What a gift it is to feel that way with total sincerity. Rarely, if ever, do we recognize such a gift while feeling it. Only through hardship can we fully appreciate its sweetness. More to the point, the euphoria of my enthusiasm and vibrancy put me in a kind of bubble, my instincts and intuition notwithstanding. I wasn't blind or unaware, but my happiness sheltered and shielded me, causing me to forget the most important thing of all. I was in Afghanistan. Rosy outlooks are fine in peacetime, but in war zones, not so much. In a war zone we need to be shrewd. We need to keep our eyes sharp and our wits sharper. In those early days the people around me had such different attitudes than I did. The environment had toughened them, and they had allowed it to because they knew it would enable them to survive.

My attitude and demeanor baffled them. They were individuals, different in their own way, but they had one thing in common and one shared purpose—to earn money. People would look at me in disbelief when I told them that money was secondary to me. Job satisfaction and adventure were my dual primary objective. That was rather difficult for most people to accept. "Are you serious? We're in Afghanistan! This is a war zone where people get killed or kidnapped!" The exact verbiage might vary a bit from person to person, but this was the gist of people's responses to me. I pretty much shrugged it off in the early days. Yes, of course it was a war zone. I'd known that going in. It was also an environment rife with corruption and deception. It was drowning in both, to be honest. I hadn't imagined the extent of that going in, but it didn't take long for me to see it. The best way I can describe it is to say that I was aware that it existed from the beginning, but I didn't *feel* it. I was simply swept away by the country's magnificence—the harsh beauty of its landscape, the grandeur of its history and culture. And the challenges of building a business in a unique environment swept me away too, albeit in a different way. The former captured my imagination, while the latter captured my entrepreneurial spirit. Both absorbed me utterly, body, mind, and soul, eventually captivating my heart as well. Simply put, the positive aspects of being in Afghanistan resonated deep within me. This was where my heart was, and so it was also what I wanted to focus on. I put my intention there, and then I let myself follow it.

Cultivating Resilience

Part of my role as GM was not only to oversee all retail operations on the ground in Afghanistan but also to control TerraTota's most volatile commodity and greatest resource—alcohol. With the exception of fuel, alcohol was the most sought-after product on the black market. We were living in a land where 95 percent of the world's opium supply came from,* and where alcohol was strictly prohibited. I couldn't help but think about my school days when we learned all about the era of Prohibition in American history. Corruption and deception had been rife then too. The situation I found myself in here in Afghanistan was not really much different, not essentially anyway. I was living in a country where it was AH 1385 (the year in terms of the Islamic calendar, as opposed to our then 2007) and where the people claimed to live and die by their strict Muslim religious and cultural beliefs. But did they? I pondered that often. It seemed to me that the only difference between the days of US Prohibition

* Independent Women's Forum, *Stabilizing Afghanistan: The Case for Not Legalizing Poppy Cultivation*, http://www.iwf.org/files/70d535f137e8c101995e72f4b3d646ee.pdf.

and contemporary Afghanistan, though separated by ninety-odd years chronologically, was that Afghanistan had no speakeasies. Alcohol was permitted as long as it was supplied behind the wire and under the watchful military eye of ISAF. Contrary to the Muslim religious beliefs that prevailed throughout the country, alcohol was also easily available in the dark backstreets of Kabul and in the surrounding bazaars.

Inevitably, this led to as much opportunism as bathtub gin, to borrow again from Prohibition. But people are people, and most of them will have hidden agendas no matter where they are; it's part of human nature. In reality, I didn't care about other people's hidden agendas. Determination was and always would be my driving force, and it would propel me to survive in Afghanistan and to fight the injustices I encountered by seeking and defending the truth and by fighting for and upholding human dignity. Through the course of this journey, I learned a very valuable lesson. The truth is never on the surface. We must look hard and dig deep in order to find it.

I've said that my background didn't really prepare me for Afghanistan, but part of it did in a way. I grew up under a strict disciplinary regimen established by my father. He was ex-army, as I've mentioned, and he served for twenty-eight years, which represented most of my life up to that point. As a result, I was quite accustomed to the strict military culture. My father, a Vietnam vet and ex-Special Forces member, had trained me long ago. Without even realizing what my vocational destiny would be, he had nonetheless prepared me for this journey. The longer I remained in Afghanistan, the more I recognized this. My appreciation of my father deepened, and I sought to make him proud. (Like all children, even in adulthood I wanted my father and mother to be proud of me no matter what I did in life. Seeking to make my father proud in this instance, however, was at a different level than this natural desire.) My father taught me the importance of self-respect and self-discipline, as well as the importance of respect for others. He also taught me the importance of having the courage to fight for what I believe in, to have the personal grit and fortitude to not be swayed by other people's opinions. All that takes courage and discipline, yes, but it also takes flexibility; we have to learn how to bend but not break. Together, all this comprises what I think of as *resilience,* a core of inner strength and self-reliance. I diligently cultivated and nurtured all this, all the while remaining mindful of all that my father had instilled in me.

As I said, the early days in Afghanistan (that is, the first six months or so) would prove to be something of an unexpected challenge and a call for resolution. There were of course the day-to-day events of operations—the so-called business as usual—but I would soon learn that the murky gray areas that had never seemed quite right to me were far worse than I ever could have imagined… and a daunting challenge that would become a journey of no return.

Face-to-Face with Corruption

Remember that my closest call with a suicide bomber happened just six weeks after I first arrived in theater, as described in chapter 1. My assistant, Nicholas, and I were in the process of moving warehouses when that brush with destiny occurred. Over and above that incident, which we obviously had no idea of in advance, we were up to our necks in stress and hassle because of said warehouse move. Such a move would be less than pleasant in the best of circumstances, but it was all the more difficult when it involved moving a prohibited substance, namely alcohol.

Everyone in the area knew what we had in our warehouse, and so the trick was to move it without being intercepted by the local Afghan police, most of whom were corrupt. We therefore spent hours every night in the warehouse once the local Afghan staff had left for the day. Using only a torch for lighting, we black-pallet-wrapped all the alcohol, labeling the goods as such innocuous items as toilet paper and tampons. We put anything but alcohol on the labels. We had been warned by our own security company that we needed to do this because these individuals wanted to bypass our regulations in order to obtain a few beers to drink during a rugby match. They told us that we couldn't move the alcohol out of the warehouse without a permit/license from the MoI. If we had followed our security company's advice, we would have probably lost our entire stock.

I thought about the conversation I'd recently witnessed between Kurtis and the MoI official, and so I knew a permit/license was not an option. We'd have to pay all the duty taxes, and Kurtis would not be agreeable. Even though export was out of my hands—aside from my having to sign the documents—I was still responsible for our stock, and there was not going to be an inventory problem on my watch. Excellent job performance was still high on my list of priorities. Recognizing how great an evil corruption was in theater, I had to come up with a plan to move the stock without involving our local Afghan staff. That meant Nicholas and I had to work at night in order to prepare the stock for transport the following day. This way our local Afghan employees were none the wiser as to when we actually moved the alcohol.

The long and short of it was that it was impossible to trust anyone in the environment where we worked in Afghanistan. There was no way of knowing "who's who in the zoo," as Tucker, my warehouse manager, always phrased it. It was possible that our local Afghans would pass on information to the Afghan authorities, who in turn would give them *bakshish.* Bribery was rampant. Our local Afghan staff would eagerly offer information in exchange for the money the police would readily provide. All this meant that the police, upon receiving this information, would be able to intercept our trucks transferring the alcohol, and then that would be the last time we'd see our stock.

In addition, Dr. Asadullah, the landlord of the warehouse we currently occupied, had threatened us. He was a typically corrupt Afghan businessman who, although a doctor by training, chose a different path for earning a living. He wanted us to buy potatoes from him as part of the food supply to the troops. As this never would have passed the food safety regulations, there was no way that we would consider him as a vendor. He also wanted me to supply him with whiskey, informing me that Kurtis had promised him a case. This was more than likely a trap designed to catch us selling alcohol to a local Afghan, which not only would have landed me in an Afghan prison but also would have jeopardized TerraTota's contracts with ISAF.

I wasn't prepared to compromise my moral values. Nor was I keen on continuing to have to deal with Dr. Asadullah on a regular basis, which I would have to do for as long as he was our warehouse landlord. We knew that Dr. Asadullah was, for lack of a better term, "in bed with the government," so he had more than likely organized the would-be trap with his influential friends. I will never forget the day he came to visit our warehouse for an inspection prior to our vacating the site. His wife, Mina, accompanied him, and she was almost hysterical with rage, as she had come the day before to check the premises only to discover that there were no doors, windows, or partitioning. Tucker had decided to remove all these materials, which infuriated our landlords to no end. It was their belief that regardless of whether the building had been modified by us or not, any refurbishments should remain on the premises. I now had the privilege of appeasing the situation, dealing with both Dr. Asadullah and Mina, whose rage-whipped hysterics had turned her into quite the harpy indeed.

After I saw the warehouse for myself, I decided to meet our landlords outside the warehouse gate. I later learned that this was a very brave move on my part. I had originally wanted to go outside with my operations manager, Sean, but he disappeared just before we were ready to go. In the end Tucker and I went to meet them.

Dr. Asadullah and Mina were both very astute, well-educated people—a doctor and businessman and a businesswoman. Not only was she involved with all sorts of property dealings, she also participated rather visibly in programs for Afghan women.

I greeted them at the gate, playing up the fact that I was new. "I'm here to rectify any issues," I informed them, keeping my tone courteous but firm. I knelt on the gravel, taking notes on what transpired and writing down their concerns.

Dr. Asadullah appeared to be receptive to my responses and demeanor. "Please… come," he said, offering me a seat in the back of their car.

As I was still relatively new to this environment and quite naive, I didn't realize at that time how dangerous accepting this offer really was. Tucker later confessed to me that he had visions of them kidnapping me by simply driving off with me in the back of the car!

Thankfully, nothing that dramatic ensued.

I perched on the backseat, continuing to speak in a calm tone of voice. "Everything will be put back in its rightful place," I assured Dr. Asadullah and Mina. I had learned earlier that Mina had already put a previous GM in an Afghan prison as a result of a dispute, and anyone who asks Dr. Asadullah will learn that he used his political influence to have the man released. Dr. Asadullah takes great pride in both using his political influence and letting those in his midst know just how much influence he wields.

Skirting corruption—or maintaining balance while on its slippery slope—remained a full-time job, but the more I cultivated my resilience, trusted my intuition, and fine-tuned my moral compass, the more confident I remained that I would not succumb. It was a tough environment, but I kept telling myself that I was tougher.

And all my dad's training in strength and discipline served me well. I'm certain I wouldn't have made it through intact without the core of resilience and self-reliance he'd taught me to build up deep within myself.

4

ALCOHOL

With each passing day in theater, I felt my resilience and self-reliance strengthen, and I achieved greater competency in my position as GM. These happened simultaneously for the most part, and that bolstered my confidence and deepened my faith in my intuition. My inner compass was getting quite keen by this time, and I fine-tuned it continually. During this process I discovered the essential difference between knowledge and wisdom. Explaining this in terms of my job with TerraTota, knowledge was what I gained by doing my day-to-day work as GM, whereas wisdom was what my intuition already knew and therefore directed my moral compass to prompt me to question and explore. That said, I learned about alcohol's role in Afghanistan both by gaining knowledge and trusting wisdom.

It's difficult to have a clear understanding of alcohol's complicated role in the Afghan theater. For starters, life in Afghanistan is complicated in and of itself, full of the gray and shadowy areas I've described all along. Nothing is cut-and-dried or completely clear, which is why intuition and a fine-tuned moral compass are so essential to survival. In addition, even though alcohol is illegal in Afghanistan, most of the NATO/ISAF troops and civilian expats are accustomed to consuming alcohol to whatever extent they choose, as alcohol is not an illegal substance in their native Western environments. In short, alcohol's illegal status in Afghanistan is something that is difficult for Westerners to adjust to, especially in the extreme environment, when many of them are accustomed to using alcohol to relax and reduce stress. The Afghans, on the other hand, have a far more convoluted relationship with alcohol. They are accustomed to its being illegal in their country, but they find ways to obtain it anyway. It's a bit like the speakeasies and bathtub gin of American Prohibition, and I found myself making that correlation time and time again as I described earlier.

I continued to ponder both the Western and Afghan moral perspectives. My dilemma was that I had to live with these diametrically opposed viewpoints, and maintaining the neutrality necessary to be an effective and responsible businessperson was extremely challenging. The key to achieving this neutrality, I decided, was to understand the perspective of both sides—to find a way to balance the equation, so to speak. I came to realize that in order to do this I would have to accept that there is a difference between what is illegal because it is wrong in and of itself and what is illegal because it is prohibited by law. My correlation of Afghan laws with American Prohibition helped me clarify this within my own mind. However, this all went on during my first few weeks in theater prior to my acquaintance with the MTAs, and so it remained rather ambiguous for some time exactly what was and was not legal. (The MoI's insistence on TerraTota's owing duty tax notwithstanding, because neither Kurtis nor anyone else really explained the legalities, much less showed me an MTA, I was pretty much in the dark, with only my intuition and better judgment to guide me.)

In other words, still new to the job, the company, and the local environment, I focused on doing excellent work, and I continued to find out the truth about alcohol in the Afghan theater as I went along. This chapter will relate my discovery of that truth, which unfolded bit by bit throughout each passing day during my tenure as GM with TerraTota.

The New Warehouse

Remember that we moved the warehouse barely six weeks after my arrival in Afghanistan, and so I was still in a kind of sensory overload as a Western civilian living in Afghanistan in addition to my learning curve as the GM of a multinational supply-chain organization. Adjusting to the constantly required hypervigilance demanded unrelenting focus, and it was unbelievably enervating. In addition, the climate was rough—intensely hot and fiercely cold as only desert areas can be—and I had yet to experience my first Afghan winter. (Spoiler alert: they're brutal!) It was not easy by any stretch of the imagination. There were all sorts of unexpected sources of inspiration, though—the ruins of ancient palaces, with their harrowing histories and enduring grandeur. Their magnificence still haunts my memory. On a smaller scale there were the variety of goods in the open markets, their fabulous colors, fragrances, and tastes. The locally baked breads, for instance, had an aroma and flavor I'd never encountered before or since (caveats about not ingesting local food and water aside). The dried fruit and nuts (which usually sold for three US dollars per kilo) were utterly mouthwatering. Part of the sensory overload was less than pleasant, of course—children playing in the streets amid garbage and worse, what we referred to as the "organized chaos" of the airport and other public places, the police checkpoints searching for insurgents at every turn, and so forth. Overall, however, it was unforgettable in a way that captures the imagination and pierces the soul, at once breathtaking and sobering.

Suffice it to say that my cultural education expanded and my inner learning increased as I went along. My process of gaining knowledge and trusting wisdom was just beginning, far from complete or even well underway. And the sights, sounds, and smells all around me heightened my senses and increased my awareness, honing my intuition all the more.

My adventure with our previous warehouse landlords, Dr. Asadullah and his wife, Mina, was over, and I was ready to roll up my sleeves and get to work. Our new warehouse was perfectly situated, as it was in close proximity to the rest of our business operations. Unlike our previous warehouse, the premises were brand new and spacious. The warehouse had two large buildings divided by a long, tarred road leading to a large guesthouse at the back of the premises. As we didn't require the use of both buildings, it had been decided that we would take the building situated farthest from the main gate, given the sensitivity surrounding some of the contents of our warehouse, namely alcohol.

Before we decided on this location, there were many factors that we had to consider. For instance, even though we had many Afghans working inside our warehouse, it was imperative that we took the precautionary measures necessary to ensure that we would reduce the risk of outsiders having any knowledge of our operations. Even the local Afghan drivers who would enter our compound to deliver containers were not permitted to enter our warehouse, and we required them to stay inside their vehicles while the containers were unloaded. (Similarly, as described in the last chapter, we wrapped all the alcohol, labeled it as other goods, and moved it under cover of night after the local Afghans had finished work for the day, all in order to ensure security.)

I previously quoted the favorite saying of my warehouse manager, Tucker. "You never know who's who in the zoo." These were words worth taking to heart, and over time the rest of the team came to value and live by them as much as Tucker did. The long and short of it was that we were constantly dealing with unknown quantities. We all tacitly understood that this was potentially dangerous; we would only learn later on just *how* dangerous it actually was.

Although the new warehouse was a positive move from my perspective, it was not universally popular. There were questions and concerns as to how our new warehouse location would handle export. In our old warehouse apparently this had been less of a problem. That venue was somewhat removed from the prying eyes of individuals both local Afghans and otherwise—our politically connected former landlord and the MoI's shrewd customs official all notwithstanding.

As it had already been decided that I would be excluded from the whole operation concerning export (other than signing the documents), I was happy that this entire matter was something that my boss would be the one to deal with. Kurtis had no issue with this, of course, and he took charge of ensuring that there would be an operational solution. After all, it was in his best interest to find an appropriate solution.

However, I soon learned that it would not be that simple to find such a solution. The secrecy enabled by our previous location had likely been deliberately engineered or at least used to maximum advantage. I learned from a colleague that export pickup in the old warehouse sometimes occurred in the wee hours of the morning. I had a funny feeling that this practice would cease to continue in our new location. I later discovered that one of the reasons for the middle-of-the-night pickups was to ensure that the goods would have a safe passage to their destination, as fewer police checkpoints existed at that time of the night. In any case, the previous arrangements of export pickups would now be an issue in our new warehouse because there were more guards posted on the gate. This meant there would be questions in the future as to why delivery trucks were entering and leaving during the middle of the night.

Again I had only been in theater for less than two months at this point, and I still only had limited information regarding export operations. I basically pieced it all together from the scraps of information I received, fitting it into a semblance of order by trusting my intuition and using my business acumen and common sense. Even that early on it seemed odd to me that very few people knew of the existence of our export operations; our warehouse staff and management were really the only ones who I was sure were aware. I suspected there was more to the MoI customs official's warning than met the eye. I couldn't shake the feeling that something just wasn't right and that export was at the root of that something. Over time these suspicions and intuitive feelings deepened into dismay and worry, but let's not get ahead of the story.

For a few months I kept my nose to the grindstone and worked, worked, worked. Little by little I unearthed tidbits of information, some of it very instructive and illuminating. I would soon discover what happens when a person who is trying to be a good employee in a dangerous environment—more precisely, a war zone—must simultaneously develop a plan for self-preservation, both personal and professional, in an atmosphere where corruption seems to manifest itself with increasing frequency. I relied on my intuition and moral compass more and more, as they became the key to my survival, powered my inner core of resilience, courage, and self-reliance, as inculcated by my father in the deepest levels of my being.

Lost Containers in Kabul

Recall my previous description of business as usual. Global logistics or turnkey supply solutions comprised the core of TerraTota's business, and we operated essentially in conflict regions. All this is corporate speak for providing the supply-chain and site services to troops in war zones. And that means nothing is ever simple or hassle-free. Challenges and stress were part of each and every day, but I had expected as much, was prepared for it, and handled it competently (if I may say so).

After I had been in the theater for almost three months, we were on the lookout for a few containers that we had been expecting. One of these containers held valuable stock—namely beer, wine, and spirits—and all the containers were to travel through Karachi (Pakistan), across the border, and into Afghanistan. As usual, there were delays in the transport, but this was not cause for concern. Our containers were often delayed because of increased fighting at the border, which resulted in ISAF closing the borders until the troops had brought the insurgents under control.

This particular time, however, things were a little unusual. According to our logistics department, the containers had arrived in the yard and been recorded, but then they had mysteriously been driven out again. To add to the mystery, this departure had taken place in the middle of the night, and no one seemed to know where the containers were now. The container of greatest concern was filled with assorted spirits and wines, and the market value was likely as much as four times greater than the value on the local Afghan black market. To lose this whole container would have a serious impact on our business, as our supply chain had recently experienced major delays with the processing of exemption certificates (customs documentation allowing the containers to travel from Pakistan into Afghanistan). We normally expected it to take any container up to three months to arrive in Afghanistan. Anything quicker than this was considered a blessing! Thus, delays were par for the course. Vanishing, unaccounted-for containers were not.

It just so happened that I had contacted the yard manager earlier that day in order to follow up on our receivables only to learn that the yard had no confirmation of whether the containers had arrived. I found this a little unusual since we had already received reports from Dubai that our containers *had* arrived. This was either an instance of incompetence, or we had some potentially misplaced (as in *stolen*) containers on our hands.

Finally, the yard manager, who happened to be a local Afghan, admitted to me that he had no idea where our containers had gone. According to his information, which had been rather slow and hardly forthcoming, the containers had arrived two days prior and sat in the yard for hours, and then the same driver had driven them out again several hours after that. Of course, the driver was another local Afghan, and no doubt he was aware of the exact contents of our premier container. Things were beginning to look incredibly suspicious. Containers, one loaded with alcohol, arrive together and then leave together for no apparent reason—all while under the watchful eye of our security company and in the middle of the night. Alarm bells immediately started ringing!

The next day we decided to investigate what had happened to our lost containers. The whole thing was extremely strange and suspect, and it was looking more and more like a case of corruption on the inside. Corruption was almost expected in a supply-chain venue, especially in a war-torn country like Afghanistan and most especially with local Afghans involved. Nevertheless, I was totally shocked, and yet I was also determined to locate the containers with the help of our security company and retrieve the key container with all its goods intact.

The first step was to call a meeting with the transport company representative and the owner. I soon discovered that the driver had already returned to Pakistan for his next pickup, but no one could explain what had happened to the vehicle and the load he had been carrying. Where were they? After I asked many questions and got nowhere, I eventually decided that I was going to have to spell out the action I was prepared to take if we did not find our containers—and with all their contents intact.

"You have three choices," I told the transport company. "One, tell us where we can find the containers and their contents. Two, pay us $250,000 in damages, or three, spend the next several years in an Afghan prison."

I was serious, and they knew it. Perhaps I'd also gotten the attention of both my boss and the investigator as they watched me speak to the owner of the transport company and one of his managers. (Kurtis had come to Afghanistan from Dubai to assist in resolving the problem.)

My plan worked. Ten minutes later the two men sat in front of me and two former police officers, scratching the tops of their heads while sweat poured from their brows. Finally, they admitted that they knew the exact location of the containers.

"I witnessed our driver leave the compound with your containers," the transport company manager said hastily, explaining that the driver then took our containers to an area just outside Kabul.

"We were afraid to take action ourselves, as the other people involved were local Afghans and very well-connected," the owner added, the latter point a stipulation designed to prevent his bearing any culpability.

This confession was a major breakthrough, not to mention a tremendous relief. We now had a chance of locating our containers, and with any luck, the one container's goods would all be intact. I was overjoyed but would have to postpone celebrating my triumph. We couldn't waste even a moment.

Like a scene out of a police movie, we spent the next two hours driving through the backstreets of Kabul, following the men from the transport company who swore they knew the location of our containers. By the time we reached our final destination, we had traveled almost twenty miles, the majority of which we had driven in circles. This was normal. Afghans seemed too used to taking the long way around as a result of driving amid all the traffic and chaos that pervaded their environment.

In any event, we arrived just as it was getting dark. It appeared that we were in a semi-industrial area, and our containers were behind a huge wall secured by a guard's tower above and several padlocks on the gate. We now had a different challenge—how to get in undetected and how to get out with our goods! Fortunately, the guard had gone for his dinner, so now we had to make good use of our time in order to break in and find our containers, the most important one especially. We could see that there were several containers stored in the yard, so perhaps we weren't the only victims of theft. We had security personnel with us, all of whom happened to be ex-police well versed in the art of breaking and entering. The men from the transport company had already beaten a hasty retreat, so we were on our own.

After we broke in, we were in complete darkness. Our only light source was the illumination from the handheld torches we used to search the area for our lost containers. We had entered what appeared to be an old storage yard housing only three containers. The first container we broke into belonged to our company, but all it held was bottles of hand sanitizer (which we supplied to the troops). The second container we opened had what looked like approximately five hundred cases of beer along with a few bottles of spirits sitting just inside the entrance of the container. There was an immediate sigh of relief. Now we just had to open the last container, and we crossed our fingers that the rest of the stock would be there.

As we opened the last container we could see that apart from the five hundred or so cases that had been removed and placed in the second container, the rest of the stock appeared to be intact. It was an absolute miracle that the goods weren't already available on the local Afghan black market, much less not even unloaded.

Using only the lights from another vehicle, we spent the next two hours repacking the entire container. (Guards in such venues are rarely diligent, and Afghans do not set much store in doing things quickly, so meal breaks of this duration are typical. All of this was quite fortunate for us in this instance.) The pressure was on to get the container organized as quickly as possible—before the guard returned and/or the local Afghan police were alerted. There were about ten of us until extra reinforcements arrived. The guys on the ground formed a human chain, passing the cases to each other one by one in order to reload the container as quickly as possible. I'll never forget that night. It was about nine o'clock, and we were almost finished. As I was the smallest, I had the task of repacking the top of the container, which had very little space and very little air. Days later I still had numerous bruises as a result of the experience.

Once I'd completed my task, we were ready to depart. As we were waiting out front to leave the yard, we noticed two unmarked black GMC vehicles. They drove up and down the road several times, passing us each time. They were obviously interested in our activities. Later on we drove past them when they appeared to be located in a guesthouse two blocks away. We had no idea who they were. The whole situation was somewhat eerie, but this was a sense perception with nothing to actually indicate that anything was amiss.

Our subcontractor arrived with his flatbed and crane to transport the two containers back to our warehouse. By the time we arrived at our own guesthouse, it was almost midnight. Retracing the way back to our accommodations was a bit like winding our way through a labyrinth, and the return trip alone took us almost an hour. We were all exhausted and still a little nervous about the two black vehicles that had been monitoring our movements.

But all's well that ends well! The gist of that saying proved its truth to me after that experience. I remember sleeping very well that night, relieved that we had found our lost containers somewhere in the backstreets of Kabul.

The Business of Export: Legitimate Enterprise or Deep, Dark Secret?

The longer I worked as GM, the more I realized how much of TerraTota's business depended upon alcohol. Operating a business that sold alcohol to expats in a country where that substance was illegal presented all kinds of challenges, specifically because it opened the door to on-selling, racketeering, and the black market. Even early on when I had no knowledge of the MTAs, I recognized the multiple dangers of this situation. For starters, it was impossible to police the whole distribution network, which caused me great concern. Kurtis downplayed all this, and because he was my boss, I didn't want to push the issue too hard. Besides, whenever I brought it up, he reminded me that I was not involved in export. This was true, of course, aside from my having to sign the documents. That remained in the back of my mind, always vaguely unsettling, but I had so many other things to handle and learn that I couldn't let it preoccupy me, especially during my first few months in theater.

Regardless of my isolation from the logistics of export operations, I did not agree with the procedures Kurtis had in place for alcohol sales. By that I mean our legitimate alcohol sales, the ones I'd known about prior to signing on as GM and the ones that were legal in terms of the MTAs (unknown to me at the time but discovered later on). Basically, his attitude was this: Once TerraTota sold alcohol to an authorized person, what happened to the goods thereafter was neither our problem nor our responsibility. This never sat right with me, *legal* or not. We sold the hottest item in a war zone (other than fuel), and that entailed a certain level of responsibility in my opinion. Kurtis disagreed, and I quickly discerned that it would be in my best interest to keep my thoughts on the matter to myself.

The alcohol side of the business was a huge moneymaker, from which all the complications related to it arose. Authorized expat customers were allowed to purchase alcohol in large quantities. The rate of consumption was impressive, leading to the cash-cow status of our alcohol enterprise. To say that our alcohol business was booming would be a gross understatement. It was so lucrative that it would often boost sales by 50 percent, making it a key contributor to a healthy bottom line. Sometimes an entire container of spirits would sell out in two days, while a container of beer could easily sell out in four. Consequently, our supply chain often struggled to keep up with our customers' demands for alcohol, particularly the call for hard liquor. This was why the business of selling alcohol became a full-time business separate from our normal operations.

This full-time, separate business had a darker side, one filled with secrets. This was, of course, what I have referred to throughout as export, the enterprise that my predecessor had supposedly engineered and then been fired for because of his corrupt dealings. The same export that I myself had to sign the documents for, creating a paper trail and likely allowing me to become a scapegoat just as the GM before me had.

But all that is what I came to realize. During my first few months in Afghanistan export was a shadowy realm that very few people even knew about. It was a deep, dark, dangerous secret that had been carefully guarded and still was at that point. Even I knew very little about it then, my required signing of the documents notwithstanding.

"No Questions Asked"

It would be many months before I actually pieced together the truth behind the secret of export. What I had managed to learn within the first few months of my tenure was that export now consisted of only one customer referred to cryptically as 110 (pronounced "one-ten"). This code name had been designed to protect his identity. It worked. I had no clue about who he might be. All I did know for sure was that he had been given exclusive access to our warehouse on a monthly basis. All the rest of the details were closely guarded, which told me that a "no questions asked" policy applied. Acknowledging that, I proceeded accordingly. I knew that if I was to discover anything, I would have to carefully chip away until all the facts revealed themselves.

Chipping away was easier said than done, and it took far longer than I had anticipated. His identity would remain a mystery for several months, but I did manage to glean some essential information. Firstly, I learned that he was Afghan-born and in his early thirties. Soon after that I discovered that he had his fingers in several pies, which included selling alcohol on the black market. Kurtis did tell me that supplying 110 was a long-standing arrangement, and we actually owed 110 a large amount of stock that he had paid for in advance. Kurtis never did tell me the exact amount of stock we owed 110; however, he did emphasize that he would handle the associated inventory control. I mentally recorded all the information I gathered about 110 while I simultaneously chipped away to discover the rest, as I sensed that it would assist me immeasurably in illuminating the shadowy depths of export as a whole. I had yet to learn what 110 stood for, but I did wonder why they had chosen it and not some other number. It seemed both random and strange.

I continued along with my day-to-day duties, which included signing the documents. Where any sales to 110 were concerned, I usually received the paperwork a week or two after the stock left the warehouse. I remained in the dark as to when he arranged to pick up his goods. I didn't allow myself to become bent out of shape over this, hoping that I would eventually learn more either through my own chipping away and subtle investigating or once Kurtis came to trust me. Failing either of those, as I became more involved in our warehouse operations, I reasoned that Kurtis would either provide me with all the details or I would discover them on my own once I had full access to all the data. Regardless of which way things played out, I knew I had to appear nonchalant about all of it. I would never get anywhere close to all the facts—or the truth—if I made my curiosity obvious.

I remained low-key but vigilantly aware for several months after our warehouse move. Once a month a blue folder would arrive on my desk for an approval signature. This folder contained a document detailing the stock that had been collected by 110. Also about once a month a truck would turn up in our warehouse to collect a thousand cases of Heineken. Kurtis would coordinate with the warehouse and 110 via text message, and this would ensure that the delivery was ready for dispatch.

Following the strict controls established by Kurtis and adhering to the "no questions asked" policy that I had intuited, I pretended to ignore what was going on, and in doing so, I also conveniently forgot to sign the documents. I was able to do this for some time because no one actually looked for the signed documents. They were simply a paper trail to account for inventory if needed down the road. In addition, I had an extremely hectic schedule and was always traveling and rarely in my office. At that point, as far as I knew, neither Kurtis nor anyone had asked to see the signed documents. By this time, even though I was no closer to uncovering the truth, I had started to feel powerless as a result of this part of the business, and my concerns had begun to deepen. I feared that someday I could find myself in serious trouble with the Afghan authorities—not to mention the higher-ups at TerraTota—if this practice was not authorized.

The first time I felt serious concerns about export actually occurred not long after Lloyd, a senior manager from another part of our organization, had questioned me over our unusual spirits business. I had no way of knowing who I could trust, and

I feared that whatever I said could be used against me, so I chose to keep quiet until I had some solid facts to back me up and also until I knew who I could count on to be on my side. Nevertheless, this senior manager's comments rattled me, as *unusual* would not apply to any enterprise approved by company management.

As time went on, those words became more of a wake-up call to what was really going on. But the fear that information might fall into the wrong hands kept me from discussing my situation with anyone. After all, if I discussed my theory with the wrong person, it might not merely be detrimental to my career but even my very life! Afghanistan is a dangerous place, and its black market is even more so.

Thus, although I continued to appear nonchalant and calm on the surface, deep down I was extremely worried. The more I discovered and the more I thought about my situation, the more I worried. The restless, sleepless nights soon followed. My predicament was constantly in the back of my mind, moving front and center at a brisk pace. The wake-up call that had been soft at first was getting louder with each passing day. My moral compass was spinning, and my intuition was working overtime. Only my resilience kept me going. I had no intention of fulfilling the role of scapegoat, and so I dug in deep, willing myself to stay focused and strong and promising myself it would all turn out okay in the end. If ever I needed my self-reliance, this was the time, and I knew it wouldn't fail me, thanks to my dad's training. That would serve me well indeed.

The General's Visit

I tried to keep the wake-up call in the back of my mind, but this proved a fruitless endeavor. The more I tried not to think about it, the more it popped into my consciousness, unbidden, demanding my attention. In addition, things far beyond my control continued to crop up, all of them signaling that I needed to find a way to address my concerns quickly—or at least as quickly as I could.

The general's visit was what can only be called a red flag, especially in hindsight. It had started out to be just a routine visit by ISAF, much like ranking executives touring an outlying site so they can deliver an operational report when they return to corporate headquarters. General Scott, a high-ranking military representative with ISAF, was interested in learning more about TerraTota's warehousing operations across our business as a whole.

Kurtis sent me an e-mail about the general's upcoming visit. "We'd like you to provide the general with a basic overview of our business unit's operations, per his request."

I groaned inwardly while I read the corporate-speak that didn't tell me much of anything. And then just as his e-mail signature block came into my line of vision, Kurtis phoned me.

"You received my e-mail about the general's visit?" Kurtis asked in his typical brusque fashion.

"Yes, it just came through," I replied.

"You're on board then," he said, but it wasn't phrased as a question.

"Of course," I said, striving to seem my usual compliant self, always the company woman, but rapid-fire warnings were going off internally. The wake-up call seemed to be telling my intuition that zero hour was approaching far more quickly than I wanted to acknowledge.

"Great, MJ," Kurtis said. "I knew I could count on you."

"Anything in particular you'd like me to show the general, Kurtis?"

"No, just a basic vanilla tour," he replied, and then he paused. "It's more what you're *not* to show him that interests me." His tone on the last part was exactly the same as the one he'd used when he told me that I was out of the operational loop with export, that all I had to do was "sign the documents."

"Do go on," I said, all brisk efficiency. "I'll be sure to bypass whatever you wish."

"I'm certain you will, MJ. That's why I've chosen *you* to give the tour."

"That's grand, Kurtis. Thank you."

"Don't show him the alcohol," Kurtis said with his customary abruptness. His tone was innocuous enough, but it had an undercurrent that was leaden, almost threatening.

I felt my stomach churn and immediately do a somersault, but I told myself I was likely imagining it all. There was nothing even vaguely menacing about my boss. I would accomplish nothing by overreacting to a simple statement. More likely than not, my imagination was working overtime. Perhaps it was nothing more than our senior management not wanting ISAF to feel that we considered alcohol so significant. Maybe my so-called wake-up call was nothing more than a reflection of that.

These thoughts rushed through my mind within mere seconds, and I quickly recovered myself. "Whatever you wish, Kurtis. But then we can only show the general half of our operations."

"Precisely."

"All right. I'll take care of it."

We said our good-byes, and then we each hung up.

My mind raced. No time to think about wake-up calls or anything else. I had to use all my mental powers to craft a solution to this problem. Half of our warehouse contained the alcohol stock that was our premier moneymaker. The difficulty with this was that in order to do what Kurtis wanted, my staff and I somehow had to devise a plan, a reasonable explanation for why we could only show the general half of our warehouse operations. Most important of all, we had to be careful not to raise any suspicions—least of all the general's.

I assembled the key members of our team. After we put our heads together, we reached a consensus on the most ideal solution. We would place a sign on the door of the second chamber in the warehouse (the one housing the alcohol) that would read, "No Entry—Under Construction." The product of our brainstorming was quite ingenious, as no one would find it in any way suspicious. After all, military personnel were used to seeing signage displaying rules and regulations all the time.

We set everything up accordingly and well in advance of the scheduled date of the visit. The general arrived along with Lloyd, who served as liaison between TerraTota management and ISAF headquarters. As planned, I served as tour guide of our site.

The general was a friendly man, and he was very interested in understanding our operations. As I led him around our facility, giving him the planned tour of half the warehouse, he made a rather interesting comment to me in front of Lloyd.

"On several occasions the Afghan government has made numerous accusations that your company sells and supplies alcohol on the black market," General Scott stated matter-of-factly.

In that instant I froze.

Lloyd dismissed this without missing a beat. "Such claims are unfounded, General. They might have been an issue in the past, but all that was resolved some time ago. ISAF has nothing to worry about."

I was in shock, to say the least. Words cannot adequately express just how deeply shocked I was. It was my understanding that export was a deep, dark, closely guarded secret. After all, customers went by enigmatic code names like 110, which only reinforced the cloak-and-dagger aspect all the more. Now I wondered whether it was really such a big secret… or any sort of secret at all. The general's comment certainly indicated that based on accusations made by the Afghan government, the military had their suspicions. And mere suspicions were the least of it. This could be the beginning of things getting a lot worse.

These thoughts filled my mind, but I forced myself to push them back until I could consider them calmly and in solitude. In the meantime I swallowed hard, afraid that I might actually choke on my response if I spoke too soon. I made it seem that I was just giving my superior the time and space to answer, according a level of respect that the general, as a military man, would appreciate. Again I silently thanked my father for all he'd done to prepare me for this increasingly challenging dilemma, in which I found myself ever more deeply immersed.

While Lloyd continued speaking, I struggled to formulate a response I could use if required to give an answer myself. I couldn't possibly give the general a direct and honest answer. In the first place I was still in the process of gathering and sifting through all the facts. I still didn't know whether the black market sales and supply had derived from specific individuals up and down the ranks of TerraTota or whether it was the fruit of corruption that was on a scale far larger—which meant that it might stem from something sinister and too powerful to control.

All that I did know was that whatever was going on was a blatant conflict of interest.

Now I knew that the wake-up call was real and all my intuitive promptings were right on target. The time of pushing them aside had past, no matter what reasons for continuing to do so might arise. I had to find a way to act, and soon. There was no other option.

I stood there, letting the conversation between the two men float around me so that I absorbed enough of it peripherally to follow the thread, but my mind worked feverishly. I couldn't help but feel some sort of guilt—the guilt of innocence, of naïveté, of ignoring the potential dangers entailed by being part of something I had no control over. Yes, I had recognized the danger and the wrongdoing, but I hadn't done anything about it. And even though I had reasoned away my concerns—convincing myself that I had more pressing obligations and might even be overreacting—in my gut, I had known it was wrong. I had known, too, that I could easily be implicated, "guilty by association," as they say. Finally, I decided it would be better to let my superior handle it all. If I said anything to the general, he would know I was hiding something. Just as my father had always known. Perhaps military men were just made that way. Discerning the truth was part of their training, a survival skill no different from knowing when to take cover and when to fire at will.

The more I thought about it all, the worse I felt. The guilt overwhelmed me.

Eventually, the conversation ended, and my superior signaled me to proceed with the tour. I never did find out whether the general really suspected anything. I often wondered if he might have sought my response as an indication of the truth. But I'll never know.

Fortunately, my many dealings with all facets of the military had allowed me to practice my diplomacy throughout what remained of the general's visit. I saw to it that he left our facility feeling utterly charmed. My staff and I often marveled at how easy it was to be a female civilian in this war-torn environment. The military men would often let down their guard, making special concessions to women. Female company was something that most males in the military clearly appreciated. It was amazing how a little application of lipstick and soft feminine dress would result in receiving their undivided attention. To be honest, it was actually quite flattering to be in the minority receiving pleasant attention from the majority. What woman wouldn't enjoy and thrive on that kind of special treatment?

That said, I of course didn't flirt with the general or do anything even remotely untoward. I simply allowed him to feel he had earned the undivided attention of a civilian Western woman who respected his military achievements. It was a great relief that this enabled me to bypass scrutiny related to the issue of alcohol, but I promised myself that I was going to heed my own instinctive warnings and prompts to action. I no longer had a choice.

After Lloyd and General Scott left our facility, their visit continued to play out in my mind. Constantly, in fact. I couldn't stop thinking about it, and I couldn't help but ask myself the same question. Were we supplying the entire Afghan black market? If we were, who was responsible for it on our end? Regardless of what my predecessor's level of involvement had been, he was no longer here, and yet export was still a booming business.

It didn't make sense. I still needed answers and data and facts, and then maybe I'd be able to solve the mystery. I'd managed to assemble some of the pieces; however, export was a jigsaw puzzle, and I had a long way to go before all the pieces fit together.

A few days after the visit Lloyd sent a report detailing the general's tour of our facility. This report provided me with a few more clues, as it highlighted the general's comments about our supply of alcohol to the Afghan public, as well as the reassurance he had given the general that this issue had long been resolved.

That might be all well and good on the surface, and I had no reason to distrust Lloyd; however, the report made me realize that for the sake of my conscience and peace of mind I had to clarify exactly who was at fault, who was responsible, and who was trying to cover it all up.

I couldn't avoid it any longer. I had to uncover the full truth—and let the chips fall where they may.

Police District 9

While I was formulating my "uncovering the truth" plan, I still had a lot of work to do as GM on a daily basis. I had not lost sight of the tremendous responsibility I bore, and I still felt keenly that doing my job to the best of my ability would serve me well regardless of what the truth proved to be. No matter how many angles I examined the situation from, I always reached the same conclusion. If I'd been earmarked a scapegoat, I'd be the one left blowing in the breeze once the truth was out. The best I could do for myself was to have an unimpeachable performance record. As that was within my control while finding and revealing the truth was not, I continued to focus on delivering top-notch work. All the while I convinced myself that the means to doing what I had to do would present itself it to me. Perhaps I was simply trying too hard to find an answer. Sometimes we have to just stand still and let the answer find us.

One day not that long after the visit of the ISAF general, my team and I had quite a hectic day. We had already visited several military camps when my cell phone went off.

"Sorry to bother you, Boss, but it's urgent." It was my operations manager.

"All right, Sean. Bad news first."

"One of our delivery trucks was stopped at a police checkpoint."

"On J'bad Road again?"

"Yes," Sean confirmed. "On its way to one of the embassies."

"I see," I said. "It's all bad news then, I suppose."

"Worse," Sean said, and the details he provided verified it was so.

The police had arrested the driver and taken him and the truck to the infamous Police District 9. This had become a regular occurrence of late—truck intercepted and driver and vehicle apprehended usually along the notorious J'bad Road, my favorite Afghan thoroughfare. This was the second such incident in that week alone.

"Thanks, Sean. I'll head over to District 9 now."

We said good-bye and ended the call.

I instructed my driver, Hasib, to go to Police District 9.

During the drive over I considered the situation. My team and I had a sneaking suspicion that someone was leaking information about our delivery schedule and its contents to the local Afghan police. The police at that particular checkpoint along J'bad Road were renowned for being corrupt. They were always looking for ways to increase their income by means of bribery (*baksheesh*, as the local Afghans called it). The average Afghan policeman earned US$140 per month, so bribery was seen as an efficient means to generating extra income. Here again was an instance of what I described earlier as "reversed morality." Westerners found this behavior unconscionable, but the Afghans considered it normal and necessary. I strove to maintain neutrality here in order to achieve my primary goal in the moment, which was to get the police to release our driver along with our truck and its contents.

Once we arrived at the entrance to Police District 9, it was clear that this particular incident had been carefully orchestrated. The police seemed to be expecting us, and it was as if the orchestrator of the entire incident had given them clear instructions to use delaying tactics until he (or she) arrived.

The police station entrance was typical of any Afghan government building. There was an old gate surrounded by Hesco barriers designed to guard against any damage from suicide attacks. Inside the gate was a beautifully manicured old garden that led to the main building. Only the garden was unexpected, a place of sanctuary and beauty inside a fortress governed by corruption and deception.

As we drove up to the main building, there were two shabbily dressed Afghan guards awaiting our arrival. I had our driver, Hasib, come with me. Hasib addressed the guards, and they responded. At the time Hasib spoke few words of English, but he knew enough to inform me that the police district commander was in an important meeting at the MoI and would come to meet us in thirty minutes. In Afghan time this could mean three hours.

Thirty minutes later I had Hasib ask the guards how much longer the commander would be. The two guards smiled in response to Hasib's question. One of them raised his hands in front of me, saying, "*Inshallah!*" Such a comment was more intended to indicate that the delay was beyond their control than to actually invoke Allah's help. The guards were in no hurry, as it appeared they had nothing better to do. No doubt we were part of their amusement for the afternoon. Perhaps our visit was intended to amuse the police commander as well.

I decided I was not going to wait any longer for resolution to our situation, but I needed more translation assistance than Hasib's English skills could provide. Perhaps our company interpreter, an Afghan by the name of Kareem, could help. Kareem had worked in our company for several years, spoke excellent English, and had a lot of experience dealing with corrupt police. I contacted my assistant, Nicholas, and he assured me that he would send Kareem over immediately.

I tried to wait patiently, but my frustration continued to intensify. Our delivery truck was clearly visible, parked right next to the side of the police building. I walked over to check it out. Thankfully, the truck had not been tampered with, and all the padlocks were secured and still intact. I asked Hasib to find out what they had done with Aazar, the driver of our truck. After he queried the guards, Hasib informed me that Aazar had been placed in a locked cell underneath the building along with the other prisoners in police custody.

This information turned my frustration into indignation. We had been waiting for the police commander for almost two and half hours by that time, and poor Aazar had been without water in the sweltering heat of an underground prison for almost four hours. All my carefully crafted plans of neutrality, diplomacy, and the like evaporated in the wake of my mounting anger as a result of such egregious violations of human rights—basic care and concern for a fellow human being's suffering. Just as I was about to explode, Kareem thankfully arrived.

With Kareem's assistance, I informed the guards that I was from ISAF and that an ISAF convoy was on the way to assist with the release of our truck and driver. The guards looked first at me and then at Kareem, but they didn't appear to be interested or worried in the slightest. At one point I even pretended to call ISAF on my cell phone in order to let the guards think that if they didn't meet our requests, the military would enter their compound. This time they appeared to take some notice. Little did they know that I was in fact on the phone with my warehouse manager, Tucker, who played along with the charade. I asked Kareem to explain to the guards one more time what would happen if they didn't meet our request.

Within two minutes of Kareem's explanation, following the guards' overhearing my latest pretend phone call with ISAF, the apparently more senior of the two guards made a call on his phone. After a brief conversation he turned to Kareem and said a few words to him. Kareem informed me that the guard had assured him that the commander was only a short distance away.

We had now been at Police District 9 for almost four hours. It was hard to believe that our wait would soon be over. But indeed it was.

Moments later a four-wheel-drive vehicle escorted by one vehicle in front and another behind drove up to the main building. The police commander at long last had arrived. Glancing toward us very briefly, he moved past us and entered the building. We soon followed, escorted by the two armed guards who had been our courteous hosts throughout our nearly four-hour stay.

I took a deep breath, reminding myself that sarcasm wouldn't serve me any better than rage. My goal was to get Aazar, our truck, and its contents safely released, and then to return to our compound.

I looked at Kareem, and he nodded.

We moved through the so-called police station, following the commander. The building itself was derelict and appeared to be the remnants of an old school. The armed guards flanked us the entire way to the commander's office. Apparently, the commander was a target with insurgents, and so he took it upon himself to step up his personal security.

The commander's quarters resembled a living room, complete with sofas, television, and a coffee table. It hardly looked like an office at all, apart from his desk, which he sat behind as we entered the room.

The commander stood up, first shaking hands and speaking to Kareem, who in turn introduced us. We all smiled, nodded, and shook hands. As the commander spoke very little English, the entire exchange was relayed through Kareem.

The next twenty-plus minutes involved Kareem's account of the incident and attempt to achieve a resolution to it. As Kareem spoke, the commander kept looking at me as if trying to acknowledge what Kareem was saying to him. He then began to tell Kareem that he had information about our supplying the local Afghan market with alcohol. I replied directly to the commander, telling him that his information was unfounded. Kareem translated rapidly. The commander responded quickly, asking his assistant to bring him something. Kareem continued translating.

The assistant returned a few minutes later carrying a bottle of vodka. Showing us the bottle of vodka, the commander started to explain that a minibus traveling along one of the main streets of Kabul had been stopped at a police checkpoint. Upon searching the vehicle, the police discovered several cases of vodka. Consequently, the driver was arrested, and the vodka was confiscated.

Although the bottle looked identical to our stock, it was difficult to say that it had *originated* from our stock. There were no serial numbers for identification, and there were other sources it might have come from. I pointed all this out, and Kareem translated.

The commander, on the other hand, was convinced that it was our vodka. He was quite vehement actually. In addition, he invited us to have a drink with him. Raising his eyebrows and smiling to himself, he began pouring himself a generous shot of vodka into a large glass containing pineapple juice. He signaled his assistant to go get more glasses.

Kareem, Hasib, and I just sat there, stunned. It was truly an amazing sight to witness.

The commander finished the first glass within two minutes of pouring the drink, and then he immediately began to pour another. His assistant returned to the room, carrying a tray of glasses filled with pineapple juice.

Seeing the worried look on my face, Kareem asked the commander what was in our drinks.

The commander laughed. "Please taste it, and you'll find out!" he answered. "You people made the rules, and now we can't stop drinking!" he added snidely.

Kareem translated all this, of course, but I could see for myself that the commander already appeared to be a little drunk.

Fortunately, Hasib was happy to sample the drink in order to prevent me from making a fool of myself—or worse, to implicate me in any form of bribery. I think the commander had realized that he was dealing with someone who was not about to be easily led astray, and so he acted accordingly. He appeared to be quite proud of himself, in fact, and through Kareem he informed me that he had been waiting to meet the person responsible for the alcohol, the person who could help supply both the MoI and him personally.

As Kareem relayed everything verbatim, the commander's ulterior motive became obvious. However, I was simply not up for negotiating with him or his colleagues. Supplying alcohol to either party would have serious consequences on both TerraTota's business as a whole and my job specifically.

The commander turned directly to me and said in Dari, "The MoI and I want to buy alcohol." He said this after he took another gulp of his concoction of vodka with pineapple juice.

Immediately trying to downplay his request following Kareem's quick translation, I pretended to interpret his request as a joke. "Shame on you, Commander!" I said with deliberate lightness. "What will Allah think if I give you alcohol?"

Once he understood what I had said after Kareem translated, he laughed at my response, as he could see what my intentions were. But then he repeated the very same request, informing us that if we supplied him and the MoI, we would have no more problems with our delivery truck or driver.

I had to be very careful and diplomatic, as we were now dealing with an Afghan police commander. Through Kareem I made it clear to the commander that as I was still new to my role, and so this was something I could not decide on my own. I would have to consult with my superiors.

He laughed again, perhaps thinking that maybe he was asking the wrong person to play ball with him. Definitely unaccustomed to discussing business with a woman, he'd appeared a bit uneasy from the start. This was clearly evident in his body language, and I used this to my advantage. As a commander, I found him to be rather shy. An innocuous smile from a woman seemed to knock him completely off balance, with more than a little assistance from the vodka, to be sure.

By this time, Kareem had started to become a little impatient with the commander, who was clearly getting drunker as we sat and watched. It was now late on a Thursday afternoon, and that was when most Afghans started their weekend. Looking at his watch, Kareem turned to the commander, saying, "It's 6:30, and I have to go to a party tonight. Can we go now please?"

It was obvious that the commander had lost his chance of negotiating any deal with us, and he was now very drunk.

He responded to Kareem by waving his hands in the direction of the door. "*Burra bukhi!*" he said, indicating that we were free to go on our way.

Whether it was a stroke of luck or the simple fact that the commander had forgotten his original motive after he had had too many shots of vodka, we would never know. Regardless, we were relieved to be out of there and to reclaim Aazar, our truck, and all its contents intact.

Several days later, we learned that our friend the commander had gotten himself into serious trouble with a high-ranking Afghan official because of a long-running dispute between the two of them. This landed him in an Afghan prison. Quite ironic actually.

The other twist to this saga was that we never again experienced any issues with our delivery truck where Police District 9 was concerned.

The positive outcome of this entire episode shored up my confidence, and I told myself that the time for truth-telling had come. I'd escaped a run-in with the commander by the skin of my teeth, but I might not be so lucky the next time. I couldn't trade on being new forever, and everyone might not so keenly appreciate my smile or blue eyes. Perhaps the solution was not how I would uncover and expose the truth but rather who I could trust to help me. Finding reliable allies was essential, and so determining who among my colleagues was trustworthy and reliable might just prove to be my most effective next step.

5

IT'S NOT JUST BUSINESS, IT'S PERSONAL

My internal struggle with the dilemma of the truth about export continued. I knew that time was not on my side. I had to act decisively and quickly, but I still felt so alone in it all. My intuition grew ever keener and my resilience continued to deepen, and I knew I could count on them both. My self-reliance had never been stronger. Nevertheless, I still needed a friend or friends I could trust. Camaraderie and loyalty are essential in a theater of war for military and civilians alike.

From this point on, I knew without a doubt that personal resilience, true friendships, and trustworthy relationships were the most valuable things I would ever find in Afghanistan. My recognition of this led me to understand that the situation I'd found myself embroiled in "was not just business but was personal," reversing the traditional phrasing of the popular expression.

I had come to understand just what happens when a hardworking, dedicated employee must choose between doing the job right and doing the right thing. I was between a rock and a hard place because of the ever-deepening moral dilemma entailed by export. As I said, I knew I had to act in order to avoid becoming the scapegoat, but my responsibilities as GM weighed heavily on my conscience. If I chose my professional obligation over my conscience, I knew I would live to regret it, probably for the rest of my life. If I chose my conscience over my job, I didn't know what would happen. Certainly I'd lose my job, but I didn't know what additional repercussions might ensue, professional and otherwise. Was uncovering the truth and exposing the corruption worth ruining my career? Beyond that, was it worth my life? The dangers in Afghanistan were legion, and I still didn't know who the true mastermind of export actually was.

Eventually, after much inward pondering and debate, I decided that I would reach no clearer conclusion than that it was necessary for me to trust my intuition, remain resilient and brave, and find one or even a few trustworthy friends to support me in my efforts. I couldn't go on with things the way they were. Sometimes that is our best and even our only motivation. The only way out of this situation was the way through it. I had to face it with valor and fortitude, relying on my moral compass, which would never let me lose my way. This is what we all must do in such extreme circumstances if we are to survive physically, psychologically, and emotionally. In short, my moral compass, intuition, resilience, and self-reliance saved me.

Accordingly, I escalated my mission of determining just which individuals I could trust from among the people I knew in theater. This was not an easy task because of all that was at stake professionally and personally. I was not being unduly dramatic in recognizing that revealing too much to the wrong person(s) could easily put my very life in danger. As a result, even though I knew I couldn't waste time in discovering the truth, I also knew that I had to take the time to cultivate trust and loyalty carefully. They would be worthless if they weren't genuine.

I eventually found friends to trust and rely on, and that took developing and nurturing of mutual trust and camaraderie on their part and mine. Trust and friendship in the Afghan theater are not things to give or take lightly. I learned that lesson well. Above all, I came to recognize that no matter how resilient and self-reliant we may be, no matter how strong and keen our intuition becomes, we each need someone to count on and be supported by. Quite simply, I couldn't have done what I did without my friends. They were my colleagues and companions on an unimaginable journey. But I'm getting ahead of the story again. (The next chapter will focus on the building of these friendships.)

All-Too-Fragile Peace, All-Too-Frequent Suicide Bombings

Concurrent with resolving my ongoing dilemma was the day-to-day challenge of survival in the war-torn land of Afghanistan. Looking back, I can't really say exactly how I managed two stressors of such extreme significance. The more I trusted my intuition, the more it deepened. The more I relied on my resilience, the more it grew. Simply put, I just did it. I didn't have a choice. It's amazing how keen and strong our survival skills and instincts are when we have to use them every day. This is a source of amazement to most of us in the Western world, but to people living elsewhere—the majority of the world's population—this is a self-evident fact accepted without question. Doing what is necessary to survive is automatic. Some grapple with their conscience and moral compass afterward; others don't. Perhaps it varies from one instance to another even where the same individual is concerned. When in extreme circumstances, we have to do what we need to do in order to survive. This doesn't mean that we eschew or ignore our consciences or our values; it means we use them to get ourselves through the situation, knowing that survival comes first. Morality and philosophy are vast topics, of course, and they are filled with gray areas. I would not dream of attempting to even scratch the surface of either one, much less claim to have all the answers or purport that I never made mistakes or fell short of my own expectations. I have made mistakes. I have fallen short. I am still learning. This is true of every human being everywhere. It's why we're here.

What being in Afghanistan taught me in regard to my conscience is that it is pointless to judge the behavior of others. We usually judge others because of what we choose to avoid or ignore in ourselves. For example, the longer I stayed in Afghanistan, the more it seemed to me that those who bribed government officials in order to help their own families were acting in a way that I could condone in light of the circumstances, whereas those who accepted said bribes seemed somehow reprehensible. Why? Did immersion in a morally ambiguous environment permit me or anyone else to bend/break rules? Or did it merely impact my judgment and assessment of right and wrong? This internal struggle tormented me, and in a way the daily fight to survive kept me from sinking into the despair that such forms of deep thinking often bring about. Perhaps the clearest answer is that as long as we see the difference between right and wrong and question what seems amiss, we know our conscience is intact and our moral compass is working just fine. It's when we feel nothing or don't care or stop questioning that we are truly lost, that we have fallen into the abyss—evil, immorality, or whatever word we use to describe it. So I did what I could to remain strong and brave, and I let my inner compass continue to guide me. The moral dilemma engendered by export continued, of course, but more often than not, the frighteningly ordinary moments of life in Afghanistan simply took precedence over it.

I was committed to doing the right thing, but above all I had to survive.

And survival was not an automatic accomplishment in Afghanistan. It was a place where it was impossible not to appreciate the fragility of life, the miracle of each day. Horror and beauty were so frequently juxtaposed in this landscape scarred by war on top of its naturally stark features and harsh climate. I remember the soft sounds of birds calling me to wakefulness on many a morning. One morning in particular the birdsong awoke me quite early. I can still recall the moment with vivid clarity. At the time I thought about how peaceful Afghanistan could be even amid all the challenges of a war-torn environment. It was as if the day was about to start fresh and the birds were announcing that peace was possible. Perhaps that was just the way nature wanted it to be.

My peaceful, optimistic thoughts were soon to be overturned. Within a few seconds of their passing through my mind, I felt a strange movement of the bed where I still lay under the covers. Alarmed, I bolted upright, swung my legs over the edge of the bed, and felt a tremor vibrate through the floor beneath my feet. It was unlike any other earth tremor I had ever experienced. I soon learned that such tremors were an automatic response to explosions. The earth absorbed the force of impact and then reacted to it. These scientific explanations aside, and even before I'd been schooled to understand them, it was an awful moment. The innocence of the day had been destroyed by the so-called sacrificial act of a suicide bomber. Nicholas's and my close call with the would-be suicide bomber had been chilling, but this was far worse. I hadn't seen it or been in imminent danger, but I'd felt the reverberations. Worse still, as I soon learned, this bomber had carried out his mission successfully.

Posing as a member of the Afghan National Army (ANA), the bomber had stepped onto a crowded bus, self-detonating his vest, which held about ninety pounds of explosives. This senseless act tragically ended twenty-seven innocent lives—men, women, and children starting out to begin their day, on their way to work and school. All innocent. Whatever that actually meant in Afghanistan. Certainly the bombers had no comprehension of or interest in the word. I never understood how these suicide bombers fulfilled their missions. I never will.

The following day, by sheer coincidence we drove past the area where the bus had exploded. The aftermath of the horror endured. All that was left were the remnants of a burnt-out bus severely mangled on impact. Beneath it was a crater in the ground.

There was nothing more that could be said or done. Neither words nor actions could do anything, and most of us were too numb to even cry. The bird of prey had already fulfilled his violent purpose, in stark contrast to the actual birds that had sung so sweetly moments before his fiery shriek of rage.

Not long after the destruction of the bus, similar incidents occurred along the notorious J'bad Road. On one particular morning our security company informed us that there was to be no travel, as all the roads had been blocked by the Afghan military. They had anticipated a series of insurgent attacks, having received several intelligence reports indicating that there were at least ten suicide bombers driving around the streets of Kabul. This was not unusual, and it was simply a matter of waiting until the military police intercepted and captured them… or until they found their target and self-detonated. Tragically, the latter was the result too often, although the ANA did the best they could. A single successful suicide bombing is one too many. Numerous checkpoints were set up along the main arteries of transit, including J'bad Road. The ANA searched all vehicles, often finding explosives contained within them and thus ultimately sparing another life. The suicide bombers would often travel across the Pakistan border on a journey of no return. Hence, Pakistani plates on the vehicle were often a dead giveaway.

That day, confined to our compound, there was very little we could do except wait.

At around 11:15 a.m. we learned that a suicide bomber had finally exploded along J'bad Road. Despite the numerous checkpoints, he had managed to avoid being intercepted. He made a beeline for his target, an ISAF convoy, self-detonating on impact.

Hasib, who was with us in the compound because the roads were closed, had heard the explosion. He called his brother-in-law, Basheer, to find out where the explosion had occurred. None of us were surprised to learn that the infamous J'bad Road was the site of another act of senseless violence. I wondered how many casualties had resulted from the sacrifice of yet another extremist.

Immediately thereafter a hailstorm ensued, lasting at least ten minutes and unleashing tremendous hailstones. Was God above crying tears grown hard in the face of so much horror and grief, or was it an intentional cleansing of the earth following such heinous violence?

Fortunately, every suicide bombing did not succeed (including my own near miss thankfully). I learned of another would-be attack that had a much happier ending. A suicide bomber had wired his vehicle with explosives, and he went about posing as a taxi driver in a yellow and white Corolla. After he drove around for several hours, his vehicle failed to explode—miraculously—so he and his passengers were spared. The unsuccessful bomber told one of his passengers that he had survived by a sheer miracle. This passenger was so relieved to hear how lucky he had been to survive such a brush with death that he visited an Afghan bakery the very next day, purchased their entire inventory of bread, and spent the rest of the day giving away loaves of bread to the public. I thought of this as "pay it forward" Afghan-style! Such moments, though rare, inspired me to remain in theater, doing the work I had originally set out to do and fighting the wrongs that I found myself caught up in by no fault of my own.

Destiny and the Serena Hotel

Extreme stress and fatigue were part of my new normal, the routine of business as usual in Afghanistan. I had adjusted to this the best I could, but I don't think anyone can ever really *adjust* to such circumstances in the same sense that we do in our ordinary lives. War-zone normalcy is what leads to post-traumatic stress disorder (PTSD) and all sorts of challenging and unpleasant symptoms and syndromes. It isn't normal to always be waiting for the other shoe to drop, but when that becomes what we have accept as normal, we learn to adapt because adapting enables us to survive. So perhaps I should say that I had *adapted.*

Part of the way that I adapted was to just keep going—one foot in front of the other, one day after another. Perpetual motion is of great assistance in adapting. It works like a charm. Nevertheless, after long hours day after day, innumerable sleepless nights, and many months without taking a day off, I finally reached the point where I needed to take a well-earned rest. I had actually relished the idea of taking a day off, as I sorely missed my once-daily regimen of spending a couple of hours working out at the gym. Once in Afghanistan, the best I could manage was a few hours every week or two. It was extremely difficult to even carve out those measly hours. I did my best to do whatever amount of exercise I could, though, because I found it extremely important as a stress release, a balance between my dedication to my work and my commitment to my health and well-being. These few precious hours were only possible because Sean and I stumbled across a gym located in the Serena, one of Kabul's most luxurious hotels.

"Let's check it out, Boss," Sean urged. "I'm sure it's fantastic!"

My operations manager was as much of a fitness enthusiast as I was, and he couldn't have been more right in his preassessment of the gym. Fantastic was the understatement of all time. Once within the grounds of the Serena, it felt like any part of the world other than Afghanistan. Complete with day spa and sauna, the gym had all the typical amenities of any other luxury hotel catering to a wealthy international clientele.

"Fantastic indeed," I said. I was hooked. The gym at the Serena Hotel became my oasis for a few hours every week or so.

After many months of nonstop work I had wanted to go Serena Hotel's gym for several days, particularly because I had started to feel lethargic, which I knew indicated that I was becoming unfit. Since I had arrived in Afghanistan, I had done a complete turnaround with my health regimen, and I knew that it was not a good choice in the long term.

Finally, I decided to put it off no longer. I'd earned a few hours off, and so I planned a visit to the gym. I arranged for Hasib to pick me up at around one o'clock in the afternoon, as I had some business to take care of first, and then I planned to go to the gym later on.

The business involved my female staff. I had promised to spruce up their staff uniforms, which required the services of a tailor. We'd already chosen the perfect blouse to provide as a sample, so we visited a renowned tailor inside an ISAF military camp to discuss colors and fabrics.

This turned out to be a grand bit of fun for all of us, a real girls' day out. It also made me realize that some of these ladies had not been outside the warehouse compound for several months, and they were delighted by the change of scenery and quite excited to be going on an outing with their boss. I was happy to see how much it meant to them, and I wasn't about to spoil the special occasion for one minute. An afternoon with the ladies on my staff would have to supplant my longed-for gym time, but I knew it would be worth it. I would find a way to make some time to go to the gym another day.

Aside from not wanting to put an end to their fun, I was also benefiting from the opportunity of getting to know them on a less formal basis. One of the challenges of working in a multinational organization was having to interact with people from all sorts of countries and disparate cultures—Filipinos, Nepalese, Indians, and Zimbabweans, to name but a few. Most of these women had very hard lives often filled with tragedy, and they viewed working in Afghanistan as a passport to a better life, a chance for a better future.

I decided it would be a great idea to take them out for lunch after we finished up at the tailor's. It would be a nice change from the usual food served at our dining facility in the compound.

"How would you girls like to have pizza for lunch?"

A chorus of glee arose in response to my offer, and I was glad to see the ladies so happy and excited as a result of such a simple gesture on my part.

We went to a pizzeria inside the ISAF camp for a late lunch.

The ladies and I had a wonderful time eating and talking, and this was perhaps the first time we had ever discussed anything other than business. It was like we had really connected as friends in addition to being fellow team members. Perhaps we had forged a bond close to that of family, which we all sorely missed when in the midst of a war zone and so far from our own homes.

My understanding of the reasons why they each had chosen to live and work in Afghanistan deepened as we talked that day. Life wasn't easy in any of their own countries, and most of them had many mouths to feed back home. It was a given for each of them that most of their salary would be sent back home, which underscored for me what a privileged upbringing I'd had and what a charmed life I'd led in comparison to theirs. I already knew this, of course, but hearing the personal details they shared made it clear in an altogether different way, a way that was undeniably all too real. Like me, they had chosen to come to Afghanistan for the opportunities that working there afforded; however, the opportunities were of excitement and adventure and entrepreneurism for me but were for ameliorating the unending exigencies of poverty and dire need for them. The reality of that brought me up short. It was imperative for them to endure life in this harsh land for as long as possible, all for the sake of the many mouths they had to feed back home. One of my employees had to support her entire family of five, which included providing two of them with schooling. I had been far removed from their situations, only vaguely aware of their life circumstances. This opportunity to connect with my staff on a deeper level was invaluable to me, and I was grateful for it.

After lunch we decided to take a leisurely walk around the rest of the military camp, visiting several stores and the local Afghan bazaar, a typical open-air market selling everything from handmade carpets to marble ornaments to copies of designer watches and more. (Such copies often looked like the real McCoy, but after a week or so in the harsh environment the effects of the wear and tear proved they were not premier timepieces.)

It began to grow dark outside by this time, and the issue of security and travel were my main concern now. No sooner had I mentioned to the girls that it was time for us to go back to our compound than I received a rather anxious phone call from my HR manager, Hannah, who was based in Kabul. She joined TerraTota after I did, and we subsequently developed a good friendship. Originally from the UK, she had lived in Australia for several years, which made us compatriots. (Although I had not yet determined that she was someone I could trust, I eventually discerned that she was, and our bond grew even stronger over time.)

As soon as I answered the phone, Hannah burst out, “Please tell me you’re not in that bloody gym!” I’ll never forget those initial words and the concern in her voice.

Not knowing what all the fuss was about, much less the reason for her concern, I explained, “I changed my mind at the last minute and decided not to go to the gym. I spent the afternoon with the ladies on my team instead.”

“Oh, thank God!” she breathed. The relief in her voice now was as clear as the concern had been when I answered the phone.

“What’s happened?” I asked, alarmed now myself.

She then began to tell me about what had happened just thirty minutes prior to her call. The Serena Hotel had become the latest target of a suicide bomber. Of course, I felt a bit of shock while I listened to her, as it was only by sheer luck and a last-minute change of heart that I had escaped that day’s tragedy. Suppressing an involuntary shudder, I counted my blessings for not being among the several casualties that had resulted from the attack. I had narrowly escaped this tragedy because of a choice of seemingly little significance made in a split second. And doing what I felt was the right thing with my staff had turned out to be even more valuable for me than for them, though I couldn’t have known that at the time I had made the choice. Yet again trusting my intuition saved the day… and my life.

Later on another source informed me that a suicide bomber dressed as a businessman and accompanied by two armed guards had apparently walked through the first security checkpoint of the hotel and then, upon entering the compound, had self-detonated the vest that held the explosives, taking out the hotel security guards at the entrance. The men posing as the guards of the businessman were actually Taliban, and they proceeded through the hotel along with other insurgents already inside and masquerading under different disguises. They used grenades and AK-47s to carry out their attack on the hotel, hitting as many international targets as possible. Apparently, hotel guests exiting elevators into the hotel lobby were also targeted as they innocently walked into the insurgent gunfire spraying bullets. My beloved, once-magnificent gym had turned out to be one of the main focal points of the insurgent attack. I later learned that a guy using the elliptical at the time of the attack had his iPod's earbuds in his ears and didn't hear the din outside the gym. His back was to the entrance, and the gunmen shot him from behind, putting a bullet in the back of his head.

Ironically, four nights after the Serena Hotel bombing, an Afghan business associate invited me to dinner. Coincidentally, he chose to take me to the very same hotel for their buffet dinner. The hotel itself was heavily guarded, and there was an eeriness pervading the atmosphere. Scaffolding had been erected alongside the exterior windows of the spa and gym area. Several side windows facing the main foyer and entryway had been peppered with bullets during the insurgent attack. The glass looked scarred. And yet somehow this visit to the Serena Hotel not only calmed me following my shock from the day of the attack, but it also helped me to move on, overcome my fears, and continue to survive because I knew that by trusting my intuition, which often means no more than honoring a split-second hunch or choice, I *would* survive.

The Fate of Aazar

"Every day we are going out, and we don't know if we're coming back alive."

How often had I heard Aazar, the driver of our delivery truck, say those words? I'd always considered them philosophical and wise in the way that those living in war-torn areas become philosophical and wise beyond their years. Now those words, which he himself accepted as a part of daily living and did not consider anywhere near as deeply as I did, will haunt me forever. For on one day pretty much like any other, Aazar was shot dead. He had been driving back from Poli Khomri on the way to Mazar-e-Sharif when the Taliban shot up his delivery truck. I was devastated. He had been working with us for more than a year by that time, and he had become a part of our team. Worst of all, he left behind a young wife and two children. He was only twenty-four years old.

When I received the news of his death, our interactions flashed through my mind. There was the incident in Police District 9 related in the previous chapter. He had been with me a few other times when I had to get our delivery truck released from the police as well. Perhaps I thought about these events now because it created the illusion that he was still here, still with us. Perhaps I just needed something to distract me. Either way, I let the memories flood me.

There was another exchange with the Afghan authorities that was every bit as memorable as the encounter with the commander of the infamous Police District 9 (please refer to chapter 4 for details). This other episode had also involved poor Aazar.

Even though I was removed from the logistics and procedures related to export, as GM, I was still responsible for TerraTota's alcohol stock in Afghanistan, which was why Kurtis required me to sign all the documents. This also meant that handling any other issues that arose relating to our alcohol stock fell under my purview as well. Consequently, dealing with local Afghan law enforcement was one of my primary responsibilities and a frequently recurring one at that. During part of 2008 I made the rounds of the Afghan police stations at least once a week.

On this particular occasion our delivery truck was detained at police headquarters along with Aazar. As usual, Hasib accompanied me on this visit, and because the police spoke no

English, Kareem came along as well to offer his skills as interpreter once again.

The police took us to where they had left the truck. It was still locked, and all our security seals were intact. Four armed policemen surrounded the vehicle, and they appeared to be rather relaxed. They had set up camp around the truck, complete with chairs and a television that they were watching. It was actually quite amusing to observe them. They were clearly bored with their task and were just following the orders of their superiors. Short attention spans were common among some of the Afghans, and we even had the same challenges with our own local Afghan staff.

Kareem asked them why they had decided to detain our truck, but they couldn't provide us with a straightforward answer. Through Kareem, I insisted on speaking with their head of command, demanding the immediate release of our truck and driver. (Once again, Aazar had been locked up in the prison cells underneath the police building.)

After about an hour of pleading we eventually met with their head of command, who was accompanied by several plainclothes detectives known as CID (Criminal Investigation Division). One of them spoke English.

"We are special police," he informed me. "We insist on your allowing us to open the truck to inspect its contents."

When I hesitated, he added, "We have been informed that there may be dangerous goods inside your vehicle, and we must investigate."

This was a total fabrication. They knew exactly what was inside our truck. They just wanted confirmation, and checking it themselves was the only way to get it.

We spent the next hour arguing, but then eventually agreed to allow them to open the truck with us present as witnesses. The detective who spoke English nodded his thanks but remained inside the office, instructing other officers to take us to our truck.

Once the police broke the seal and opened the truck, they would see exactly what was inside—cases of spirits! This was quickly becoming a very dangerous and volatile situation, but we'd really had no choice but to agree to a concession. They had no intention of just releasing the truck and its contents to us, much less Aazar. Whatever else happened, I was not leaving him to rot in an underground cell.

Hasib, Kareem, and I stood there behind the truck as the police commenced breaking the seal, surrounded by a dozen Afghan guards armed with AK-47s pointed in our direction. As I had my camera phone with me, I made the brave decision to take some shots of them entering the truck and checking the goods just in case we needed this later on as evidence. I made sure I got clear shots of each of them. This made them very nervous and agitated, and they asked Kareem what I was doing. They then proceeded to go through each pallet of goods, checking for what they continued to call dangerous items.

I instructed Kareem to tell them that they had better hurry up, as the goods belonged to a very important commander and we had to deliver them on time for a VIP event. (This was actually true. The client in question was one of the embassies. Consequently, the alcohol sale was not technically illegal because of the embassy's diplomatic status. The corruption of local law enforcement and governmental agencies is so pervasive in Afghanistan that what is legal and illegal is often extremely difficult to discern even when in possession of the appropriate documents because individuals bend and break rules to suit their own needs and agendas. Therefore, the long and short of it is that what is legal and illegal is quite often flexible at best and capricious at worst.) I further told Kareem to inform the detectives that I was taking photos of them to give to ISAF to put on all their bulletin boards if we didn't get our truck and driver released.

They appeared to be rather concerned and a little nervous when Kareem told them this but simply laughed in response. After they inspected the goods, they allowed us to reseal the truck and then asked me to go back inside their office with them. Now things were getting a little more serious; however, I had no choice but to comply with their request, as we were on their soil and they had all the weapons. I wondered if we were about to join Aazar in an underground cell. They could have easily locked us up, as no one outside these walls would have a known a thing that had transpired.

I was asked to enter the office alone, take a seat, and wait.

The detective who spoke English entered the room, and I struck up a conversation with him.

He was pretty friendly but remarked, "You should not have taken photos of the police."

"The police had no right to take my truck and arrest my driver," I replied, keeping my voice firm and my tone agreeable. "This incident will be further investigated," I added, still speaking evenly but a little less pleasantly.

I then noticed that the suit he wore still had the label attached to the sleeve, Hugo Boss, but it was clearly a copy. "That's quite a nice suit," I told him. He smiled and nodded his thanks. And then I added, "But it isn't fashionable to wear the label on the sleeve." We both laughed. He only wore the label so people would think it was Hugo Boss, even though it wasn't.

A moment or two later he told me, "Another detective is preparing a special letter in Dari stipulating that you will delete the photos of any police. In return, we will release your truck and driver. All you have to do is sign the letter."

It sounded like a reasonable deal, so once the letter was ready for signing, I asked for my interpreter to come in to translate the letter. Kareem assured me that I wasn't signing my life away. The English-speaking detective handed me a pen, and I signed the document. I then began deleting the photos one by one while the police watched me.

Once they were satisfied that all the images had been deleted, they released Hasib, Kareem, Aazar, and me along with the truck and its contents. We then made our way out of police headquarters as quickly and as calmly as we could.

I later realized that what I had done was crazy, but it was all I could think of at the time to get our goods back and our driver safely released. Miraculously, we came out of it unscathed and alive.

I was lucky, and so were those with me at the time. As Hasib had told me early on, "Boss, the day of our death is already written." Tragically, Aazar's luck ran out the day that he and his truck encountered Taliban gunfire. Or perhaps that was simply the day that his death was written. Nevertheless, for the short time he walked this earth, he made it a better place, even while in the midst of all the chaos and terror of war-torn Afghanistan.

The Incident at the Indian Embassy

After several months as TerraTota's GM in Afghanistan, I was summoned to attend my first official meeting in Dubai. It was also the first time I would leave Afghanistan since my arrival. I was torn between feelings of excitement and melancholy, having now become conditioned to living in this land of turmoil and to surviving in its harsh environment.

Nevertheless, I looked forward to my trip to Dubai, which, among other things, would offer me an opportunity to scout for new recruits. Many staff were unable to endure the conditions in theater for more than a year, and after they completed the twelve months agreed to in their employment contracts, they often never returned. We joked that their so-called first vacations became permanent. Those who had no choice but to return because of financial commitments were often subjected to paying bribes to their own customs' officials, as their home governments had officially banned them from living and working in Afghanistan. I called them "the soldiers of fortune." But they were not exactly the same as the mercenaries of yore. It was as if their families had sent them off to war to seek their fortune because the rest of the family back home depended on their financial support. It was the behavior of those from traditional cultures that had captured my attention, and such individuals earned nothing less than my unqualified support and admiration. Their resilience and adaptation to the environment was formidable. (All this certainly applied to my multinational female staff, as described earlier in this chapter.)

However, my headcount certainly suffered attrition as a result of the twelve-month curse, and I needed to fill the staff ranks. As I said, Dubai was the ideal venue for seeking new hires. Having decided to embark on my first recruitment exercise, I had also taken the initiative of preparing a fresh batch of business cards. These would have to be sourced locally, but that was not a problem. Finding a printer in Kabul was quite easy. The two main issues were quality and price. Fortunately, I was able to rely on Hasib's ability to source a network of contacts that we could visit in order to negotiate the supply. Hasib's talents and contacts seemed to know no bounds, and I relied on him tremendously.

When the cards were ready for pickup, I decided to go get them because I wanted to ensure that they were exactly what we had ordered. My assistant, Nicholas, accompanied me. Hasib drove, of course, and would be on hand for any translating needs, as such an exchange would not require Kareem's interpreting skills.

As we drove along, the streets that were so often chaotic and bustling with enterprise seemed unusually quiet for a Sunday. It actually appeared to be more like a Friday, the Muslim day of rest. As we approached the small group of shops where the printer was located, there was a designated parking area in the middle. At first glance, I could see that this complex was perhaps no more than two or three months old, and there were still a couple of vacant shops on the first level. By Kabul standards, this was quite a modern shopping complex! Hasib decided to park away from the rest of the cars, as was his usual practice. He always parked as close as possible to the shop we had to enter, which would also provide us with a quick exit strategy if need be. In this volatile environment, an emergency exit plan was a necessity, and Hasib was very experienced in this area. Yet another of his skills that I had come to rely on.

As an aside, I had recently learned that Hasib had worked as an assistant to the former President of Afghanistan, Dr. Najib,* until the leader's death at the hands of the Taliban.

Hasib had accompanied Dr. Najib everywhere, just as he did me. The position of driver entailed so much more than simply transportation. When I found out about Hasib's working for the late Dr. Najib, I imagined that the man had relied on him as much as I did. When I visited Hasib's home for dinner, he showed me an old black-and-white photo of him and Dr. Najib in Moscow.

---

* Dr. Mohammad Najibullah Ahmadzai (a.k.a. Najibullah or [Dr.] Najib) was President of Afghanistan from 1987 to 1992, when he was assassinated by the Taliban.

It was obvious how much loyalty and love Hasib still had for the man some thirty years after his death. I felt this keenly after he described having found Dr. Najib's body hanging from a rope after the Taliban had tortured him and left him to die. A tragic end for Dr. Najib and a horrific experience for Hasib, who had to release his fallen leader from the gallows of such a torturous demise.

"I am like Dr. Najib, Boss," Hasib had told me upon finishing the gruesome tale. "I am a Communist, and I believe in all people having the same."

I'd felt Hasib was sincere in his description of his beliefs at the time. He'd worked for Dr. Najib since the late 1970s. Whether thirty years of supporting a family while enduring constant exposure to hardship and corruption had persuaded him to change his beliefs and practices was something I had yet to determine. Perhaps I would never know for sure. Without having an in-depth conversation in Dari, I could not really confirm one way or the other. Besides, it wasn't really any of my business; however, in a theater of war, we have to know who we can trust, and knowing a person's true beliefs and ideals helps us build that trust. My ability to rely on Hasib was crucial, and I needed to rest assured that I could completely trust him. Often he was all that stood between me and certain danger, even death.

I kept this in the back of my mind more often than not, and these pressing issues were the source of many sleepless nights. But back to the visit to the printer. My mind was on the business cards and my upcoming trip to Dubai, not Hasib's political ideology. It seemed like a pretty ordinary day, which is never really the case in Afghanistan.

As we left the vehicle, I remember being overwhelmed by a very strange feeling. A sudden sense of awareness, and I could feel that something terrible was going to happen. My intuition was in high gear. This strange intuitive awareness overpowered my confidence and rational thought. I stopped in my tracks, telling my staff, "Something terrible is going to happen here!"

Nicholas looked alarmed, but Hasib just leveled his gaze on me. We moved toward the printer's quickly.

Such an alert was not uncommon in Afghanistan. Everyone's instincts were different, and we warned one another in this manner quite often. Acting on instinct, trusting it was the only way to survive in this environment. We all knew that. My months in theater had broadened my perspective, sharpened by senses, and honed my instincts and intuition. Letting my inner compass spin, I proceeded to conduct our business as quickly as possible, and my staff knew that my alert indicated this was my plan.

We entered the small shop, and Hasib asked to speak to the printer with whom he had placed the initial order. Fortunately, he spoke some English and started to explain that there was a problem with their machine. Consequently, our business cards were not ready. This did not explain why we'd received a call that they were ready, but this was Afghanistan!

For me, this was just another excuse among countless others we had previously received from Afghan suppliers. Nothing ever was completed on time. I soon learned to take the approach of holding them accountable for the original deadline, believing that relentless persistence would achieve my desired outcome. In that particular instance, I managed to persuade the printer to commit to providing the cards by six o'clock that evening, explaining that I had to have the business cards ready for my trip to Dubai the following morning. I then arranged for Nicholas and Hasib to return to the shop at six to pick up the cards.

The second batch of business cards, which were for my operations manager, Sean, would be ready for pickup after eight the following morning. Because I would be on the plane by this time and Hasib would be on his way back from the airport, I decided to have Nicholas have one of the other drivers take him to pick up the second batch of cards.

That night I barely slept. Sleepless nights had become far too routine, but in this case, it was simply nervousness at the prospect of being out of theater for the first time in months. Living in a war zone can feel a bit like living in an asylum, I suppose—not that I've been institutionalized. However, adapting to the normal of any extreme environment requires so much of our energy on a continual basis that we fear leaving it, not sure we will be able to readapt once we return.

Hasib picked me up at o'dark thirty (5:30 a.m. to be precise). It was still very dark all the way to the airport and even once we got there. I then had to face the convoluted process of airport security, which started at the entrance. The police had set up several checkpoints complete with an armored tank and several machine gun posts. As part of the Muslim culture, it was normal practice for all females to be individually body searched by a female security guard in a separate room. This part was actually quite easy, as more often than not the female security guards were Afghans and they were more interested in finding lipstick than anything else. On this occasion as the guard looked through my handbag, her eyes immediately lit up. Holding the lipstick out in front of me, she asked, "Gift for me?" This was a part of Afghan culture that I wanted to avoid as much as possible. It was the kind of custom which, once formed, would end up becoming a habit.

After almost an hour of constant checking, we travelers eventually made our way into the check-in area of the airport terminal. There was a certain sigh of relief after we completed the many checkpoints, and in the airport lounge several other expats waited to board the same flight I was on. The lounge was also crowded with the Afghan merchants and educated businessmen who frequented

Dubai. We eventually boarded our plane at around 8:30 a.m., which was almost on time by Afghan air traffic standards.

When I landed in Dubai, I soon learned of what had transpired at the same time as I had boarded my flight. Nicholas had been prepared to pick up the final batch of business cards from the printer. He was running a little late that morning, so he called one of the drivers to pick him up at around 8:45 to take him to the printer. (I already described Nicholas as middle-aged, balding, and paunchy. He was also habitually running late, a shortcoming I chided him for on more than one occasion.)

The driver said, "Impossible!" He further explained that the shop was *callas*. (Upon hearing this, I once again wondered if Nicholas felt that his decision to work in Afghanistan in order to avoid familial responsibilities was one that he ought to reconsider.)

Perhaps what had occurred was mere coincidence, but I don't think so. My awareness, intuition, third knowledge, premonition—or whatever description fits—proved to be on target. The sense of "something terrible is going to happen here" tragically became a reality. At approximately the same time I boarded my flight to Dubai, a suicide bomber drove his car into the entrance of the Indian Embassy, killing fifty-eight people and injuring more than a hundred innocent bystanders. Among those casualties were the people working in the shopping complex next door, the one where the printer we had visited the day before was located.

But for a few hours it could have been me; but for a few minutes it could have been Nicholas. Life is so fragile. Thank God our senses, instincts, and intuition all grow stronger in the harshest of places. Humans would have died out long before now if that were not the case. I am living proof of that.

6

THE TURNING POINT

I mentioned having been at a crossroad in my career prior to accepting the GM position with TerraTota. My excitement about the opportunities offered by a supply-chain career in the Afghan theater had not diminished, but my moral dilemma over export made doing my job increasingly more complicated. After being in Afghanistan for a little more than a year, I arrived at the turning point, the center of a different crossroad from which there would be no going back.

The preceding months in theater and all the events described up to this point worked to coalesce my observations, thoughts, and feelings. They sort of simmered on my mental back burner while I focused on the daily professional routine of being GM and the daily personal challenge of surviving in a war zone. But while in Kandahar working on a special project, all that simmering suddenly reached a rolling boil. But instead of allowing it all to boil over, I used the heat to supercharge my focus and clear away any detritus that wouldn't serve my purpose—rather like annealing metal in order to purify it.

None of this was easy. In fact, it was incredibly difficult. And I suppose much of it worked on a subconscious level, as intuition often does. In the same way that the simmer intensified to a boil seemingly all at once, I just found myself knowing that the time had come at last to do what I needed to and to do it without fear or dread or regret. When intuition kicks in and we trust it, this is just the way it works. And trust it I did. I fine-tuned my moral compass, intuition, and instincts even more than I already had done, and then I used this as my center, which kept me grounded, calm, and focused. This in turn further strengthened the resilience, courage, and fortitude that I had continually cultivated and that I required now more than ever. I'd never felt more self-reliant. But I also knew that I needed to find the support and mentorship I had already started to seek. I had done a lot to develop relationships with colleagues, as well as to deepen my ties with my team, and now I felt more confident about the people I could trust.

Remember that I said loyalty and trust are among the most valuable commodities in Afghanistan. I was about to discover just how valuable they actually were. (Please see previous chapter for description of both new and ongoing relationships cultivated with staff and colleagues, as well as details on the deepening of these bonds as this chapter unfolds.)

The Issues with Export Persist

The meeting I attended in Dubai was quite a productive one. Although I gathered no earth-shattering information that would help me unravel the mysterious cryptic knot of export, I did make some meaningful connections with colleagues (which I'll describe in detail later in this chapter and the next one), pursue some new-hire possibilities, and establish myself as a valuable player within the TerraTota organization. As a result of the latter, I received a plum opportunity—the KAF project.

At that time Kandahar Airfield (KAF) was still in the development phase, but it was to be one of the biggest and most important air bases in Afghanistan under the NATO banner. Extending our retail footprint into the KAF domain was a key corporate objective for TerraTota and had been for some time. We already had catering contracts on the base, and my objective was to establish new business. Consequently, I was in Kandahar on a regular basis, often spending several days at a time there. (Just to give a brief geography lesson, Afghanistan is made up of thirty-four provinces. Kandahar, which also houses the city of Kandahar, is in the south near Pakistan. Kabul, which houses Kabul City, the nation's capital, known simply as Kabul in the West, is in the east. Please refer to the glossary for more information on both cities.)

I was eager to be part of the KAF project that was so critical to TerraTota. Just as I had done from the beginning as GM—just as I did in every job I ever had—I threw myself into the work, body and soul. It was only after doing so for some time that I experienced the revelations described in the opening of this chapter. In the meantime my adventures in the southern part of the Afghan theater were just beginning.

For now, back to logistics and practicalities. Extending TerraTota's business footprint was not an easy task. As is usually the case on any military base, a company must first acquire military sponsorship from a nation in order to justify its presence on the military compound. I had already established close ties with Captain Lenard, the French military commander in Kabul, and he had given me a point of contact to meet at KAF in Kandahar. It was a long shot, as military sponsorship would have to be approved by military headquarters in France. Nevertheless, it was worth my best effort. Morale and welfare played a large role in business in terms of providing support to ISAF and associated personnel. Negative public opinion continued to intensify, and most of the Western world strongly opposed ISAF troops being stationed in Afghanistan. As a result, any services provided for the troops and support personnel offered an opportunity to boost morale.

Boosted morale would in turn increase profitability in the eyes of TerraTota's senior leadership.

I had therefore come up with what I considered an innovative idea. My proposal was to present a French PX/bakery concept specifically tailored toward meeting the needs of the French Air Force and other military personnel based in KAF. TerraTota had tried for three years to develop our business in this region without success. Consequently, that success was now among my top priorities. As I'd done when moving our warehouse just several weeks into my stint as GM, I rolled up my sleeves and got to work.

Unlike some of the other military camps, KAF was designated as a dry camp, meaning alcohol was completely off limits. One of the main reasons for this was its geographic location in the southern part of Afghanistan, commonly known as Taliban country. (Kandahar was actually the capital city during Taliban rule. See glossary.) Understandably, KAF and all of Kandahar were referred to as a hot spot. For this reason, we would often experience rocket attacks, which meant that all personnel (both civilian and military) had to be on alert 24-7. (This was virtually the case for everyone everywhere in Afghanistan, but in Kandahar, close as it was to Pakistan, it was even more so. I'd never been so alert or vigilant in my entire life. My internal compass never stopped spinning, and my instincts and intuition were needle sharp at all times.)

As soon as the sirens sounded, we would hear the voice-over from the Joint Defense Operations Center (JDOC) repeat, "Rocket attack, rocket attack!" This meant all personnel had to take cover immediately. We had to lie facedown on the ground, with our hands covering our heads, and then make our way to the nearest bunker as quickly as possible. (Such situations were all too regular in Kandahar but not at all so in the Kabul province, where I had grown accustomed to living.) I can still recall one evening in September 2008. We had a total of thirteen incoming rockets, one after the other. It felt like we had spent most of the night in the dusty bunker, and there were about fifty of us huddled together in the dark. Through the slits in the walls, we watched the skies constantly lit by rocket flares. We could hear the inimitable hum of the rotors as helicopters patrolled the perimeter. In the distance was what looked like a shiny speck, probably a drone searching for the source of the rockets. Rockets would land randomly, and they were often mechanized to launch by the use of an Afghan clock and blocks of ice that would eventually melt, thereby launching the rocket. The Taliban used this method to avoid being detected by the drones that constantly monitored the area for any insurgent activity. This meant that the Taliban were already miles away by the time the rockets were launched.

Rocket launches were frequent, but work—and life—still went on. I focused on the project at hand, keeping the big picture of our business in mind, as was my responsibility as GM. But my time away from our compound in Kabul resulted in developments beyond my control.

Specifically, my spending periods of time in Kandahar also provided several windows of opportunity for alcohol to move out of our warehouse in Kabul. Notably, such alcohol was always earmarked for export purposes. This export business would happen randomly once or twice a month. A regular order of a thousand cases of Heineken would leave the warehouse in the truck belonging to the mysterious 110. (See chapter 4 for details on 110.) The day, date, and time were all secret, of course, closely guarded by Kurtis from his office in Dubai. He would text the warehouse a few days prior, informing the staff to prepare the black-pallet-wrapped cases of beer. He then texted the orders of the dispatch mere hours before the desired delivery time. A thousand cases of Heineken had a cost value of US$10,000 and a retail value of US$30,000. Even more surprising was the local Afghan market value, which would sometimes fetch as much as US$50 to US$60 a case (that is, twenty-four cans of beer). Demand was always greater than supply, and because we regularly received Heineken by the container load and in full swing of being sold, Kurtis had apparently made an agreement to supply 110 with a thousand cases every month.

I was not immediately aware of the intensifying export issues back in Kabul. It wasn't until I returned from spending a few days at KAF in Kandahar that I learned that another shipment had been dispatched, as the paperwork had been placed on my desk for signature of approval. This particular time, TJ, my warehouse dispatch coordinator, had left a whole pile of unsigned paperwork dating back several months. I think he was trying to protect me as much as I was trying to protect him and all of my staff. So far I had managed to dodge this paperwork, citing my hectic work schedule as the main reason for the oversight of administrivia. In reality, my oversight had been purely intentional, as I've already described. I was in the process of shoring up my allies in order to expose the truth behind export, and I simultaneously sought to gather as much data to back up my claim as I possibly could.

As I went through the latest pile of paperwork, a document caught my eye—a dispatch order for 150 cases of whiskey. Actually, it more than just caught my eye. It opened both my eyes wide. The cost of this was far greater than a thousand cases of Heineken. (I was later informed that Kurtis had made a special once-off arrangement with 110 just prior to Christmas, as our export customer had been desperate for the stock. The stock had apparently moved quickly during my several days in Kandahar, and I couldn't help but feel that this move had been intentionally orchestrated in my absence—and even more significant, that perhaps a financial incentive had been the main motive on both sides. Kurtis had a penchant for expensive gadgets, as well as merchandise from exclusive brands like Rolex and Mont Blanc. He never went anywhere without his gold Rolex.)

I soon realized that this was not an isolated occurrence. Kurtis seemed more motivated to move the stock during my absence from Kabul. This realization occurred quite by accident. I had planned to fly to KAF but had then decided to cancel my plans at the last moment because I had begun to feel concerned that if I left at that particular time, too much alcohol might leave the warehouse, and I would be the one ultimately held accountable. Consequently, I had returned to my office from the airport only to discover that, as predicted, 110 had his truck conveniently parked in our warehouse ready to receive another dispatch of Heineken. By this point, my patience was paper-thin, and my nerves were shot. On top of months of pressure from my daily responsibilities as GM, the day-to-day stress of living in theater, and the increased danger of time spent in Kandahar, I'd had it. I was quite simply over having to worry about alcohol leaving our warehouse for export purposes in addition to all the other constant challenges I had to endure.

Call it the moment of truth or the straw that broke the camel's back—whatever it was, it had arrived, and I could ignore and deny it no longer. Sometimes such a moment comes as a shout. For me, it was more of a murmur, but it was a persistent and critical one. I heeded it and acted at its behest because it was significant, not because it was loud.

I became even more diligent in my observations, and I also began to increase my collection of evidence related to export. I quickly amassed a pile of dispatch notes that I carefully hid in a blue folder under my mattress. Soon I realized these items would not be sufficient. I needed more hard evidence. Recalling the episode with the police described in the previous chapter, I decided that some photos would be a valuable addition to my dossier. Quite likely they would even be essential. I didn't realize at the time that my shutterbug adventures in this instance would prove to be even braver than they had when I was dealing with the Afghan police!

Unaware of the risk and determined to expose the truth, I forged ahead, undaunted. Pretending to have a reason to visit an office inside our warehouse, I stood at the top of the office stairs and used the camera in my trusty cell phone to take a photo. The image clearly showed the black-pallet-wrapped Heineken sitting inside the truck belonging to 110. Just as I finished taking the photo, my project manager, Hodges, who had been having a meeting inside his office, came outside. Caught off guard, I panicked, nearly falling down the stairs. It was clearly a case of coincidence, and I never was entirely sure that he saw me take the photo. I might have been lucky enough not to be seen.

It was too late to worry about that now. I took a deep breath, willing myself past the panic. I had to keep my wits about me now more than ever. I knew now that I had to continue my investigation. I had to finish what I had started. I was frightened, but I remained calm now that I'd quashed my initial panic. My mind raced, and I let my inner compass take over. It was sort of a faithful autopilot.

I went outside beyond the office gate. Standing idle for a moment, I pretended to take a phone call, and then with the truck belonging to 110 and its driver in full view, I began taking photos of the truck, showing its license plates. It was highly possible that the driver had noticed what I was doing, and this could be an issue later on.

By this time I was calm and centered again. I knew I was doing the right thing. What I had to do. The first step is always the hardest, but not taking it when we know that we must is even harder. And then we must live with the regret… and the fallout forever. It's a bitter pill when we know we could have and should have done something but didn't because we gave in to fear. My resilience and self-reliance helped me stand tall, and my intuition and wisdom shone my way forward. I swore I felt my dad's hand on my shoulder and a whispered, "Well done, MJ." That was all I needed to know.

* * *

About an hour after that I received an unusual phone call from Kurtis in Dubai.

"Hello, MJ. Are you in Kabul or Kandahar?"

"I'm in Kabul," I said, calmly explaining that my military flight had been canceled. He could check this and find out that I had lied; however, I took my chances because I knew my boss, and he wouldn't take the time and trouble to investigate. On the other hand, if I said that I'd just decided to postpone my departure, it would immediately send up a red flag.

He immediately asked some routine business questions, which I answered, and then we said good-bye and ended the call.

I was in the middle of a task when I received his call, and then I was preoccupied with inventing a reason for not being in Kandahar, so I didn't initially focus on why he would be asking where I was. Once I put down the phone, however, the reason why he'd asked the question suddenly dawned on me. Actually, it hit me like a ton of bricks. I immediately felt my heart begin to beat rapidly, thundering in my chest as cold sweat started seeping out of seemingly every pore of my skin.

Kurtis had expected me to have left Kabul far earlier en route to KAF. His asking whether I was in Kabul or Kandahar meant that someone, possibly the driver of the truck belonging to 110, had in fact seen me take the photos. Kurtis was obviously trying to establish whether I was the one who'd taken the photos. The only other person the driver might have seen was Hodges, and he (the driver) would have been able to identify both Hodges and me. I was quite certain that no one but the driver could have seen me snap the pics. Thus, that same driver had to have been the one who notified Kurtis. It was now obvious to me that my boss was aware of my suspicions, and this in itself was a threat to him and his export business!

I had entered a very risky situation, and the bonds I had forged with my trusted staff members would become more important than ever. As I had surmised, they each sought to protect me as much as I sought to protect each of them. I'd cultivated trust, loyalty, and camaraderie because these were things I prized above all else in my fellow human beings. Now that value would prove to be not just precious but truly invaluable. As invaluable as our very lives, in truth. We didn't know how the situation would end or what all the ramifications might be. We only knew that we had to do what we were doing, and all we had to rely on was one another.

We took turns guarding the evidence. Each night a different one of us would sleep with all the documentation under our mattress. Shortly after the photo incident I went to a printer in the city of Kabul to make copies of all the documents. I needed these as proof, and so I decided to keep rotating the copies under our respective mattresses and deposit the originals in a safe place until such time as I needed them. I was incredibly nervous while on this errand, concerned that someone might see me copying these documents. I hoped I had chosen a shop that was sufficiently discreet, and I ensured that I left no copies or originals behind just in case the Afghan in the shop decided to use the information for his own gain. All the notes clearly indicated that alcohol was involved, and TerraTota's name and corporate logo appeared clearly at the top of every document. In the wrong hands this could have been another serious issue.

After this episode I fully expected that every time I left Kabul for Kandahar, another thousand cases of Heineken would leave our warehouse. It was clear that Kurtis didn't want to run the risk of me or anyone else taking more pictures. Perhaps in essence he felt that the days of export were now numbered, and therefore, he had to maximize the windows of opportunity.

I was not happy to say the least, and I made my thoughts known to Hannah, my HR manager, who was my friend as well as my colleague, the fellow Aussie I described in the previous chapter as working in the city of Kabul and joining TerraTota shortly after I did. She had lived and worked in Dubai prior to that, so she understood the challenges facing civilian Western women working in the Middle East and the Afghan theater. Over the past several months, our friendship had continued to strengthen. She proved a great support, which was vital in an environment such as this. I relied on my team, and I trusted them completely—even with my very life. However, it was crucial to have an ally to depend upon and trust and to seek advice from when necessary. There were things I could tell her that I couldn't and wouldn't burden my staff with. It was for me to give them advice as their boss, not the other way around.

As HR manager, she was used to letting people vent, to listening without judging, and to offering workable solutions. This was her job, and she was good at it—thankfully for all of us. It was vitally important to have an HR specialist in our ranks because most of our work was plagued with people issues. This was not just in terms of day-to-day office politics, which of course occur in every company everywhere. We had to deal with all this in the midst of a theater of war. Hannah was adept at handling this as well, and she interfaced with all of us, reporting as needed to headquarters in Dubai.

A conflict zone has many types of casualties, and working in such an environment, whether as a member of the military or as a civilian, often takes its toll on human behavior and psychological/emotional well-being. This is the prime reason why alcohol is the number-one vice in theater—escapism. Unfortunately, because of both the local altitude and the rate of consumption, alcohol readily exacerbated aggressive behavior, often leading to immediate termination of employment and repatriation. Sometimes no more than a day passed between an employee's termination and mandatory return to his or her home country.

Drama inevitably abounded during such incidents. In fact, I can still vividly recall an event of this type. I received a phone call at around one in the morning from another business unit's senior manager. (This was actually prior to Hannah's joining our team by the way. Had she been on board, I'm sure she would have handled the incident either on her own or together with me or another of the managers.)

As I struggled to awake fully, he informed me that a serious incident had taken place in one of our main compounds that housed employees. "Can you get over there right away?" he asked after he shared the details.

"I'll get there as quick as I can," I assured him.

At that point in time, I was still residing in the guesthouse located on the outskirts of the city of Kabul, which meant that I had to travel across town to attend to the incident. Given the late hour, I decided that dress code was not a top priority! Putting on my robe over my pajamas, I slipped my Ugg boots onto my feet and hurried to meet Hasib, whom I'd already contacted. I wasn't planning on meeting anyone official, so this attire had to suffice. Besides, my colleague had roused me from a deep sleep, and I was still only semiawake.

By the time I arrived at the site of where the incident had occurred, a bar located within our compound's environs, all I discovered was a large hole in a window, indicating that someone had possibly been thrown through the glass. The two people allegedly involved were both expat managers who will remain anonymous. They had apparently gotten into an altercation after they had copious amounts of alcohol. Fortunately, no one was seriously injured, and since no one wanted the matter to be further investigated, the whole incident was conveniently covered up. There was very little I could do except to ban all sales of spirits at the bar, moving forward.

The entire incident was like a scene out of an old cowboy movie. Once I'd resolved it as best as I could, I had Hasib drive me back to the guesthouse and pretty much thought that would be the end of it. Admittedly, all this occurred prior to my deepening concerns related to export. At the time it seemed an issue centered on a couple of expat managers who had too much to drink. Certainly they should have known better and behaved more responsibly, but as it occurred on our compound, it didn't seem to be a critical issue.

The truth was that our bar staff were trained to serve alcohol responsibly, but as they were either Filipino or Indian, commonly referred to as "TCNs" (third country nationals), they were often intimidated by the expat managers. In fact, some of these managers coerced the TCN bartenders into serving them beyond the officially set consumption limits, knowing the TCNs feared losing their jobs if the managers complained about them. (Expat managers' relationships with TCN employees would prove far more complicated than this, extending to actual violations of human rights, but I wouldn't discover this until much later, as events detailed in the final chapter will describe.)

In any case, the issue with alcohol consumption among employees, both expats and TCNs, did continue, but it was not something that I had to deal with on a regular basis. Months later during my first Christmas and New Year's Eve in Kabul, the entire situation escalated dramatically, resulting in the removal of all alcohol from our employee PX between Christmas and New Year's. In addition, all parties held over this period were to be alcohol-free.

Let me back up a bit to explain the reason for these drastic measures. Leading up to Christmas, other business units had hosted numerous parties. During one particular party several Nepalese employees had consumed far too much alcohol, resulting in a number of fights breaking out. As a result, several terminations and repatriations took place the following day. The alcohol-free dictum was therefore neither unfounded nor unreasonable.

I had been fairly blessed, as the majority of my team drank very little alcohol, so holding alcohol-free Christmas and New Year's Eve parties would not be an issue. It was to be our first Christmas and New Year's together, which held more significance for most of us than did getting drunk. Besides, most of us had large families back home and missed spending the holidays with our loved ones. We looked forward to spending quality time with our adopted family—the team we had built together.

My management team and I therefore worked hard to ensure that Christmas would be a day to remember. I managed to secure a special venue on the other side of Kabul, a rooftop restaurant situated in the Intercontinental Hotel. Most of our team had spent the past twelve months away from their families, and we knew that they would all feel homesick on Christmas Day. We organized a special buffet lunch, and one of our guys dressed up as Santa, giving out the presents we had wrapped and placed under our traditional Christmas tree. Accompanying our lunch was music performed by a band provided by the hotel. We listened to the music and danced along with our local Afghan staff. It was quite likely a first for our Afghan staff to celebrate Christmas, and it was definitely a first for most of us to sing and dance to Afghan music instead of the traditional "Jingle Bells"!

The panoramic view from the rooftop was incredible. A fresh snowfall painted the rugged landscape a pristine white, making Kabul look like a perfect Christmas postcard. For a few precious moments, it was hard to imagine that we were in the middle of a war-torn environment. The festive atmosphere, joyous mood, and beautiful view all combined to make it a most memorable and delightful day. The spirit of Christmas was alive and well, making alcohol quite unnecessary. Even our fight against the Taliban seemed far away, beyond the soft white carpet of snow that made the magic of Christmas seem real, even if only for a few precious moments.

From Heineken to Vodka

Unfortunately, other aspects of alcohol were not as handily resolved as mandatory alcohol-free Christmas and New Year's parties. Issues with export continued, seemingly with no end in sight.

My KAF project with the French Air Force was well underway. One morning while I was working in Kandahar, I received a phone call from Reed, one of our people responsible for cargo arrivals received via air bridge at Kabul Afghanistan International Airport (KAIA) on the NATO base side. Reed was a fellow Aussie, an excellent operator, and above all, a straight shooter. On a few occasions, we had helped each other out with operational situations, whereby we had developed a mutual respect.

Communications was often difficult down in Kandahar, especially cell phone service. The initial message I received from Reed was quite distorted because of this, and so at first I thought he was referring to a container we had been waiting to receive from across the Pakistan border. (As previously mentioned, containers were often held up at the border for several weeks, sometimes months, as a result of fighting and quelling insurgents. As a result, there was a frequent backlog of processing exemption certificates by customs. This often impacted our stock levels, and the presence of empty shelves in our PXs was quite common, as was the limited amount of items in our dining facilities.)

But back to Reed's call. It took three return calls for me to understand exactly what had happened. One of our cargo planes had flown a thousand cases of vodka into KAIA. Finally, some forty minutes later, I received a barrage of e-mails, complete with photos of the incident. Preparing incident reports was something that TerraTota staff were quite proactive about—both constructing the documentation and ensuring that the entire organization, including senior management of course, was copied in on the incident in question.

This situation was no different, and Reed had intended to give me a heads-up before everything hit the proverbial fan. Apart from the internal politics already fomenting, I now had a potentially critical situation to deal with, both politically and contractually. If handled incorrectly, this could have serious ramifications on our company as a whole, not to mention my position as GM and subsequent career.

As for the vodka, here is a summary of what transpired: Without any notification from our support team in HQ (Dubai), one of our cargo planes flew into KAIA, transporting a thousand cases of vodka. These cases were unwrapped, just sitting on a pallet in the wide open space of the military tarmac in Kabul's international airport in plain sight. Military personnel and civilians alike could clearly see these spirits and clearly see that they were property of TerraTota Suppliers. Apparently, our ground cargo staff, who were predominantly Afghans, had refused to move the cargo once it was unloaded by a forklift onto the airport tarmac. The vodka continued to sit on the tarmac, naked bottles of hard liquor on display in the capital of Afghanistan. This went on for almost two hours until the services of the cargo-handling company arrived to assist in loading the goods into one of our service trucks.

To be absolutely clear, alcohol, let alone spirits, was not permitted to be flown into Afghanistan without a letter of diplomatic cargo indicating special circumstances. Therefore, the vodka arriving in clear-wrapped plastic and sitting on the tarmac for hours was tantamount to a political assassination.

I counseled myself to remain calm. I needed to keep my wits sharp and my emotions controlled. My mind raced nonetheless. I forced myself to be still so my intuition could take over. More than ever, I needed to let my inner compass be what guided me. My career was surely at stake, and my very life might well be too.

* * *

A few hours later, I received a phone call from Kurtis.

"How soon can you be back in Kabul, MJ?" he asked. I could hear the stress in his voice, even from all the way in Dubai.

"I'm not due to leave Kandahar until tomorrow," I said coolly. He hadn't initially explained that he was calling because of the situation with the vodka exposed on the tarmac in Kabul.

"Well, get back to Kabul as soon as you can," he said. "You're going to have to appease the powers that be regarding the incident at KAIA."

His tone of voice and choice of words implied that he had no intention of taking responsibility for the vodka's flight to Kabul. I said nothing in reply.

"Someone's head will roll for this!" he informed me just before he ended the call.

I wasn't surprised really. I'd known that it was only a matter of time before the inevitable happened. The anticipation of it had caused me so much fear and worry and angst that the actual moment felt rather empty. I knew what I had to do, and I was almost relieved that the moment had finally come. I didn't have to worry about it anymore.

Even though I wasn't surprised, I was outraged. Kurtis's unwillingness to step up and be accountable made my blood boil despite my knowing that this was exactly what he would do. It was why my predecessor had been dismissed in ignominy. I let myself rail inwardly, knowing I had to let off steam in order to be cool-headed in the critical hours that followed. How could he expect anyone to believe that he would have no knowledge of the goods flying, given the fact that all air bridge cargo required his sign-off? The steam curled out of my ears, but needless to say, there was nothing I could do about his response. It was all outside my control.

The only thing that was within my control was my own response to the situation. My main objective now was to defuse the situation on the ground as quickly as possible. Damage control and fallout management were my immediate priorities, as my performance was more critical than ever before. I had to conduct myself with personal decorum and professional aplomb.

What I'd told Kurtis was true. I was scheduled to leave KAF the following day. By default, I had been booked on a commercial flight from Kandahar to Kabul. This proved to be a blessing. I used the time to coordinate what I needed to from Kandahar prior to my arrival back in Kabul. I contacted the operations manager of the subcontracting company who coordinated all ISAF cargo on the ground, letting him know that I would be back in Kabul the following day and wanted to meet with him. Fortunately, I knew him rather well. He was another fellow Aussie, down-to-earth, and a good sport. His name was Todd, and he had previously worked for TerraTota. I intuitively felt I could trust Todd. He wasn't out to score any points. As long as he could give his boss a report of the incident as part of their internal procedures, he had no other stake in the situation.

The following day I took the first commercial flight out of KAF. Miraculously, it left on time—and not on Afghan time! I had arranged to go directly from the airport to the logistics office to meet with Todd.

We both were typical Aussies, so neither of us much cared for small talk. The meeting would be straight to the point. While en route to Todd's office, I fine-tuned the gist of my dilemma. From a ground perspective, I was responsible for the vodka flying into Kabul, which meant that I was in a very precarious situation. I couldn't point any fingers, but on the other hand, I didn't want to be seen as the careless culprit. I therefore went into the meeting apologizing profusely for the complete botch-up!

"There's a complete investigation underway to ascertain why the vodka flew in the first place," I assured Todd, further explaining that perhaps it had been intended for one of our Bosnia flights, as we had contracts in Bosnia as well.

Todd looked at me, nodding but not saying anything. I wasn't sure he was completely sold on my explanation; however, I was fairly sure he could see from the fear in my eyes and the tone of my voice that I personally wasn't at fault. Moreover, he was accustomed to the politics often played in our organization based on his experiences during his own tenure there, and more likely than not, he put himself in my shoes. He did remark, "Mate, you could have at least wrapped the goods in black plastic!"

Of course I agreed with him, but I couldn't say as much. Keeping my gaze steady, I looked him straight in the eye. "That's why I believe that the cargo was meant to travel to Bosnia!" This was definitely a better tack for me to take, and it did explain the lack of care in wrapping. It was a thin explanation, but I prayed it would serve. "It must have been a complete mistake, Todd. In fact, I'm sure it was. Everyone knows you can't fly alcohol into Afghanistan, let alone spirits!" I pronounced, finishing my tale.

He gazed back at me, and I could see him connecting the dots in his mind.

I finished the meeting by assuring him that he would receive a complete report once the investigation had been completed.

We said our good-byes, and I left his office, heading back to our compound.

I felt I had pulled off the necessary damage control, and I was greatly relieved. Nevertheless, I was extremely pissed off with our support team in Dubai, particularly my boss, since they had been responsible for the cargo flying in the first place, and yet they were now busy playing "dodge the bullet" with the senior hierarchy. Of course, I kept this to myself.

All in all, the damage control succeeded. The only fallout was a verbal caution from senior management to our entire business unit in Kabul. I breathed a sigh of relief, but I knew I had to escalate my export disclosure, as I now trusted Kurtis less than ever.

* * *

Several weeks later, after a chain of e-mails traveled up and down the corporate ladder and the internal politics hit the fan as a result, an investigation was completed. One of our supply-chain managers was conveniently blamed and held responsible. It was just a political front, and fortunately, he only received a slap on the wrist via e-mail.

One mystery still remained, though. Why had the spirits been allowed to fly into Afghanistan in the first place, and why had no precautionary measures been taken to transport the goods in a sealed tri-wall and wrapped in black plastic? Instead, the goods had been carelessly loaded onto the cargo plane, which would later be unloaded and left in clear view on a runway shared by both military and civilian personnel in a Muslim country where alcohol was prohibited. It made no sense.

I had made sure to keep Donna, our HR senior manager in Dubai, informed at every stage while the incident unfolded. Following Hannah's advice, I had already shared my concerns about export with Donna (Hannah's superior), and this incident was far too important for me not to keep her apprised. Besides, I somehow knew that this whole blunder had something to do with 110, our export customer. There could be no other reason to run the risk of flying alcohol into Afghanistan, as to supply our normal customers, a thousand cases would have been sold in a day. I therefore believed this cargo was intended for some special purpose.

Donna documented the incident, reassuring me as she had when I initially told her about export and my concerns related to it and the documents Kurtis required me to sign. "MJ, don't worry. If anything should happen, I've got your back."

The Election Campaign Incident

Afghanistan was a zone of drama as much as it was a zone of conflict. Intrigue was a way of life there, imbued into the culture since ancient times. All this went on regardless of prevailing contemporary events and regardless of the presence of military forces from other nations or coalitions. As a result, there was a lot going on in theater separate from the war, let alone my own worries regarding export!

This of course included politics. There had been a lot of speculation up to the time of the election as to who would be nominated as the next Afghan president. Public opinion was mixed, and many Afghans wanted to see their country return to normalcy—that is, without the presence of ISAF troops. Many of them felt that Karzai was just another puppet controlled by the United States, someone who, together with his cronies, was busy pocketing the proceeds of foreign aid instead of developing the country, which was rapidly deteriorating as a result of many years of turmoil. As the election drew closer, one particular contender stood a good chance of beating Karzai. His name was Abdullah Abdullah, and he appeared to be very well-educated, a doctor by profession, and his popularity continued to increase through the support of some of the local Afghan media. About six weeks prior to the election we had already been placed into lockdown mode because of increased threats from insurgents in the area, which translated to an increase in suicide attacks. We expected even more trouble in the days leading up to the election, as this was all part of the political propaganda masterminded by the Taliban.

This meant that most personnel were confined to our accommodation compound, with the option of working on their laptops from their rooms. On one particular day I chose to abandon telecommuting and to work out of my office, as our warehouse was only five minutes by car on the same road as our accommodation. Besides, I had to check on the warehouse, which held a large quantity of alcohol, as I did not want to have another explosive situation so close on the heels of the KAIA vodka incident. It was also necessary for me to go to my office because the Internet connection in our accommodation was unbelievably slow, and I knew that I would have at least two hundred e-mails requiring my attention. It was business as usual for our support team in Dubai, which meant that e-mail traffic would be normal despite their awareness of our lockdown conditions.

I gave Hasib the day off, as it would be futile for him to spend all day sitting in his vehicle while we remained in lockdown. I managed the short drive from our accommodation to the warehouse on my own.

A short while after I arrived at the office, he called me. "I have something important to tell you, Boss," he said.

"Of course, Hasib. Do you want to talk tomorrow?"

"No, Boss, I should come see you now," he insisted. His tone was urgent, which was rather unlike him.

"All right, if you like," I said.

We ended the call. His urgency both puzzled and concerned me, but I decided to wait to see what he had to say. Worrying about it ahead of time would accomplish nothing, and I'd come to learn that there was always ample time to worry once all the facts were assembled. I thought of this as informed concern, a far more purposeful approach. In this particular instance I told myself that Hasib was always excellent when it came to providing key information, especially items featured by local media, which, unless we had local contacts, we rarely learned about, as expats were deliberately kept out of the loop.

I didn't have long to wonder about the source of Hasib's concern. He arrived soon after we'd ended our call, entering my office and explaining in a rush that there had been some sort of an issue involving helicopters. As a result, certain flights had been grounded. "This could cause us trouble, Boss," he said, finishing his report.

I agreed that this certainly could have an impact on our operations. "Thank you for coming to tell me this, Hasib," I said.

"Of course, Boss," Hasib said with a nod and a half smile. He knew that I appreciated this piece of information just as I always valued all the tidbits he shared with me.

"Is there more to the story?" I asked. Judging from his facial expression, there had to be more.

"Yes, Boss."

Actually, there was a lot more. The situation was actually much worse than it had first appeared. It seemed that the day before there had been an incident potentially involving a helicopter owned by TerraTota, and this was now all over the Afghan media. Apparently, this helicopter, which was filled with propaganda materials, had flown over the entire area of Kabul, dropping thousands of flyers endorsing Abdullah Abdullah as the next Afghan president. This had occurred after one of the Afghan generals, with whom our aviation department regularly liaised, had obtained permission "as a favor" to use the helicopters for special purposes. This general was an avid supporter of Abdullah Abdullah, and like most of the Afghan military and police force, he hoped that a new president might increase the salaries of members of the military and law enforcement.

Needless to say, this general's initiative had far-reaching consequences, as many of the flyers also landed in the presidential palace, completely covering the grounds and setting off the intruder alarms. After his security alerted him, President Karzai came outside to see what was falling from the sky and littering his grounds. He was fairly pissed, to put it mildly, upon discovering the helicopter-deposited Abdullah Abdullah propaganda strewn all over the property of his own residence. This was not unwarranted really. Besides, Karzai was renowned for the occasional outburst of rage, and this incident had certainly hit a tender nerve. Apparently, he was observed screaming obscenities from his office, demanding to know who was responsible.

"He kept asking, 'Who owns the helicopter?' He wanted all the details, Boss, and said action was to be taken immediately," Hasib summarized.

I thanked Hasib again for the valuable information, and we concluded our conversation.

Over the days that followed, more details came to light. Ironically the person who had given the Afghan general approval to use the helicopter had not asked the general what purpose he intended to use the helicopter for. This was clearly a key question, as the subsequent events proved. Consequently, the helicopter was grounded. The Russian crew was arrested, and their passports were confiscated.

This blunder was considered a great insult to Karzai. If proof of TerraTota's involvement manifested, this incident would likely have serious ramifications on our company's future. In essence, there were two possible scenarios. If Abdullah Abdullah won the election, we would become heroes overnight. If Karzai won reelection, we could easily become part of a conflict of interest! Only time would tell.

Meanwhile, the election was almost at hand. Elections were very trying times. Many Afghans, including women, were voting for the first time, and despite the normal threats of intimidation carried out by the Taliban, thousands still voted. Even in some of the most remote regions, people exercised their right to be heard, and donkeys were used to carry boxes containing thousands of votes from these hinterlands to the city. The efforts made touched my heart, as we in the West so easily take our freedom and rights for granted. People in Afghanistan risked their lives by voting, and yet they did it anyway. Exercising certain rights is more important than living in some ways. I suppose only those who have been oppressed can truly appreciate the gift of freedom.

Voting certainly entailed all kinds of dangers. While a donkey carrying one of the voting boxes went along a mountain trail, it accidentally stepped on an IED. This was the end of the poor beast, of course, as well as the votes. Thousands of such hard-won symbols of freedom literally disappeared into thin air. Even worse were reports of the Taliban cutting off the fingers of some who had voted in the province of Kandahar.

Karzai of course won reelection, and the whole episode with the helicopter seemed to fade into oblivion. The effects of voting, however, lingered—for good and ill. As I said, drama is eternal in Afghanistan. It will far outlast the NATO presence just as it's outlasted every foreign presence throughout its long, long history.

The Importance of "Pet" Projects

Humans were not the only ones impacted by the horrors of war. Animals suffered terribly in theater, and strays were frequent casualties left in the streets for the ravages of scavenging. It was a heartbreaking sight. Like children, animals are all too often the innocent victims of the violence inflicted by rage-filled adults. There was nothing I could do about the violence, but at least I could help some of the strays. I decided this would serve a twofold purpose. First, it would offer a nurturing environment for a few hapless creatures; second, it would add some cheer and warmth to our workplace. Accordingly, I introduced some pets into our admin compound. As I suspected, the animals thrived under our care, which in turn boosted employee morale and emotional well-being.

To further assuage the grief I felt every time I saw a stray, I decided I needed my own dog. I might not be able to help every sad animal I encountered, but I could shower my own pet with all the affection I had to give. It was love at first sight between Daisy and me. I found her in an animal shelter run by an American woman, a veterinarian, and several Afghan volunteers in Kabul, and I adopted her immediately. Daisy was not your average dog. She was a Heinz, with the body of border collie and the legs of a corgi. She was also the smartest dog I'd ever seen. She took her own precautions while she lived in a conflict zone, which included digging herself an underground bunker when the threat of insurgent attacks increased during election time. Unlike most stray dogs in Afghanistan, who never even got to a shelter, she was one of the privileged few to actually have a real home, not to mention a residence in a warehouse compound where she was trained by our Nepalese guards. The guards, most of whom were former Gurkhas, adored Daisy, and they trained her to keep any intruders out of our compound. Daisy disliked Afghans, probably because she sensed their fear and dislike of dogs. (Dogs were considered dirty animals in Muslim culture, and they were often subjected to cruelty as a result. Some Muslims raised a special breed of dogs known as Coochi dogs, purely for fighting purposes against other dogs, a sport Afghans enjoyed watching and placing bets on.) Daisy, smart as she was, could easily distinguish between our local Afghan guards and civilian Afghans. Sometimes the Nepalese would test Daisy by asking the Afghan guards to enter the compound wearing only half their uniform and donning their Afghan slippers instead of their military-style boots. Daisy would immediately pick up on their scent and chase the Afghan guards out of the compound.

On one particular occasion she saved our lives. The main distribution board had caught fire, and Daisy immediately alerted us by barking uncontrollably to warn us that the equipment was ablaze. Unfortunately, like most electrical work carried out in Afghanistan, the board was overloaded, and it short-circuited. In addition to this, one of our own workmen had placed our warehouse generator within close proximity to the distribution board. The generator had a large several-hundred-gallon tank of diesel, enough to cause serious collateral damage. To make matters worse, our offices were a stone's throw away, and if an explosion had occurred, it would have resulted in about thirty casualties. The Afghan fire safety officer who responded to our emergency call did put out the fire, but it was Daisy that had saved the day!

Her status as a literal lifesaver notwithstanding, Daisy was not our only pet on the compound. One of our HR specialists had a dog that stayed on the opposite end of the compound. Daisy immediately befriended this dog, aptly named Visa (because of HR issues that will be described later on), and the two were partners in crime in all sorts of adventures. We had some stray cats in the back of our admin offices, including one kitten that became the admin staff's mascot. I suppose I was really to blame, having been the one to actually adopt said kitten, and I accept full responsibility for this.

Several stray cats had taken up residence in the back of our admin office in the compound. One very cold and wet wintry morning, I happened to be using our ablution toilet when a tiny kitten no more than four weeks old popped its head under the toilet door. A pitiful meow soon followed, one at a decibel far louder than the small furry form seemed capable of emitting. It was the cutest thing I had ever seen, and so of course I had to find it some food. The little ball of fluff was shivering and clearly starving.

I picked up the kitten, went back to the office area, and asked the admin staff to give it some of our leftovers from the previous day's lunch. The admin staff fell in the love with the kitten as easily as I had, and soon the little fur ball was the center of attention, adoring the affection as much as the food. It seemed our compound was about to have a new pet.

But as much as she seemed to love all the stroking and fussing, the little kitten was every inch a cat. After she'd had enough to eat, she gave a contented purr and stretched out on the corner of one desk. While she settled into a catnap, we all resumed working, smiling to ourselves because of the adorable interlude. An hour or so later I brought her back to where the other strays were, and she took off like a shot. Apparently, she was only interested in being a part-time pet, but we were fine with that. That kitten was so cute, the staff and I would let her do whatever she liked. It was as simple as that.

A few days later the same kitten reappeared, looking very sick. It was bitter cold out, and so I was worried that she might be in the early stages of influenza. Blood dripped from her tiny pink nose, and she seemed rather weak. Without veterinary care, I doubt she would have lasted more than two or three days.

"Don't worry. I'll take care of you," I whispered to the little ball of fluff quivering in my hands. I couldn't help but feel that I at least had to try to save this poor little kitten. Grabbing the last fifty US dollars I had in my purse, I immediately arranged for one of my admin staff to take the kitten to the nearest animal clinic. I use the word clinic quite loosely here, as these facilities are not what they are in the West—not for animals or humans. Veterinary clinics in Afghanistan had only the barest essentials for treating sick animals. The veterinarian gave the kitten an injection, as well as some antibiotics to take over the few days that followed, and the admin staff ministered to her constantly, providing round-the-clock nursing care with utter devotion.

The vet had only given the kitten a 30 percent chance of survival, and so we were all very concerned, taking turns to ensure that she received her medicine and stayed warm. We knew our kitten needed a miracle, but it was a miracle that the stray cats survived in our admin office in the first place!

The admin section of our compound was predominantly concrete blocks fitted with containers that had been modified into offices. Very little vegetation surrounded the concrete, so the environs consisted of mainly dust and dirt. It was truly amazing that several cats had managed to survive in these harsh and barren surroundings. If not for the handouts from our lunches and the guards' leftover rice, the poor felines would surely have long since succumbed.

One cat in particular, known as Lady, had lived there for years, and she was more than likely responsible for 70 percent of the rest of the compound's cat population. Named by one of our longtime staff members, Lady was clearly not a lady by nature. I suspected that the little kitten we were trying to save was probably from Lady's most recent litter. As Lady was a very tough customer, I hoped the kitten had inherited some of her strength and determination. She'd need it in order to survive both the illness and the rough existence she'd been born into.

It took several days and three visits to the vet before the kitten started to show signs of recovery. It was far too cold outside to let her go back to the haunt of Lady and the other strays, so we decided to make a small bed in an office no longer in use. This nest ought to ensure that our kitten would have a good chance to fully recover. We tucked her in, and she mewed a thin but clear thank-you. The lot of us had grown fond of the tiny thing, and we all hoped she would remain our little mascot for a lot longer.

Finally, after several more days of constant nurturing, we arrived in the office one morning to find the kitten fully awake and padding about in the box that served as her bed. She greeted us with a feisty meow that was clearly a demand for food. The poor thing had barely eaten over the past few days, only enough to get her medicine down. The return of her appetite was a clear indication of recovery. We were all delighted and commenced making an even bigger fuss over her than we had when I'd first found her.

It was amazing to see how the tiny kitten's recovery immediately lifted all our spirits. Our prayers had been answered, and we were overjoyed. As I said, there is nothing like a pet to boost morale.

"Our little kitten seems quite the tiger, doesn't she?" I said, and the entire admin staff agreed.

The name Tiger stuck, and she was our office pet and mascot from that day forward.

I can't overemphasize how much Daisy, Visa, and Tiger helped us get through our time in theater. Caring for them grounded us, helping us remember that there was still love and goodness in the world. Cuddling a pet was sometimes the only pleasant and nurturing moment we had during the course of an entire day or longer, and often such a simple thing made the environment bearable. It was as essential to our survival as our bonds of loyalty and friendship.

Zero Hour

Things were moving along with the KAF project, and I did my best to keep my concerns regarding export in the back of my mind. Truth to tell, with all the work in Kandahar on top of the routine demands of my job as GM, I barely had time to sleep and breathe, let alone think. I focused on executing an excellent outcome in Kandahar, as I still believed that a first-rate performance record was essential to my emerging unscathed from the export situation, whatever the roots of the cover-up proved to be.

After the vodka-in-KAIA debacle I knew that things would soon come to a head despite the seemingly innocuous fallout of slap-on-the-wrist e-mails. I wanted to find a way to get in front of it, but I also recognized that contriving that way would not serve me well in the short or long term. So I stuck to my mode of work, work, work, trusting that an opportunity to reveal the pieces of truth I had already unearthed would eventually emerge. In the interim I let my inner compass take charge of the big picture, while my resilience and self-reliance got me through the details of my day-to-day life.

The cold month of November drew to a close, its gray chill brightened by the joy and sparkle of upcoming Christmastime. The KAF project was scheduled to launch in the early part of the first quarter of 2009. Excited as I was to see all my months of tireless effort come to fruition, by the time my second Christmas in Afghanistan approached, I decided a trip home was long overdue.

Home for Christmas

The closer Christmas came, the more I realized that an Aussie Christmas was exactly the tonic I needed. No matter how strong our bonds with one another were and no matter how much we loved our Afghan pets and office mascots, nothing took the place of home and family. I had been in theater for fifteen months by that point, and the constant stress (particularly the past months of juggling my regular responsibilities as GM in Kabul and managing the new KAF project in Kandahar) made it feel more like fifteen years—if not longer. Once I made up my mind to spend Christmas with my family, I practically started counting the days until I would be home.

Prior to flying home to Australia, I spent two days in Dubai coordinating logistics with our procurement team. This was necessary because the brand-new French PX/bakery concept was scheduled to open in KAF in just six weeks. After I spent a whole day in headquarters, I decided to take a day to do some Christmas shopping for family and friends. Dubai is something of a shopper's paradise, so I had a grand time indeed. I was scheduled to fly from Dubai to Australia early the following morning. As I would be in the air for the good part of a whole day, I decided to pop into the office one last time that evening to check to see if I had received any urgent e-mails.

As it happened, I chose a desk that was not far from the desk of our HR director, Katherine (Kat for short). A few minutes later Kat passed by on the way back to her desk, and she stopped to chat with me. This was typical of her. She was quite bubbly, a "people person," as the saying goes. Originally from the United Kingdom, she had spent several years living and working in Dubai. I'd had occasion to interact with her shortly after I was hired and then again every time I came to headquarters.

"How's it going, MJ?" Kat chirped, perching on the edge of the desk I sat behind while I was going through my e-mails.

"Well enough, thanks. And you?"

"Fine. Looking forward to Christmas at home?"

"Indeed," I said with a grin.

"I see your shopping trip was successful!" She laughed, indicating the collection of bags and boxes I'd deposited beside the desk.

I started to answer but then came across an e-mail from Kurtis related to our alcohol business. Perhaps this was the perfect moment to casually mention my concerns regarding export. Hannah always said that it was best to find a neutral time to bring up sensitive issues like this, as it would necessitate less defusing. I quite agreed with her.

"The shopping was grand," I said.

She smiled.

"There's actually something else I'd like to talk to you about if now is a good time." Perhaps that wasn't my best attempt at avoiding defusing; however, I only had a small window of time, and I didn't want it to slam shut before I had a chance to utilize it optimally.

"Of course, MJ. That's what I'm here for," she said amicably. Her demeanor was unchanged, so I couldn't tell if she discerned I was concerned about a major issue.

"It will be easier if you just read it for yourself," I said, moving to the side as she pulled up a chair and sat before the computer I was using. I opened a key e-mail from Kurtis from several days prior, and I watched her face as she read.

She arched an eyebrow. "Interesting," she said evenly. "Is this unusual?"

I felt certain she suspected it wasn't, perhaps because of the history surrounding my predecessor. I shook my head no.

"Show me," she said, and I complied.

Fortunately, I had asked Tucker to copy me on all e-mails related to the authorization of alcohol for 110, so I had several weeks' worth of correspondence saved. Previously, I had been purposely excluded from such e-mail correspondence—at Kurtis's directive—but I explained to Tucker that from an accountability perspective it was necessary to include me. He agreed. Here again, I knew my team was trying to protect me as much I tried to protect them, and I was grateful. But I also knew that if Tucker included me in the e-mails regarding export, Kurtis would then have to think twice about approving the movement of alcohol, as he would realize that I was now being kept in the loop and had documented proof.

This had seemed wise to me at the time, and Hannah and Donna had agreed. I was now even more thankful that I'd initiated this procedure with Tucker because I now had hard evidence to show our HR director. After Kat finished reading a few e-mails, all of which clearly demonstrated that we were currently supplying a nonauthorized customer (i.e., 110) with alcohol directly from our warehouse, she turned in her chair to face me. I had carefully watched her reaction the entire time she was reading, but it was difficult to gauge what she actually thought about the situation. After all, HR people are trained to be diplomatic and neutral. However, I could see that she felt my concerns were legitimate.

"I understand your concerns, MJ, and I'm not minimizing them by any means. Please keep an eye on all of it, but park it for the moment."

"All right," I said, staying calm. That answer could mean a lot of different things, and I wasn't going to read anything into it. It was possible that she didn't want to enter this situation until there was further evidence to support what I had told her and shown her. Perhaps she wanted to seek further advice from senior management or even from our legal department or ISAF liaison team.

At the very least, I felt relieved that I had informed our head of HR that there could be an issue concerning the illegal sale of alcohol and, most important, that I was not involved and that my team members were acting under the direction of Kurtis, their manager's superior, so they had no choice in the matter. Despite my relief, I was also a little concerned that perhaps I had made the wrong decision by informing her at this stage. Did I now run the risk of her in turn informing the wrong people, who might also even be involved in the whole scheme? It was too late to worry about it now because the truth was out. I'd set the wheels in motion, and now I had to just go along for the ride. This was a relief too, though. I'd done what I felt was right. No matter what happened, I'd be able to live with myself, and nothing was more important than that.

I wasn't going to let it ruin my time with my family—the first time I'd seen them in more than a year… and Christmas to boot. I filed it away in the back of my mind and willed myself into a festive holiday spirit.

* * *

I flew out to Australia early the following morning, enduring an eleven-hour flight with a day's stopover in Singapore. I was exhausted after several months of traveling back and forth between Kabul and Kandahar, with visits in between to Dubai. I had been averaging six flights a week, working twelve—and fourteen-hour days, often seven days a week and rarely fewer than six. I was awfully glad to be among family and friends again, especially at Christmastime; however, I couldn't hide the stress and strain I carried, and I worried that my visit likely caused them more concern than joy. In a way I was unable to de-stress and unwind and found myself still in Afghanistan mode, which was difficult for anyone who's never been in a conflict to fully understand. My dad and I exchanged a few wordless looks, and I had no doubt he empathized completely; however, I'm sure everyone else decided I'd turned into an incurable workaholic, frayed around the edges by my war-torn surroundings.

I didn't have the luxury of spending too much time thinking about popular opinion. Kurtis e-mailed me several times, all regarding issues that required my immediate response despite my being on vacation. There was even one related to export, which rather perturbed me; however, I contacted Donna, and she helped me craft a reply to him. At Donna's insistence I copied her on the e-mail for CYA purposes. I had to sweat it out, waiting to see what fallout there would be once Kurtis realized I was keeping HR in the loop, but it was worth it to know someone with authority had my back. (There was fallout, of course, which I'll describe in deeper detail a bit later.)

My greatest preoccupation during my Christmas holiday back home concerned general operational logistics and, even more than that, the KAF project. Manpower had been strained by the challenges we were having in getting staff visas (more about that later on), and I had very little time to waste, as our KAF project was scheduled to launch in early 2009. Most projects in any part of the world rarely run according to plan, but in a country that posed daily logistical challenges, every task became even more difficult than it ought to have been. The KAF PX/bakery concept was no exception.

As a result of all these combined factors, although this was to be my first Christmas home—and my first vacation in over a year—my trip was to be an abbreviated one. All things considered, returning to Afghanistan early was kind of a blessing. I was simply unable to wind down, and my restless energy disturbed those around me at home. Besides, there was far too much riding on this project for me to risk any problems arising simply because I'd taken a longer vacation. I arranged to arrive in Kabul on the afternoon of December 31.

Ringing in the New Year

We had planned a team New Year's Eve party, which was another reason I was glad to return to Afghanistan in the midst of the holidays. Our whole group was to attend because we hadn't celebrated Christmas together. Complete with DJ, disco lights, and plenty of food and refreshments, we partied until the wee hours of the New Year. The combination of eleven hours of oxygen from the flight and several glasses of champagne was enough to keep me in high spirits all night, but it hit me like a ton of bricks once the sun came up.

Unfortunately, I had an important meeting with Lieutenant Bisonte, the French contracting officer, on New Year's Day. Not one of my best acts of planning, I admit! Sporting a case of jet lag *and* a severe hangover, I struggled to understand the lieutenant, who only spoke French. The purpose of the meeting was to translate our sponsorship agreement from French into English, a project that was sheer hell in the midst of jet lag turbocharged by a vicious hangover. Luckily the lieutenant was young himself and completely understood my predicament. He even seemed to sympathize. After all, the night before had been New Year's Eve, and I'm sure I wasn't the only person who'd had too much champagne.

"Do not worry," Lieutenant Bisonte assured me. "There is no rush. I will be happy to e-mail the agreement to you."

Perfect! My procurement manager, Félicité, was French and could easily translate the agreement. I thanked him profusely, and we ended the meeting.

The next day I was booked on a commercial flight to Kandahar, as handover of the project from the construction company was scheduled to commence. One of our project managers was at the helm, overseeing everything in my stead. Having not been to KAF for a few weeks, I was keen on seeing what kind of progress they'd made during my absence.

As per usual, the small team I brought with me and I spent several hours waiting for our flight to arrive into KAIA, which meant, in effect, another waste of a day. Flights in and out of Kabul seldom ran on schedule, so every day of air travel was a washout. Eventually landing in KAF, we traveled with several bags, anticipating that our visit would be for the next few weeks, depending on whether we were able to open on the date planned. And what a few weeks it would be.

Opening a Bakery Is No Piece of Cake

My immediate priority after I arrived on base was to visit the site of our KAF project. Since handover was to be the following day, I had anticipated that 98 percent of the tasks would already be completed, with only the usual minor few tasks left to be done at the end. After just a few steps onto the site, however, I realized that this was not the case. In fact, reality was about as far from what I'd envisioned as it could possibly be. So much so that I nearly fell backward in shock. With less than twenty-four hours until handover, the project was nowhere near ready. There were still no doors, no floors, no windows, no internal ceiling—and these were just the areas that I could readily see. I had no idea how many less obvious but nonetheless essential items might still require attention. Welcome to Afghanistan!

Unfortunately, the project had been managed from Kabul during the preceding four weeks, part of which time had comprised my vacation in Australia. The construction company had of course taken advantage of our project management in absentia. This was a valuable lesson learned the hard way. At the time, however, I definitely did not see the value. All I saw was red! During the month that followed, which was the amount of time it took us to finally complete the PX/bakery and commence operations, I continued to see nothing but red. No doubt my blood pressure doubled, and I lost a good ten pounds from a combination of stress, lack of sleep, and the long hours we were working. As hectic as things had been before Christmas, now they were scarcely bearable. How we endured this in the midst of the ongoing chaos of Kandahar is something I cannot explain, even after I had experienced it firsthand. As for the project itself, everything that could have gone wrong did go wrong. It was like a comedy of errors—a *bad* one.

My first priority was to arrange for a ton of linoleum flooring to be flown from Dubai into Kandahar. It wasn't an easy task to undertake because the construction company couldn't give us a solid answer as to when they were likely to do this; therefore, I took it upon myself to organize everything. There was talk of the construction company flying in an Antinov 124, the largest airplane in the world, in order to transport all their materials as quickly as possible. This sounded good, but the question of when was still up in the air.

I simply had to take matters into my own hands, as I'd deemed the construction company worthless by this point. First, I had to line up some trustworthy and reliable assistance, and I decided to work from the bottom up—that is, start with the floor and finish with the ceiling. So with the amazing support of my colleague, nicknamed simply "G" by me, we arrived at a solution for the flooring problem in just three days. G was also a fellow Aussie, and he worked in another part of our organization in Dubai. Specifically, he controlled all cargo flights of our fruits and vegetables into Afghanistan. If anyone could help me, it was G.

He was on vacation in Australia at the time, but I managed to reach him on his cell. While the signal went in and out during our call, I literally fell to my knees, begging for a mammoth favor. "I'm on my knees, G," I assured him. "I need your help and promise I'll make it up to you."

"No dramas, MJ," he said (Aussie-speak for "no worries"). "I'll see what I can do on my end from here."

I thanked him profusely.

"That's all right, mate. I may yet take you up on that promise!"

"By all means," I said.

We both laughed and ended the call.

I already felt worlds better. G and I had met on a couple of occasions in Dubai, and he knew how important this latest project was to the business… and to me. Trouper that he was, G proved as good as his word. The linoleum flooring arrived on a 747 into KAF direct from Dubai just three days after I talked to G. I gave a silent prayer of thanks for as stellar a colleague and staunch a friend as G.

Thus, one huge problem among many was thankfully fixed, and now we just had to deal with the remaining ones.

There was no easy solution for the doors, as the construction company had unfortunately forgotten to order them until the last minute. Equally ridiculous logistic issues pertained to the windows and ceiling. As a result, we had no choice but to play the waiting game. The majority of the construction-oriented issues were out of our hands. I consoled myself with the fact that at least we had a great floor, thanks to G!

There were so many other obstacles to overcome that I didn't have too much time to sweat the building details. We had a team of employees scheduled to arrive in several days, but we had yet to find them accommodation. It would take pages to enumerate every difficulty we faced and had to surmount. Suffice it to say that we encountered a new problem at every turn. No sooner did we find a solution to one issue than yet another challenge would arise. To make things even more difficult, copious rain and bitterly cold weather further slowed the construction progress.

Finally, some fifteen days after my team and I arrived at KAF for the handover, the project was complete. This feat had only been possible because of lifesaving G, as well as my team and I working virtually round the clock, doing as many tasks as we could without interfering with the work of the construction crew.

Despite all the challenges and hiccups along the way, we managed to commence operations less than two weeks (thirteen days to be exact) after the initial handover date. Again, even having been there and participated in pretty much every activity, I still cannot say for certainty how we were able to achieve this. All the hassles aside, the launch was fantastic, complete with an official cake-cutting ceremony presided over by the Captain Lenard. That evening we had a fashion show to rival Paris. It was all a big success, and the following day we were open for business!

My long-anticipated project had finally come to fruition. It was quite a gratifying feeling to envision a concept, work to create it, and then see that vision become reality. I felt pleased and proud. I hoped for at least a breather after many months of such a hectic pace, especially the last few weeks of nonstop stress and toil, but alas, that was not to be.

* * *

The night before the cake-cutting and fashion festivities, we had experienced a tremendous amount of rainfall. Many parts of Kandahar, including KAF, quickly turned to mud. I had to make several trips between our accommodation and the site, as we had required the use of an additional oven for our official opening. Having made a wrong turn on a road adjacent to the runway, I decided to turn around and go back. What I didn't realize, however, was that the excessive rain had softened the earth alongside the road, turning it into a huge patch of sludge. As soon as my wheels entered this sludge, my vehicle immediately started to turn over. About two hundred strawberries intended to decorate a three-tier fruit flan immediately bounced about the vehicle. Through the haze of cascading crimson, I observed the panicked expressions of my two chefs who were in the vehicle with me. I tried to keep them calm despite my own mounting concern. The vehicle appeared to be stuck in the sludge and was now sitting on one side. Luckily, we had been only traveling at about forty miles per hour, so the actual accident itself wasn't life-threatening. Needless to say, it was quite a shock and definitely a bit of drama we could have done without on the eve of our opening!

This was no time to panic. The top priority was finding the quickest solution to get us out of the mud. Being adjacent to the runway and in clear view of the control tower, it wasn't long before military police arrived on the scene with a tow truck. There was only one way they could get us out of the mud that we were now deeply entrenched in. They put a winch on the front bumper of the car, one connected the tow truck, and then went full-throttle to pull us out of the sludge. The continuous pelting of rain and the constant buildup of mud made it extremely difficult for them to pull us out.

The MPs then began to direct me to steer so that the wheels would turn as the tow truck pulled the vehicle out of the mud. At precisely the moment when I began to follow these instructions, my cell phone sounded. Gripping the wheel, I took the call via hands-free mode because it was Kurtis calling.

"MJ, where are you?" he said rather abruptly. He was waiting for me at the site, unaware that we'd had an accident.

I quickly explained the situation, wanting to end the call so that I could focus on what I needed to do in order to help the MPs get us out of the mud. Nevertheless, Kurtis persisted in following through with the original reason for his call. I answered tersely, ending the call as soon as I could and resuming my focus on the matter at hand. Thankfully the MPs' rescue was successful, and soon we were back at the site.

Once out of the mud and certain that my chefs were unharmed—just distraught over the strawberry casualties—I began to ponder what had transpired via cell with Kurtis. Clearly, my boss didn't care that there had been an accident. In fact, he didn't even bother to ask if we were all right. All he cared about was himself and whatever he happened to need or want at any given moment. In this instance, what he wanted was to make sure that he received a heap of credit for the KAF project despite the fact he had done none of the work, offered no solutions to the critical problems, and taken no responsibility whatsoever. This was typical. He never wanted to offer assistance. He only wanted to have control—total control. In addition, he had the unerring knack of asking me questions at the most inappropriate times! This time was the perfect example.

This was more than just typical Kurtis, though. This was about the e-mail exchange during my vacation in Australia—the one in which I'd copied Donna on my reply to him. Obviously, I'd touched a nerve. This was the fallout. I'd suspected this might happen, that it likely would happen, but I'd also reached the point where I no longer cared that much about his reactions, even though he still was my boss. To expand on what I described briefly earlier in this chapter, Kurtis had e-mailed me about several issues while I was on vacation, and one of them was in regard to export. I didn't reply right away, as I had explained that cell and Internet in the part of the country where I was staying were spotty at best. It kept nagging at me, so I called Donna in the middle of the night (when it would be a decent hour in Dubai), and I asked her advice.

"I think it's time you start addressing that unsigned paperwork for export, MJ," Donna said over the phone.

"Kat said to park it for now, Donna," I reminded her, having already let both Donna and Hannah know about their department head's reaction.

"I know what she said, but it's time. Just trust me on this. I'll take care of everything on this end." Donna also knew how hesitant I'd been about signing the documents all along. She, Hannah, and I all had hoped that my hectic schedule would serve as sufficient explanation for why the documents had piled up and remained unsigned. Given the tone and content of Kurtis's note, however, this was not going to fly for much longer. "If you have e-mail confirmation from Kurtis specifically instructing you to affix your signature of approval on these documents, that will serve as absolute proof that your involvement was at your direct manager's behest," Donna finished.

What she said made perfect sense. An e-mail chain would clearly show the exact extent of my involvement and the reasons why. If it came down to it, I would require no further proof of my role in export, and it would be clear that my participation was mandatory because of my boss's insistence.

Donna and I then worked together to carefully craft my reply. "Remember to copy me on the reply, MJ. CC, not BCC, so he knows that I received it," Donna said. "I'll see to it that everyone who needs to be in the loop is apprised."

I confirmed I would follow her instructions, thanked her for her assistance and advice, and said good-bye.

Too wired for sleep at that point, I prepared the reply, copying Donna as she'd specified, and then sent it off. Kurtis initially replied a short while later via his BlackBerry, which meant that he hadn't noticed Donna as a CC. This was a brief "yeah, go ahead"—typical terse Kurtis. The following day I received a second response, a rather ambiguous one at that, and this one was sent from his computer, which told me he had realized that I had copied Donna. He therefore knew that HR was in the loop, and that it was because of me. Perhaps this had confirmed his suspicions that I knew there were irregularities occurring or that HR had found out in some other way and designated me their informant. Either way, I would have to steel myself for rough waters with my boss.

I had no regrets. My e-mail reply had intentionally put him on notice that I was aware of what was going on and that I wasn't willing to be his next scapegoat. Nevertheless, it was still a very stressful time for me, as I wasn't sure what his long-range plan would be. I waited patiently for several days to see if there would be any fallout from my initial reply e-mail. None came. No surprise there. Kurtis favored the silent treatment. I had long since become accustomed to his style of management of divide and conquer. It was this very style that had created a huge communication problem between Dubai and Afghanistan. The ongoing operational issues that had evolved as a result eventually spelled the end of my predecessor, and they were the reason for my current unending stress related to export. In the bigger scheme of things, it meant that our time spent on problem solving in Afghanistan was doubled because of the lack of support and cooperation from Dubai. The environment we lived and breathed in was challenging enough without the challenges orchestrated by those above us.

In the end, my team and I had learned to build up our resilience by believing in ourselves, by setting goals we could achieve on our own. The KAF project was the culmination of that. We had built a tight and loyal network, and we knew who we could trust and rely on. We also knew that giving up meant that Kurtis and whoever else was at the bottom of the corruption we fought to eliminate would have won.

Looking back, Kurtis's reaction to that e-mail, the typical silent treatment combined with utter lack of regard for me as epitomized by his response to the accident, was the turning point—the place and moment from which there would be no going back to the way things had been. This would have irreparable impact on the illegal alcohol trade in Afghanistan, and it was essential to preserving my conscience and well-being to the very depths. With my trusted colleagues beside me, I was now determined to fight the corruption I'd suspected but never been entirely certain of. Now I was certain, and I had to fight. I didn't know the full extent of all that I would actually have to battle, but the game was on. The time to take action had come. I was ready. It would be the fight of my lifetime.

7

TAKING ACTION

Although it was a relief to have finally reached the turning point, the moment of truth, and the point of no return, the actual process of taking action was anything but a relief. In fact, it was quite an ordeal. The process of revealing the truth I had uncovered about export seemed to pull me deeper into its web until I wondered if the whole truth would ever come to light or if the lies and deceptions would remain a tangle that was never unraveled.

I had sought to expose the truth by displaying the incontrovertible facts, feeling certain that the TerraTota senior management would then design and execute swift resolution and that only those truly guilty of corrupt dealings and unethical behavior would be held responsible. I was about to discover that responsibility and accountability are rather tenuous and extremely difficult to define in such situations. In many ways, it is far easier to learn how to survive in a zone of conflict than to maintain integrity when thrown into a conflict of interest!

As I found myself inexorably caught up in the chain of events completely outside my control—all with drama and intrigue galore—the best I could do was to rely on my resilience and intuition, to stay true to myself and my values. I learned more about courage and internal strength during that time than at any other point in my life. My inner compass kept spinning, and I continued to just let it guide me. I would surely be lost otherwise. I inwardly thanked my father for all he had inculcated in me, as this kept me strong and, just as important, helped me determine who I could trust and rely on. Some of my allies in this part of my journey had been with me all along; others were people I had yet to get to know. They were all essential to my ability to endure the situation at hand. I cannot overemphasize what the support of my friends and colleagues meant to me. They supported, nurtured, and inspired me, and I only hope that I reciprocated.

The pages that follow chronicle my most challenging experiences in Afghanistan—the fight for truth and fairness, which is always the hardest battle of all. As I mentioned in the introduction, taking action was a lengthy and complex process, circuitous and challenging. While I was writing this chapter, I had to relive all the effort I had to expend and all the difficulties I encountered. I felt worn out all over again, but I also felt grateful for the wisdom I gained. It was hard-won, but its light shone my way forward, which I have tried to capture in the retelling here, an illuminating and purposeful reflection.

Meeting in Dubai, Round Two

The recent opening of our new KAF project had highlighted a number of operational deficiencies within our business, specifically on the procurement level. KAF was now considered to be our number-one site in both turnover and profit. Logistically, our business was in grave need of a shake-up. Our procurement team had lived on easy street for too long, and given the amount of skepticism we'd originally received from them regarding the KAF PX/bakery concept, they were now in a bit of a pickle. In essence, the success of KAF had proved them wrong on all levels. KAF's undeniable success had pushed the project into the limelight, and now procurement had no choice but to take our team's business initiatives seriously.

Despite my concerns related to export and taking action to expose the truth, this was a time of positive excitement from a business and career perspective. As always, I threw myself full-bore into the project, determined to be successful and to prove my value through my excellent performance record. First on my agenda was overhauling the KAF inventory. As absurd as this will sound, one of our biggest challenges was the lack of French products offered. Yes, in a French PX/bakery, we had an insufficient number of items that were distinctly French! Setting aside the obvious business reasons for why this was utterly unacceptable, it was also completely ridiculous in my opinion, given that our procurement manager, Félicité, was French. That's correct. The person responsible for purchasing was born and raised in France, and yet she refused to buy the items necessary to cater to the needs of our latest and highest-priority project, a *French* PX/bakery. Ludicrous. However, what was even more ridiculous and more puzzling too was the fact that Kurtis did very little to address or improve the situation. By this point, I did not expect my boss to do anything to help me personally, but I knew far too well how readily he capitalized on the success of his team, so it seemed extremely odd that he was not doing so in this instance. We were on the verge of recognition for an enormously successful project, one with both short- and long-term positive results, but Kurtis was not making the most of it. He wasn't really doing much of anything. The combination of his atypical behavior in and of itself and its timing caused me quite a bit of consternation, needless to say. I felt intuitively that there was something underlying it all, but I would have to let things play out in order to find out what that might be. I'd already had more than enough of this sort of intrigue, but I didn't have any choice but to wait.

As it turned out, my wait was shorter than anticipated. The higher-ups convened a marketing meeting in an attempt to rectify all the challenges we continued to face since the opening of KAF. I knew that I would have a political battle on my hands, with no backup from my boss, and so I arranged for Lloyd, one of our senior managers to attend the meeting with me. He fully supported the KAF project and valued my contributions. I felt much more comfortable about it all just knowing he would be there. (Remember that Lloyd was the same senior manager from the ISAF general's visit to our Kabul compound.)

The meeting was scheduled to last for three days in order to allow all involved parties to present their respective issues.

The meeting was typical, but I had known what to expect and so wasn't at all surprised. It was the classic scenario of the corporate procurement team covering their butts and trying to point the finger at the less-experienced personnel working in theater. Reality was that we relied upon their support to sustain our business, and consequently, the lack of ongoing support resulted in our having to find other ways to obtain the stock we needed. This meant that local procurement increased. It wasn't a case of us spending our time less wisely ("ineffective time management," as corporate-speak would call it) or a drop in our sales margin, which miraculously we were able to maintain. Ultimately, it was about the undue risk they continued to require us to take, putting our lives in jeopardy, as we had to travel as many as three times a week to areas of Kabul that often experienced suicide attacks. This behavior on the part of procurement was grossly and unnecessarily selfish, and all it did was create angst and resentment among those of us in theater. In essence, we were not only performing our agreed-upon roles but also the roles of our buyers, who sat quite comfortably in their offices in Dubai, earning good salaries with little effort and no risk. Certainly they didn't take their lives in their hands on a daily basis.

Suffice it to say, this was a sore point that I found hard to digest. In fact, it stuck in my craw. And this was not merely because of all that constant danger entailed for my team and me physically, emotionally, and psychologically but also because it was a poor business decision that made absolutely no sense. Knowing full well that Kurtis had the ability and authority to influence the necessary changes in regard to this situation and yet did nothing only served to inflame my indignation. It should have been his responsibility to resolve the issues with procurement, if not for my and my team's sake, then for the sake of the sustainability of our most successful project. Since when did a lucrative venture that Kurtis could find a way to take credit for not take priority? It was baffling. And yet there continued to be some sort of ulterior motive for him to keep our team divided from procurement instead of stepping up to his leader status and forming an alliance, which would be best for all of us and for the company.

The more I tried to figure it out, the more the answer eluded me. Intuitively, I felt it was all tangled up in the export knot, and now was the time to take action while simultaneously ensuring the continued success of the KAF project. If this sounds like a tall order, it was. But I might not get another chance, so I had to take this one.

Since Lloyd accompanied me to the meeting, I had also organized a dinner with our director of finance, Niels. He was incredibly talented, highly intelligent, and a complete gentleman. We had hit it off immediately, largely because of his wicked sense of humor, which I adored. During the past several months of my frequent visits to Dubai in between juggling routine work in Kabul and the KAF project in Kandahar, Niels and I had developed a friendship. (Events following the marketing meeting would thankfully forge it into a solid bond.) Originally from Germany, Niels had joined the company about six months after I did. Through several conversations I came to see that he was someone I could trust and eventually confide in. I had come to see this about Lloyd as well. This was why I felt my chance was this moment, one that would likely never come again.

Neither Donna nor Kat seemed to have done anything in response to the e-mails regarding export, so I had decided to travel with the folder containing all the documentation. I had discussed this with Lloyd prior to leaving Kabul, and we agreed to jointly inform Niels of our concerns about export. As finance director, he wielded considerable authority and might have more freedom to take action than HR did (if they were hesitating because of trepidation, not apathy, which I hoped was the case). I was 99.9 percent sure Niels had no involvement in export, even if there were other higher-ups who did. In the first place, he'd started after I had. In the second place, his demeanor made it clear that he would never give in to corruption, either by temptation or coercion. Consequently, it seemed that Kurtis and his conspirators (whoever they might be) had chosen to keep Niels out of the loop. This in turn made us even more suspicious of the behavior of the export contingent.

Accordingly, we had chosen to meet with Niels after the marketing meeting ended, which was also the night before Lloyd was scheduled to fly to the Philippines for vacation. Niels had asked to meet us at the regular German eatery in Dubai. It was a buffet-style restaurant serving traditional German food with German beers on tap. I had decided that the best time to approach the subject of export was after we had finished our meal, including a few beers and some wine.

Approaching the subject was rather easy. I began with, "Niels, there's something we'd like to talk to you about."

"*Ja*. Go on," he said, his eyes merry with the effects of good German beer.

"I'm afraid it's rather serious," I warned.

"Money is always serious, MJ," Niels said, his German accent making it sound formal, but then he laughed. We often joked about how no one ever came to the top finance guy unless it was serious, which it always was because it was always about money.

I smiled but didn't laugh. I then launched into the best description of export that I was able to provide.

The next two hours were spent explaining the details of export, what it was all about, how it traveled in our business, and how it involved my team and me. Gauging Niels's reaction, he had no prior knowledge of export, neither its purpose nor its execution within TerraTota. Lloyd and I looked at each other, and Niels looked at both of us, his utter shock giving way to subdued outrage. His reaction confirmed my long-held suspicions. Export was an irregularity in our business, a blatant conflict of interest unsanctioned by corporate management. I was so relieved and gratified that I had chosen to take action in this way, at this moment, and with these men I trusted.

I patted the folder resting on the table between Niels and me, relieved that it proved my team and I had no involvement other than the tasks that Kurtis, the head of our unit, required of us.

The Audit

My team and I were in the midst of preparing a celebration of TerraTota's sixth anniversary of operation in Afghanistan. Our preparations kept us quite busy. Ordinarily, six years might not be considered such a great accomplishment by a company, but in the extreme environment of a war zone, six years could easily equate to sixty if not more. Considering how many things could and often did happen on any given day or week as compared to a normal environment, it was easy to understand this.

The hectic pace kept my mind off the export issue. Ever since meeting with Niels in Dubai, I had expected that an audit would follow. In his role as director of finance, it would be his responsibility to call for such an audit, so I didn't anticipate its eventuality with any trepidation. It was the logical next step—inevitable but not worrisome. If anything, I was relieved that an audit would force "everything to come out in the wash," so to speak. An official e-mail from our principal director soon confirmed my expectation. An external audit would take place in the coming weeks, and I should prepare accordingly.

Coincidentally, I then received an e-mail from Kurtis informing me that I had accumulated an unacceptable amount of annual vacation time and needed to make arrangements to take my time ASAP. I had been working as GM for TerraTota for about two years by that point, and this was the first time I had received an e-mail from Kurtis instructing me to take time off! I was surprised, to say the least, and not pleasantly so.

Hannah was under tremendous strain by this time, so I didn't want to burden her further with my problems—our friendship came first. (In truth, all that personnel management entailed in theater resulted in a tremendous turnover within HR.) I was not at all certain I could trust Kat or Donna, so I decided to forward Kurtis's e-mail to Niels. As soon as he read it, he called me. "Things are progressing, but it is going to take time, MJ. Be patient. I will keep you posted." I thanked my friend, more relieved than ever that I had confided in him and that I had set the wheels in motion. Taking action had definitely been the right choice.

It turned out that Kurtis's and my e-mails with HR copied had triggered a chain reaction up the ladder. Ultimately, this resulted in the owner of the company questioning Kurtis. I suspected that the documentation I showed Niels served to further reinforce the higher-ups' assessment of my boss, but I did not receive specific confirmation of that. It didn't matter. I was able to connect the dots on my own. All that mattered was that the truth was out and those who needed to know and act would now be able to do so. In addition, I now had confirmation that export was not sanctioned by upper management. The conflict of interest was not company-sponsored. I was greatly relieved to know this for sure. It had never made sense to me that a company with several billions of dollars in contracts with the government would involve themselves in the business of export.

The sudden relief I felt was like Mount Everest moving off my back. I had made it crystal clear that I was not involved in export other than signing the documents. The worst was over. All I had to do now was to wait for the auditors to investigate and submit their report.

* * *

Back to the sixth-anniversary festivities. Like any other day in Afghanistan, my team and I had several things going on at once. It just so happened that the auditors arrived on the very same day as our celebration was to take place. They had been scheduled to arrive earlier; however, issues with processing their Afghan visas had caused a delay. (It had become increasingly more difficult to obtain visas for certain countries, particularly those considered to be TCNs.)

Because I wasn't worried about the audit, I focused on the anniversary festivities. We had several specials guests arrive from Dubai, and a couple of representatives from our Bosnian operations were there too. Kurtis had arrived the previous day, bringing Rachel, our new HR senior manager, with him. Needless to say, communications between Kurtis and me continued to be strained, to say the least. This was to be expected and so came as no surprise. The new HR senior manager, however, was not expected and was quite a surprise indeed—and not in a good way. I soon learned that Donna had been recently reassigned to another business. In addition, Hannah finally reached the end of her tether, resigned as HR manager, and left Afghanistan. This meant that my HR contacts now consisted of this brand-new manager and Kat; I knew nothing about the former, and I found the latter rather suspect… or at least someone whom I could not wholeheartedly trust. I was more grateful for Niels than ever.

On the day of their arrival the three of us sat down in my office to catch up. Bear in mind that my office was an old forty-foot container that had been modernized for use as an office. Kurtis appeared to be a little more laid back than usual during our brief meeting. He was even jovial. I found this odd, given that the auditors were working away all the while, a fact of which Kurtis was well aware. In spite of this or maybe because of it, I decided to play along with his banter and simultaneously take the opportunity to let him know I was on to him and had no intention of being his scapegoat in case he hadn't yet figured that out. (With Kurtis, it was hard to tell.)

"You know, it took me a long time to figure you out, Mr. Smart!" I said lightly.

Kurtis stood with his back against my office wall. He laughed, smiling proudly to himself at my comment and appearing to take my words purely as a lighthearted joke. But I had hit the nail on the head, and I knew it. His laughter was merely a cover-up for his guilt, particularly in front of Rachel. I reasoned that he might remember our conversation later on, and combining it with the e-mails and everything else, he would realize that my words held a deeper meaning. Rachel was completely oblivious to what was going on. She smiled and appeared to take my words in the same lighthearted manner. Most people present would have done the same… unless they knew the history.

* * *

The evening's anniversary celebration went uneventfully. There was a nice awards ceremony for those who exhibited outstanding performance, and all attendees partook of traditional buffet-style food and refreshments. All in all, it was a pleasant and successful event.

However, despite my confidence in my obvious innocence as documented by my precious paper trail, I had been consumed by stress and worry throughout the time leading up to the audit, and so I failed to enjoy myself at the celebration.

All I could think about was the audit scheduled to commence the following morning.

Niels was at the event, both to participate in the celebration and to ensure that the auditors were settled in and had all that they needed. This was the first external audit of our business unit's warehouse operations, so it was long overdue, even without the concerns related to export. Niels told me to expect the audit to take at least a week, but he reassured me that he would stay for a couple of days to see to it that everything began smoothly. He wouldn't leave until the auditors were comfortable and the process was well underway.

Kurtis remained for the first two days of the audit, and while Niels and I were in another part of the compound, he arranged for the auditors to move into the warehouse among our staff and next to one of his closest allies. Had this gone unnoticed, even if only briefly, it could have compromised the entire audit, as Kurtis would have been able to monitor the auditors' progress and receive constant updates. Fortunately, Nicholas became aware of it and quickly brought it to my attention. Niels and I agreed that it would be best for him to address this issue. Discreetly, he arranged for the auditors to sit in another office location adjacent to the warehouse, which would ensure that all their findings remained confidential. Everyone perceived this as a standard operating procedure because Niels had initiated it, and he'd done so with a completely neutral demeanor, a tone that was firm but unperturbed. I silently blessed him. If Kurtis was disappointed, he didn't let it show. He stayed a day beyond that and then returned to Dubai. Niels stayed another couple of days, and then he, too, returned to headquarters, leaving me as the auditors' point of contact.

For days, the auditors carefully sifted through the numerous boxes of archived paperwork. The audit had to be incredibly thorough, and the auditors certainly kept our warehouse staff on their toes. Every document was carefully examined, and the individuals involved in the events described in each document had to answer a series of questions put to them by the auditors. Naturally, everyone involved was nervous, knowing full well that a detailed analysis report would follow the completion of the audit. This final report would travel up the corporate ladder. Concern was a normal reaction for me and everyone else, but the purpose of the audit was to leave no stones unturned. Ultimately, it would expose the truth, good and bad.

Every desk in the warehouse offices was completely covered with piles of archival paperwork, presenting another challenge for our dispatch team, who had to take extra care not to mix their current paperwork in with the old. They handled it admirably, and I praised them for it.

I cooperated fully with the auditors, providing whatever they asked for as quickly as I was able to. My team followed my lead. It all seemed to be going along well enough other than the expected and unavoidable interference with our day-to-day routine. We made the best of it, knowing it wouldn't last forever. Meanwhile, I patiently waited for the subject of alcohol to arise. It was inevitable. Consequently, I had postponed my next trip to Kandahar. I had planned to meet Wing Commander Papineau, who was to replace Captain Lenard as our French Air Force liaison, following a recent troop rotation and change of command. This was all part of our contractual obligations, and even more important, it would maintain our strong rapport with our French military sponsors.

But I explained that I needed to provide support for an ongoing audit and would come to KAF as soon as I could.

I didn't have long to wait for alcohol to enter the limelight. The auditors soon had it under scrutiny, particularly our key-accounts business, which was the department that handled the sale of all alcohol to the military and expat community. This was also the information that would open Pandora's box! The auditors wanted to know the entire history of this part of the business going back several years, which would include such export clients as 110.

The days that followed would prove to be critical in understanding both the original operations and its current setup. Over the past eighteen months the key-accounts business had grown. It now had a membership base of approximately two hundred clients. Membership was subject to approval based on strict criteria. The individual must be non-Muslim, have expat status, possess ISAF ID (which allowed entry into the KAIA military camp), and so on. All criteria had of course been set by Kurtis. Our delivery truck would supply beer and wines to the air force bar in KAIA, and Kurtis had decided that key-accounts customers would collect their orders in the same camp, as they already had approved access. So KAIA was used effectively as a safe drop-off and collection point. In addition, our key-accounts truck was able to deliver to some of the international companies' compounds, all of which had adequate security. There were embassies among the key-accounts clients as well, and their compounds also had adequate security.

Business was booming, but with the high level of success came the same high level of risk. Key accounts was a complex subject. The auditors now had the mammoth task of peeling back the layers of cover-ups that had been cleverly engineered by at least one and possibly two masterminds, namely the tangled web of export.

I soon found myself faced with several rather intense days of questioning. The relief I had experienced was to be short-lived, as the nightmare I had endured for so long now seemed to perpetuate! The auditors now asked me to justify every action I had taken and every decision I had made. I was now the one on center stage. I felt like I was on a slide under a microscope with an intense spotlight glaring above it. It was horrible. My mind came close to the brink of imploding. I felt mentally tortured, and at one point I even wondered if perhaps I had made a mistake by exposing this whole issue in the first place. Despair and confusion overwhelmed me, finally pushing me to my limit. How could they question my involvement? I was at the breaking point. Having remained outwardly composed despite my inner turmoil, the continual repetitive probing finally took its toll. I exploded, releasing every feeling of frustration, anger, and hurt, casting my words directly at the auditors. At the same time that I was screaming, my emotions dissolved into tears of rage, and with every word, I threw one of the documents that I had collected over the past several months. I didn't care anymore. I had gone past the point of worrying. I was adamant that I had gone beyond the call of duty, having painstakingly taken all the associated risks, and yet I was now the one subjected to all the questioning.

I sat in front of them for hours, seething while they pieced together every document I had thrown in front of them. Having to justify my innocence took everything out of me. The irony of becoming the focus of the investigation and the victim of the interrogation was lost on me in the throes of my righteous anger and helpless despair. In time I would understand and grow wiser from it, but in the moment the rage and pain I felt were raw and visceral. I just wanted it all to be over.

After I handed over the last piece of documentation, I finally received a nod of acknowledgment from the head auditor. Shortly thereafter, he smiled kindly. "I'm sorry for all we had to put you through, MJ, but we had to question you as part of the elimination process and also to ensure that we had all the necessary evidence."

I nodded in understanding. As much as I was relieved to hear his explanation, I was also at the same time incredibly pissed off. In truth, I wasn't sure if I wanted to hit him or hug him! Yes, he was just doing his job, but in so doing he had forced me to relive months of mental torture in the course of a couple of days, which made it even more intense to the point of being unbearable. How could they be so cold and callous?

The key-accounts manager, Morris, had also been subjected to a spate of intense questioning and was also close to the brink of tears. In the end, we both were cleared of any involvement in the irregularities reported in the audit. Most of the evidence had pointed toward one person in particular; however, one crucial piece was still yet to be found, and this would ultimately nail those who were responsible. The next few days would be vital in uncovering the evidence that would ultimately prove that a person (or persons) had acted independently and for personal financial gain in terms of supplying alcohol to 110.

The evidence we required would possibly date back two years, which would prove to be more challenging because many personnel had either left the company or had moved to another department. In addition, we hoped to contact our previous finance manager, who had been based in Kabul two years prior and who would also be able to verify when export officially ceased operations. He was a highly experienced, well-respected accountant who had worked in our organization for several years and who was also incredibly transparent.

This contact was vital, but it might take several days to reach our former admin people and our finance manager. It was a long shot that any of them would have kept documentation dating back over two years, but it was worth a try. After we made several phone calls to South Africa, we were successful in contacting the previous finance manager. He confirmed that export should have ceased around the time I started in the business or just thereafter—September 2007.

In addition to this, the previous accounts person in Dubai was able to retrieve an old e-mail sent by Kurtis confirming that no more money would be received from export sales, meaning that export should have ceased in operations.

It was now clearly evident that those persons involved were acting purely for personal financial gain—a blatant conflict of interest!

The e-mail was the saber that had carved out the final fate of those involved. Kurtis had fallen on his own sword of corruption. Technically, he was terminated for irregularities in the business, a term that was common practice in such a desperate environment. It was now the job of the auditors to establish who else was involved since it would be highly unlikely that my boss had acted alone. How would it be possible for him to carry out export without support from a higher level, especially after export operations officially ceased? The thousand cases of Heineken, which were written off on a monthly basis, required director-level approval. There had been a provision created, which was used to camouflage the alcohol supplied to 110 on a regular basis. Written-off stock was common in an environment such as this, often as a result of stock expiring or sustaining damage during transport. Consequently, more terminations occurred several days later, including the termination of Kurtis's boss, Adam, who was the director of our business unit. We all assumed that these subsequent terminations were also related to the recently found irregularities in the business.

The days of export were finally over. The news of the recent terminations sent shockwaves throughout the company. (Niels later told me that when he first informed the owner about the irregularities, the man was shocked. To report this accurately, complete with Niels's German accent, "He looked at me like I vas from zee moon!")

As expected, the owner of the company probably had visions of his entire empire crumbling. He had so proudly built TerraTota Suppliers as a reputable organization, and the public exposure of the alcohol issue (i.e., export) could ruin him and the company.

It also remained to be seen how 110 would react, as we had cut off his supply chain and his regular source of income. We anticipated that there would be some sort of retaliation. I suspected that some of the local Afghan staff might have been on his payroll as well. This might have included some of our local Afghan guards, who failed to record when the truck belonging to 110 entered and exited the warehouse compound, even though such logging was part of standard operating procedure with any vehicle. It was at this point that I also learned why 110 had been given the code name in the first place. After I questioned a previous employee who had been involved from the start of export, he explained that the number one represented the letter A and the number ten stood for the letter J, which happened to be the first two letters of the man's name. He was actually not 110 but one-ten.

* * *

Once the brouhaha subsided, I decided it would be a good time to travel down to Kandahar for a few days in order to keep a low profile. I needed to tend to business in KAF, but I also needed to physically take time out to focus on another subject, a distraction that would take me away from the last few weeks of madness. KAF was a feather in my cap in addition to being our unit's top priority, and it was immensely rewarding to see it develop.

Two days after I arrived in Kandahar, I received a rather distressing phone call from Nicholas, who had originally accompanied me to

Dubai to meet with Niels. He was hesitant to discuss any details over the phone. I knew it was crucial that I return as quickly as possible, and so I opted to take a military flight. I had been placed on "Space A," which meant that should any seats be available for civilian personnel, I would be able to fly. This also meant that I would have to spend the next three hours waiting in the terminal in case my name was called. This was often the case with most military flights, as all members of the military were understandably given priority. After I arrived in Kabul, I immediately went to my office to meet with Nicholas. Clutching his laptop, he showed me a Skype message he had received the day before from 110. He had sent a message asking how he could purchase between US$50,000 and US$100,000 in alcohol. It was understandable that he was both shocked and surprised to be contacted by 110, but even more worrisome was that he had any of our contact details. It was obvious that 110 knew that Nicholas had played an important part in uncovering the irregularities and in stopping the business of export. This also meant that someone on the inside was updating 110 with information that he would stand to benefit from. It was more obvious now that I was possibly the next person he would target and that perhaps my life was in danger.

I was exhausted. The past few weeks had taken a toll on me both physically and mentally. I felt like I had run a marathon with rationed supplies of water. Fortunately, my thirst was about to be quenched by a phone call I received from the HR director, who suggested that I should take a few days R & R in Dubai. Wearing a bulletproof vest as a precautionary measure, I traveled in my vehicle, lying on the floor at the feet of the auditors, who were also flying out of Afghanistan back to their home country. I now felt like I had to cower like a hunted animal because of the corrupt activities of others. It all seemed incredibly unfair. I felt as if I had been totally used by my boss for his own selfish reasons. Even though he was no longer in our business, his actions continued to put our lives at risk. My anger ignited at this, and it burned hot deep within me.

The next few weeks would show if any retaliatory measures would be executed by 110 or his allies. I was quite relieved to be flying out of Afghanistan for a few days.

At the airport I had managed to bid farewell to the auditors. The one who spoke the best English said, "This was the worst case I have ever uncovered."

This at least reassured me that I was not alone. Others had faced what I had. I was a trouper, and I knew I would survive. But the battery in my inner compass was all but burnt out, and my resilience felt worn thin. I needed recharging in the depths of my being, and I welcomed it with all my soul.

Rest and Relaxation—Sort Of

Within moments of the plane taking off, I fell into a deep sleep. I awoke just as the plane's wheels came down in preparation for landing. The plane taxied to a stop, and I stood up, collected my things, and exited the plane as soon as the crew gave the go-ahead.

I was looking forward to the next few days, which I intended to spend resting in an executive hotel suite. (Of course, once I'd recuperated following some solid sleep and time in the hotel spa, a bit of retail therapy in Dubai would be quite pleasant and enjoyable too!) Before commencing with Operation Relax and Rejuvenate, I had to make a quick detour to the HQ office. I'd promised to drop off a box of water samples from Afghanistan.

I felt like I was on autopilot as I entered the office. The young woman who greeted me had spent some time in Kabul several months prior.

"Hello, Sonia," I said tersely. As I handed over the box of water samples, I noticed my hands were visibly shaking. I was still in shock from the whole incident.

"Hello, MJ," Sonia replied agreeably enough, but she watched me with careful eyes.

Sonia and I had sort of bonded during her time in Kabul. She, Hasib, and I had been caught in muck and mire during a rainstorm, which had required waiting for hours for a tow. (Yes, I experienced that quite often in theater!) But I just didn't feel like talking to her. I didn't feel like talking to anyone who hadn't experienced the export situation firsthand. It was too soon. Anyone who didn't really know the details would likely bombard me with questions, and I was yet unsure of what I could and should say. On the other hand, if Sonia or anyone else said nothing, I would only think that the questions were there, just unasked. So I decided to isolate myself from anyone who had not been directly involved. I didn't have the stamina for explanations. The interrogations I'd endured had been the last straw, and I simply could not deal with anything further.

I felt briefly sad about this, as Sonia was a fellow Aussie (based in Dubai and tasked with reinvigorating our corporate brand), so a catch-up would have been nice under ordinary circumstances. Now it just made it seem as if many years had passed since our last encounter. The recent sequence of events had completely changed the dynamics of time, relationships, and everything. Nothing was ordinary in Afghanistan, particularly where export was concerned.

After I dropped off the water samples, I left the office and quickly made my way to the hotel. Kat had booked me into one of the more comfortable rooms, the executive suite. I had the eerie feeling upon entering the room that I was somehow being watched. Given the recent chain of events combined with my total exhaustion on every level, it's highly likely that my senses were working on overtime and paranoia had started to set in. I was fragile physically, emotionally, and psychologically. Regardless, I wasn't prepared to take any risks, so I requested for the front desk to assign me another room. They did so, and I immediately felt my tension and anxiety ease. I rested the entire balance of the day and felt my well-being slowly start to return.

* * *

The following day I had an informal meeting with my new direct manager, Vaughn. Originally from Belgium, Vaughn was an expert in the stock market, but he had very little knowledge of our business unit.

"Good to see you, MJ," he said, greeting me with a smile and a firm handshake. "I'll need to rely on your input quite a bit till I get my feet wet."

"Count on me," I said agreeably, feeling as good about his firm grip as I had when we'd met initially. Growing up, my dad had always counseled using the handshake as an indication of the person's sincerity. I suppressed a shudder while I considered all the times I'd talked myself out of sticking to his wise advice. *I'll never forget your counsel again, Dad,* I promised myself inwardly. Kurtis's handshake had been like a wet fish.

I'd actually first met Vaughn about a year before during our first annual conference held in Dubai. He had just joined the company as one of our business development experts. Much like Niels, he was soft-spoken, articulate, and every inch the gentleman. The firmness of his handshake in the moment therefore served more as a seal of approval. I'd needed to make sure I hadn't remembered him erroneously. On top of everything else, the spate of recent events had caused me to question my ability as a judge of character and to second-guess my sense of judgment entirely. It was a terrible feeling, and I had to exert a tremendous amount of energy and determination to move past it. Knowing I would have a boss whom I could trust and admire was a tremendous blessing, and I was exceedingly grateful.

"Catch me up on KAF… if you would," Vaughn said, and I obliged, glad to have something concrete and business-related to turn my attention to.

Vaughn had visited KAF a few months prior, accompanying the owner on a tour of TerraTota's operations in Afghanistan. I provided Vaughn with details about the recent MWAC (Morale and Welfare Assistance Committee) that I had attended, explaining that I had presented our KAF PX/baker to the committee, complete with a taste test of over twenty items from our menu. With amazing support from the incredibly charismatic and strong-willed Captain Lenard, I had garnered enthusiastic responses to our concept.

"That's great news, MJ," Vaughn said, understanding full well what a top priority KAF was to our business unit and the company as a whole.

I went on to explain the importance of maintaining our excellent rapport with the French military. Captain Lenard had understood that without his support we would run the risk of negative reactions from some of the other nations that were avid supporters of our competition. (I hoped Captain Lenard's replacement would be equally supportive, but only time would tell.) To add a bit of comic relief, I relayed an exchange with one representative at the MWAC who had made her initial skepticism known rather emphatically. She was a rather thickly set American soldier in her thirties, and while she was stuffing a freshly baked chocolate éclair into her mouth, she had remarked, "I don't know. This could be seen as a conflict of interest!" (The subsequent irony of the specific term she used was not lost on me, but I did not share that part with Vaughn, of course!)

"It all ended well, though, Vaughn," I assured my new boss. "Clearly, no one else shared that opinion, and by the time all twenty food items had been sampled, it was a unanimous thumbs-up for approval!"

"Well done!" Vaughn said and grinned.

"Thank you." I smiled to myself, recalling how Captain Lenard had congratulated me but pointed out that I should always remember to thank the éclairs, for they were what had clinched the deals. I couldn't agree more!

"French support has been nothing less than formidable," I told Vaughn. "We got through the first round of approvals successfully. The second round was much tougher." I explained that the second round required a presentation to the BCPB (Base Camp Planning Board). Winning this round was a huge feat, and I filled Vaughn in on why this was so.

Land on base was becoming as scarce as water, meaning that every inch counted. Thus, the mission received top priority for all land allocated, and all morale and welfare activities were understandably secondary. We'd faced the challenge of justification, as all proposals were met with extreme caution, and consequently many submissions were rejected.

"Our basic approach was that morale and welfare are essential to effective performance in the field, and what better way to boost them than with the comforts of home—regional tastes and so on," I explained.

Vaughn nodded his agreement. "Makes sense."

"Thankfully, the BCPB concurred. We sweated bullets till it was all over, though."

He smiled. "Keep filling me in."

I explained that exactly four weeks after we received approval from the MWAC, we were scheduled to attend the BCPB meeting, which was held at the Chai House. The Chai House was essentially an old concrete building with one main room set aside for board meetings. The tables were placed in an L shape with all chairs around the outside. As with all military meetings, one had to arrive early to ensure timeliness, and since we were first on the agenda, it was crucial for us to arrive extra early. No sooner had we all sat down and the commander had officially opened the meeting than we heard a loud *thud*. Within five seconds, the rocket-attack siren sounded. We immediately got off our chairs, hit the floor, and lay under the tables, with our hands covering our heads. We stayed there for about thirty seconds, and then as the siren continued to sound, we began to make our way outside to take cover in the nearest bunker. As we made our way inside the bunker, two more rockets landed inside the base. It was clearly not to be our day, and the meeting was adjourned to the following week. This was common practice during rocket attacks, often negatively impacting productivity. This meant another week would go by, delaying the go-ahead of our project and necessitating my spending the next seven days in Kandahar.

As it turned out, I had to return to Kabul to give the owner a tour of our warehouse, making preparation for the meeting rather difficult. I had already spent several months prior to that point living and breathing the KAF project, and the pressure was already mounting from above for us to succeed. I didn't share any of this with Vaughn, of course. He was aware of that part, and besides, I didn't want to get into all that had transpired with the owner. He had insisted I fly with him. Quietly skeptical about flying on our own aircraft, as on previous occasions I had experienced delays and cancellations, I nevertheless had no choice in this instance, as it was at the owner's request. I could only hope, pray, and cross my fingers that there would be no delays with the flight this time. Our 747 had recently been modified to take passengers along with the cargo. We had originally been scheduled to fly directly from KAIA into KAF; however, the pilot had somehow missed the prior permission request (PPR), and we were forced to land in Tarin Kowt (TK) until we could be given new landing approval. It was kind of ironic. I had initially been reluctant to fly on the 747, and after I was reassured we would arrive on time, I now ran the risk of missing the presentation as a result of flying with the owner. My blood began to boil. Of course, on the outside I had to remain calm and downplay the situation when asked by the owner if there would be an issue with my being late. I hated being late, and I also knew that lateness was something the military seldom tolerated. I could feel my hands beginning to sweat as I struggled to think of an alternative solution should I not make the meeting on time.

As we sat waiting patiently in TK (well, *impatiently* in my case!), I inwardly cursed those who had been so careless in organizing this flight in the first place. How could they be so lax with their flight schedule, considering we had our leader on board? I fought to not involuntarily mutter these thoughts out loud, even sotto voce.

Time was ticking away, and I knew that if I was to make the meeting on time, we would have to leave in the next thirty minutes. Whether it was a stroke of luck or the gods once again on my side, we received a call informing us that we had been given a new landing time and would depart in the next ten minutes. I exhaled with relief, as this meant I still had a good chance of making the meeting in plenty of time.

Fortunately, upon landing in KAF, I learned that the meeting had been rescheduled to two hours later than the original time. It all turned out well in the end, as we received the approval we needed, resulting in the success the project now enjoyed. This was known throughout the company, so Vaughn was well aware.

"I'm glad we spent some time together at last year's annual conference and during my visit to KAF," Vaughn said now. "It reassures me to know I've got someone so solid on my team."

I thanked him. He couldn't know how much that reassured me, but I didn't want to appear overly emotional, so I said nothing further.

Suffice it to say I was deeply relieved that someone I already knew would be my new boss and, better yet, that he was someone who would appreciate my support and input. I intuitively felt I could trust him, but I kept my guard up just in case. My role would now become larger in order to encompass some of Kurtis's former duties. Vaughn was only a stand-in until a suitable permanent replacement could be found.

Vaughn had requested that we meet on a Friday, which was the first day of the weekend in Dubai. Consequently, the office was deserted, which allowed us to speak frankly.

"I'd like to discuss some of the audit findings surrounding alcohol… if you're all right with that," Vaughn said, once the KAF business talk had ceased.

"Of course," I said, not happy to have to delve into the topic but knowing I'd only be forestalling the inevitable if I didn't. Perhaps it was best to get it over with.

Moving forward, our alcohol business had to change, and this had to be decided as quickly as possible. Our export business was clearly over; however, there was still a big question as to how we would continue to run our key-accounts business. Its current operational model put us at considerable risk.

Vaughn and I discussed this at length, and ultimately, I suggested he seek Niels's advice. As finance director, he certainly needed to weigh in, and I felt secure knowing he was involved. Beyond that, I needed the meeting to end so I could resume my recuperation process. I had just begun to feel better, and this meeting had ended that abruptly. I in no way blamed Vaughn, of course; he was only doing what he had to do. But the effects on me were brutal nonetheless.

That evening as I entered my hotel room, my head seemed about to explode. I had felt the beginnings of a migraine a few hours earlier, but I'd hoped it wouldn't develop fully. This was a clear sign of the stress trying to remove itself from my body. I made a beeline for the bathroom, spending the next twenty minutes with my head over the toilet bowl, throwing up. I hadn't experienced a migraine like this for several years. I felt disgusted that I had let myself get to this stage, that I had allowed the stress to overwhelm me.

I knew I had done my best, but at that moment I felt weak and worthless, a far cry from the resilient, self-reliant self I counted on and admired. More than anything else, this taught me that I needed a full rest in order to recover.

I felt better after a good night's sleep, though my head still felt the aftereffects of the migraine. Donna called me to meet her and another colleague for drinks that evening. I reluctantly agreed, as the last thing my poor head needed was alcohol! Besides, I was a little apprehensive, surmising that they were more than likely fishing for information. I had been told not to discuss the audit findings, as investigations were still going on. Considering how little she had actually done on my behalf, I was adamant not to tell her a damn thing!

The audit findings had clearly exposed the deficiencies in our HR department among other things. I had no way of knowing what kind of connection Donna maintained with Kat or anyone else for that matter. Knowing full well her intentions, I purposely hedged all their questions, declining alcohol because of my recent migraine, a handy and legitimate excuse. I had come too far to give in to such foolishness as gossip. I knew that I was alone in terms of support from HR. They couldn't be trusted, and I wouldn't put it past Kat to have Donna do her dirty work, especially since she no longer wore the HR hat and so couldn't be easily held accountable. Perhaps it was in Kat's best interest to find a way to have me removed from my position by digging up dirt! I thought about my first step inside my hotel room—that feeling of being watched—and was gladder than ever that I'd changed rooms. Kat's offer of R & R in Dubai wasn't really so generous after all, I deduced, but I was going to beat her at her own game.

The lid on Pandora's box might still be open, but I suddenly recalled that in the myth in addition to all the ills that were unleashed, there was Hope, who was caught in the box, destined to remain to help mankind survive those ills. Having me around meant that those involved in export—and those who looked the other way—ran the risk that I would expose even more of the truth. I knew this was true, and I knew it entailed a certain amount of danger; however, I decided to focus on the hope rather than the ills. I had endured this much, and I would endure the rest.

Alcohol: The Plot Thickens

Because of the fallout from the audit, I would need to keep a very low profile for the foreseeable future. I also knew I would be faced with a host of new challenges when I returned to Kabul. That proved true indeed. My top priority was ensuring my own safety. Ironically, my exposing the truth about export had put me in danger. News about TerraTota's irregularities spread rapidly, which would not be popularly received by anyone involved in the black market, including 110. It also meant that the Afghan locals who worked in our business would now be aware. Not knowing where all of their allegiances might lie (and knowing that these could also shift on the turn of a dime in theater), only the few members of my team whom I absolutely trusted with my life were aware of the exact specifics of my return to Kabul.

Ensuring my safety necessitated my traveling from KAIA to our compound in the same way as I had when I went to the airport to fly to Dubai. I lay facedown on the floor of the rear of my Prado vehicle. Nicholas sat on the seat above me. Hasib had taken the additional precaution of hanging his leather jacket against the empty rear passenger window to prevent people looking inside. It wasn't the most pleasant way to travel, but safety had to supersede comfort.

Several of my staff were actually informed that I would be taking a direct flight from Dubai to Kandahar, and while Hasib drove from KAIA to our compound, Nicholas assured me that those I'd intended to think I was Kandahar bound did indeed still believe it was so. I was relieved to hear this, of course, but knew it would not be easy to continue in my role as GM while circumventing the unpopular status I'd gained for speaking up and uncovering the truth. I had no regrets, but I also had no illusions. Dealing with the day-to-day nitty-gritty details would be less than pleasant. I steeled myself accordingly.

My return to Kabul was met with surprise by all who had believed I was headed straight to Kandahar. Again I felt tremendously relieved, hoping that my status as persona non grata would quickly fade away, that normalcy would soon return—at least whatever normalcy was in Afghanistan. Unfortunately but inevitably, my popularity was destined to endure. A few days after I returned to Kabul, I received an anonymous e-mail proclaiming just how well-liked I really was. As if the subject line "Bitch! Bitch!" were not clear enough, the single line of text encouraged me to "have a nice life." This mental/psychological warfare worked its harm in an insidious way. Much as is the case with PTSD, I would not be fully aware of the effects for some time, likely because my energy was still focused on staying safe and meeting other significant challenges on a daily, hourly, and often moment-to-moment basis. My conscience was clear, yet I kept getting hit by the mud slung from every direction. Most of those slinging either had dirty hands themselves or had looked the other way in the face of obvious wrongdoing. I, the one with the integrity and courage to speak up, was now also the one being punished. Despite all my efforts to avoid it, I'd become the scapegoat nonetheless, just in a different way than I'd anticipated. Here again, the irony was not lost on me; however, it didn't make the situation any easier to deal with, and it certainly didn't seem fair.

I kept telling myself that I'd done the right thing and the situation would not last forever. Living with myself, however, was something I would have to do forever—or at least for the rest of my life. My self-respect was still intact as were my resiliency and self-reliance. My inner compass was spinning as usual, and I continued to let my intuition guide me while I forced the rest to the back of my mind. There was nothing to be gained from dwelling on what I couldn't control. This would only dilute my focus, and a diluted focus did not do much for self-preservation and survival in a war zone, especially with specific enemies lurking about.

Speaking of my enemies, my team and I now faced the gargantuan task of handling our alcohol business. Following the audit, we had to proceed with extreme caution. Every sale involving alcohol with our key-accounts customers required approval on a case-by-case basis. We knew that ultimately we would have to close the doors on our key-accounts business, but we did not know exactly how or when that would happen. (The owner and upper management were still in the process of deciding, and we would have to wait for the final decision to cascade through to our ranks.)

Our warehouse stock levels were at maximum capacity in beer, wine, and spirits, with more containers on the way. It seemed as if history was on the verge of repeating itself yet again, at least where alcohol was concerned. Upon entering our warehouse, I couldn't help but think that it appeared we had enough vodka to supply Russia. Our inventory stood at almost a hundred thousand bottles. Beer was at a comparable level, with containers arriving daily. Consequently, the contents of our pallets spilled over their boundaries. It was another case of potential commercial suicide.

No one on our procurement team in Dubai had anticipated a suspension in the selling of alcohol, and based on previous sales history, they had continued to order from our suppliers several months in advance. We had to devise a plan aimed at clearing the stock as quickly as possible but without compromising our business integrity or jeopardizing our government/military contracts. The situation we faced was enough to drive anyone to drink! (Irony and pun both intended.)

In terms of business, customer demand wasn't the issue. It was more a question of closely monitoring the situation from a risk-management perspective and designing an interim solution until a final exit strategy was put in place. Realistically, we would require three months to run our existing stock levels down to a manageable level, and this did not count the stock still in transit.

Those customers still unaware of any operational changes in our business had become increasingly frustrated, as the orders they had placed were often delayed and subject to Vaughn's approval. The situation was delicate to put it mildly, and as a precautionary measure, we had informed each of our key-accounts customers that we were currently "reassessing our processes." It seemed that our customers had anticipated that we would cease our alcohol business, as more and more of our clients increased their orders, purchasing in bulk and then stockpiling.

We knew that once we gave our customers a cutoff purchasing date, it would create a wave of panic buying. This meant that we could sell a container of beer in two days and the equivalent of a container of vodka in three days, and needless to say, our overstocking problem would improve. Without flooding the market, it would be impossible to completely resolve the issue, and that was out of the question. It was a mess, a catch-22, and a snafu all rolled into one.

After much deliberation upper management decided to cease our key-accounts business by the end of August, which would allow us to give our customers four weeks' notice and thereby also allow us to sell as much stock as possible. It wasn't as if we had to twist any customers' proverbial arms to purchasing the stock. Rather, it was more a case of having to police the quantities ordered as a way to avoid the issue of on-selling and black marketeering. This issue was rife in Afghanistan, as it inevitably is in a war zone. My team and I had come to learn this only too well, and our primary objective now was to avert anything that could further jeopardize the company.

As scheduled, our key-accounts business ceased operations by the end of August. With the exception of a couple of approved contractual obligations, our days of supplying alcohol in Afghanistan were finally over. The ramifications of it endured, though. The repercussions of corruption always do.

The decision to cease our alcohol operations had cut off the supply chain and further opened up new opportunities for bootlegging, which in turn severely inflated the price of alcohol on the black market. Sources informed me that since demand was now far greater than the supply, black marketeers would often sell a bottle of Absolut, Jack Daniels, or Johnny Walker Red for between US$100 and US$130 a bottle. Having to purchase alcohol from other sources also meant that it was difficult to establish whether the bottle was the genuine article. Consequently, approximately three months after we ceased supplying alcohol, there were reports of people going blind, becoming extremely ill, and even dying as a result of having consumed pure alcohol.

We'd had no choice but to cease alcohol sales once all the irregularities came to light, but the extreme consequences were nonetheless extremely difficult to accept. It was hard to imagine that our responsible business move had resulted in such adverse effects. People in desperate circumstances will always take desperate measures in war zones and elsewhere. In addition and quite tragically so, there is always a fine line between fulfilling the necessities entailed by living in a danger zone and just being reckless and foolhardy. Clearly, many in this situation crossed that line, and quite likely, addiction and dependence blurred it until it was invisible to many others. It was a sad situation all the way round in a prevailing environment that was sadder still.

The Visa Issue

Once alcohol sales ceased, I decided it was time to take a much-needed rest, and I went on a brief vacation. Despite this, I still had to contend with the wolves I had left behind, who were intent on seeing me removed from my position. Conspiracy was as rife as corruption in Afghanistan, and I had seen many go out on leave and never return. Some were told not to return; others simply couldn't take it in theater and only realized it once they returned to ordinary life. It thus became sort of a ritual to ensure all belongings were packed, particularly valuables, just in case the vacation became permanent by choice or decree. During the three years I had been in Afghanistan, I lost count of the number of those who simply never returned. I was technically the longest-serving GM of TerraTota's business unit in Afghanistan. Since I had become a person of interest, I made it my job to store everything in black footlockers with secured padlocks, so if the time came, I could instruct Nicholas to send my belongings home. Even more important, this ensured that no Afghans were able to pick through my belongings, which often happened to those unprepared.

Because I was a person of interest, I knew they would try everything possible to remove me—to destroy me if need be. When they saw that I would not give in to fear tactics, they shifted their attention to my staff, putting emotional pressure on those closest to me. This was even more difficult to deal with than facing concerns regarding my own safety. To know that those who supported me and helped me were now essentially being punished for their loyalty tore me to pieces. The best I could do was to stand by them as staunchly as they had stood by me. We vowed to be there for each other through thick and thin, and we were. These bonds were much like those forged in battle. In essence, we *were* in battle.

No sooner had we grown accustomed to what I came to call "fallout management" than a new issue arose that we had to deal with—what we referred to as the "visa issue." The visa issue first made its presence known shortly after Kurtis's termination and my return to Kabul from Dubai (and my meeting with Vaughn). Although it did not seem to present that much of a challenge at first, the visa issue would prove to have a tremendous impact on our operations in Afghanistan.

To give a bit of background on this, processing six-month visas in Afghanistan had always been an issue because the MoI took its time, often using delaying tactics. At one point, we had hundreds of staff members with expired visas. An option was presented to us to resolve this issue. We could renew all visas in Kandahar. This process seemed to be an easy alternative, and instead of six-month visas, they were issuing twelve-month visas for expats. Thus, the Kandahar option actually seemed better than the one we'd had up to that point.

Several other companies that had the same problem with visa renewals had also chosen the Kandahar option. This new option had worked well—at least for the first six months or so. At that point a sting conducted by local Afghan authorities discovered that hundreds of the twelve-month visas issued in Kandahar were in fact fake. They had not been processed through the correct system. This discovery practically threw our entire operation into chaos. Our business was crippled by the fact that all personnel issued twelve-month visas were unable to travel around Kabul.

The Afghan government had instructed police checkpoints to check all internationals' passports in order to ensure that all visas were valid. This meant that many personnel ran the risk of being apprehended by the Afghan police for not having a valid visa, and this could result in deportation. Consequently, the company made the decision to keep all employee passports in the company safe, and personnel were instructed to travel only with a photocopy of their passport as ID. The practice became somewhat difficult and dangerous, not to mention that there was a growing fear among our staff that in a state of emergency and/or in the case of an evacuation, they would not be able to leave the country because they didn't have access to their passports. Above all, this created an environment of fear and dread fomented by deception. It was a strike against basic human decency in my opinion. Everyone around me felt the same, whether they vocalized it or not. Morale was soon at an all-time low. Personnel were faced with not only the ongoing fear associated with the dangers living in Afghanistan but also with uncertainty about their future. The former was an expectation of living and working in theater; the latter was not, and it was completely unnecessary and should never have happened in the first place. Many staff contemplated returning home. Once the company imposed restricted movement, however, those who wanted to go home couldn't even travel.

The situation went on for weeks and eventually months. Those personnel who insisted on going home were told that they couldn't come back. In one instance, several staff from India and Nepal had traveled home on vacation, and when they arrived in KAIA, they were nearly arrested for having twelve-month visas. Narrowly escaping being apprehended by the authorities, they had to surrender their passports. They later returned to the airport to retrieve their passports only to be arrested and taken to CID headquarters, where they were detained for several hours until the company was able to negotiate their release.

Needless to say, this incident created panic across our entire business, and many wanted to return back to their homelands and a safer environment. Many questioned why our company couldn't find a solution and how they allowed the situation to continue. The TCNs in particular found it demoralizing and demotivating.

As time went on, the visa issue worsened and became more complicated. My own staff had become demotivated and depressed, as they feared for their own safety, not just in the face of ever-present insurgencies and suicide attacks but also because of the so-called legitimate authorities. The fact that our company showed no outrage and offered no support only made it worse. One of my staff, a TCN from Nepal, spent two days in bed because of acute depression. She simply couldn't understand why the company behaved as it did in regard to the passports, which caused the staff to feel completely adrift and helpless. I agreed but was unable to comfort her. As a manager, I felt doubly helpless. My staff understood that these decisions were made far above me, but that didn't make me feel any better. They were being subjected to a form of mental torture, and they knew it.

After this incident I fought even harder than I had up to that point to get our staff passports back, seeking to give my team some kind of reassurance. Not having their passports deprived them of their dignity as well as their safety. In the end, I couldn't win this battle alone and had to escalate it. With Niels's assistance, my entire team got their passports back. But the damage was irreparable. The team remained unsettled by it all, having lost not only their dignity but their faith and trust in the company as well.

I was demoralized on top of all I'd been through in resolving the export issue. How could a company as large as our multinational organization, which was able to feed and fuel the entire ISAF operation in Afghanistan, be unable to ensure the safety of their own personnel? And passport was equivalent to safety in Afghanistan. The more I thought about it, the more I realized that the visa issue had to be one that upper management could address and successfully resolve. As with sweeping the truth about export under the rug until the rug was pulled aside (by me), it seemed patently clear that only one message existed in TerraTota: "Protect the business at all costs."

There was mention of the company's unpaid taxes to the Afghan government, which was apparently at the root of the visa issue. Snapshot images of the long-ago set-to between Kurtis and the MoI customs official flashed through my mind. I recalled how I'd defused things and wondered how many other instances of Western bravado on the part of our company were now coming back to haunt innocent employees, especially the TCNs. The unfairness of it all rankled me as always. Hardworking staff should not have to suffer the effects of management egotism and blundered behavior, but inevitably they do. This is just the way of the world.

Of course the rumors about the unpaid taxes spread through our entire employee community like the plague, which only made matters worse. One way or another the Afghan government was adamant that we would pay, and it was only a matter of time before they escalated the pressure exerted. This was a war our company did not want to fight, but not unlike the Afghan government, they used delay tactics. Things became increasingly difficult with each passing day, and soon people were told that when they went on vacation, they wouldn't be able to return. Staffing became a huge problem across the business, as it was difficult to find replacements when there were no visas to mobilize new personnel. In addition, the whole visa issue was a ploy to encourage all international companies to employ more Afghans as opposed to Filipinos, Indians, Nepalese, and Zimbabweans. Clearly, the TCNs, who worked hard and sought only to improve their own lives and the lives of their loved ones back home, were blatantly and unfairly targeted.

The situation continued to deteriorate rapidly. On a couple of occasions, my employees were arrested while they were traveling between locations. One particular evening I was out for dinner with a former colleague when I received a phone call from one of my staff. Quite distressed, she proceeded to relate that she and her coworker (both my employees, both female, and both TCNs) had been apprehended at a police checkpoint only five minutes from our compound. It was a couple of days prior to Afghan New Year celebrations, and security had been stepped up because of the associated risk. I had no choice but to drive to the checkpoint where they had been arrested, try to defuse the situation, and get them released. I alerted our security and our interpreter, Kareem, instructing them to meet me near the checkpoint. Security was for extra backup support just in case; Kareem was essential. As Hasib drove up to the checkpoint, we could see several plainclothes CIDs who were relentless in their efforts to stop all traffic. It was pitch black, and one of the detectives motioned for Hasib to pull over near our bus, which was stationed inside the checkpoint area. Our two staff members had been inside that bus, but were now detained in police headquarters. This detective appeared to be quite aggressive, and he repeatedly made hand gestures asking me to show him my ID. I had been through this scenario many times, and I was adamant about only showing him my ISAF ID through the car window. I pretended to be on the phone, seemingly unaware of his precise demands. Miraculously, this charade worked. Otherwise, I, too, would have found myself in the hands of the Afghan authorities.

Eventually, our security arrived, and they deflected the detective's attention back to the two staff they had already apprehended. I was thrilled to be so ignored, but I had to focus on getting my staff safely back to our compound. Together with our security,

I prevailed upon the detective. Initially, it seemed like a kind of game for this guy. He was out to catch as many internationals as possible. In reality, he was just doing his job like any other member of law enforcement in any other country.

The truth of it was that it wasn't the detective's fault. Our people should have had valid visas, but like the rest of this turmoil-ridden country, we were caught in a web of politics, deceit, and corruption beyond our control.

Finally, we seemed to make some headway with the detective, who motioned for us to follow him. We had no choice but to proceed in our vehicle behind his police vehicle, which led us to where our staff were held. By this point, it was almost ten o'clock at night, and the police station was in an area known to be Taliban country. As described in previous chapters, I had been in many Afghan police stations, but one in Taliban territory was a first.

When we arrived, we had to park outside the police station itself, which was surrounded by an old brick wall and a wrought-iron fence guarded by the ANA. It was difficult to see in the pitch darkness, as distant candlelit dwellings were the only source of illumination. There were some stars but no moon, and the blackness of the night seemed ready to swallow us up.

One of our local Afghan security guards had come out of kindness, wanting to offer his support. Kareem, who was Pashtun, knew the area quite well. "Stay close," he said to me. It was inherently dangerous for a white female to be wandering around this area, but he tactfully didn't say that in so many words.

We had certainly attracted some attention just by parking outside the police station, as several Afghan men congregated opposite our vehicles. Their focus on our presence was obvious. I said an inward prayer of thanks for Hasib, Kareem, and our security detail.

We had yet to make our way inside this guarded fortress. Upon approaching the entrance, Kareem spoke in Dari to the police at the door, explaining to me that it was too late for us to enter. We would have to wait until daylight. Kareem didn't need to see my expression. Nor did I need to reply. He knew what my response would be. Speaking to the police further, it turned out that Kareem happened to know one of the higher-ranking police quite well, so it was agreed that he and I would be allowed to enter the station together.

Afghan police stations are far from pleasant in the daytime. A Taliban-country police station in the dead of night is an experience unto itself. I willed myself past any fear. There was no choice but to defuse the situation as quickly as possible. Two of my staff had been arrested and were undoubtedly afraid for their safety and well-being just as I was. After all, one of them was officially illegal in the country, having no visa, and she could now face imprisonment and deportation. The longer incidents like this were left to fester, the larger the issue would become. This meant that more police would get involved, increasing the likelihood of bribery.

Like every other Afghan police station I had entered, the building was dilapidated, operating with the bare minimum of resources. No electricity, only a candlelit room where the commander sat at one end, and my two staff sat alongside a wall opposite him. As we entered the room, the commander was busily going through all the contents of the backpack of one of my staff. Employed as a beautician, she had many things with her, some of which I am sure the commander had never seen before and which would catch his attention. Because it was a Muslim country, I was a little concerned that he would mistake her job for another profession, which would create a far more dangerous situation, one that Kareem and I might not be able to defuse. I could see the commander smile out of the corner of his mouth, enjoying his private thoughts. Even in a place like Kabul, whorehouses were still to be found, often referred to as "Chinese takeaways." (I learned this after once making the mistake of asking my staff if they felt like ordering Chinese takeaway [Aussie for takeout]. Of course I was referring to Chinese food, not sex. My staff enlightened me about the colloquialism immediately.)

So there were Kareem and I sitting in the police commander's office in Taliban country after eleven o'clock at night, having to explain why one of my employees had such items as massage oil, wax, and brightly colored nail polish in her bag and why she didn't possess a valid Afghan visa.

I still wasn't sure in Muslim law which was a greater crime—being a prostitute or an illegal immigrant. This situation was now looking very dangerous. Kareem kept getting up and going into another room with a plainclothes detective. Apparently, he was trying to negotiate with the police commander to get our staff released.

I kept hearing the word *baksheesh,* which could be a good thing. Police were often just after bribes, and I quietly hoped this was the case. The problem was that because of Kareem's odd behavior and coincidental connection with one of the police in this station, I had to wonder if perhaps he had somehow orchestrated this whole incident. Could it be yet another conflict of interest? I hoped not, but cynicism had become a necessary life skill.

He was adamant that offering US$200 or US$300 would secure the release of my staff. Then something changed, as if the commander had decided that it was his formal duty or some mandated protocol to send us to police headquarters for the chief of command to make the official decision. Perhaps he was worried about the consequences of letting an incident like this slide, especially since CID detectives were involved and might ask questions later.

Once an incident report had been documented, we were told that our staff would be taken to headquarters, where the chief of command would make his decision. Now the situation had escalated to a different level, which I had feared from the start. We had no choice but to follow the police vehicle transporting my staff to police headquarters, which was approximately a forty-minute journey. It was now quite obvious that any further room for negotiating had been quashed, and now the bureaucracy would take its supposed natural course—justice! I could hear the sound of the red tape unfurling in a sticky mess.

By the time we arrived at police headquarters, it was half past midnight. This was an area I had never visited before, and once again, we had to park outside the station before we received permission to enter. The outside air reeked, probably from the chicken market across the street. The stench of poultry was unmistakable.

These ancillary unpleasantries aside, the whole situation was becoming quite an ordeal. My concern for my staff had multiplied exponentially. I steeled myself for battle, praying inwardly that it would turn out all right—far better than the scenarios my feverish mind kept playing out. The police station itself appeared to be more structured, at least from the outside. Several police waited outside for us, as if we were officials of some sort. Kareem and I entered the compound while the rest of our entourage waited patiently outside.

We entered the office of the commander, which was completely different from the last station. His office was quite luxurious, more of a lounge than an office, complete with sofa, coffee table, and TV. It reminded me of the commander's office in Police District 9. Political propaganda covered his desk, and a large framed photo of the commander standing next to Karzai was prominently displayed behind his desk.

"He's the new head of command for PD 9," Kareem informed me. "This is their new headquarters."

So I'd been right to think the office décor seemed familiar. This must just be the style of head of command. I suppressed a chuckle, knowing I needed to stay focused and appear as businesslike and tough as possible, but the momentary humor had done me good. My head actually felt a bit clearer, and I was ready to do battle for my girls.

Two plainclothes detectives sat opposite us, watching the TV. My staff had been asked to sit patiently until the commander arrived. It was possible that we were in for another long wait, as it was almost one o'clock in the morning. The commander might very well have been asleep when he'd received the call to come to headquarters.

As we waited, I couldn't help but feel that this situation appeared to be more civilized than in the first station. I hoped that we would possibly arrive at a solution before daybreak.

The commander arrived a few minutes later, and he looked impeccable in his uniform, especially given the late hour.

He introduced himself to me through Kareem, explaining that he was new to his role. Although he spoke limited English, we agreed to continue to communicate through Kareem. He politely apologized for not being able to offer us tea or coffee, but they had no gas left to boil water.

There was something incredibly charming about this man. Now was my best chance to defuse this situation and get my staff released. Before I had time to initiate this course of action, Kareem began explaining the situation in detail to the commander. He asked to see the passports and then proceeded to read the report made by the previous police station.

He had just one question for me. "Why are these ladies working for you on expired tourist visit visas?"

The commander's question summarized the whole deplorable situation. I had to think quickly. If I didn't provide him with a rock-solid answer, it would be a disaster. I gave him the simplest response I could.

"We're in the process of having their visas renewed, Commander. We're waiting on the MoI to advise us when they will be processed." We had used this answer in the past, so I pulled it off well enough, better than I could have if I'd rehearsed it.

He nodded, seeming to be quite reasonable. After he listened to my explanation, he proceeded to explain through Kareem that he would have to document the incident and treat this case as a pending investigation. He would then draft a statement for me to sign stating that as GM I would act as guarantor for my two female staff members and report back to the station with them two days later. It was the best deal we were going to get, so I agreed.

"They will face deportation if their visas are not renewed," he affirmed.

I was perfectly aware of this fact. Fortunately, he never thought to ask to see *my* passport or visa. I was in the same boat as my staff. My visa had expired. Nevertheless, I had somehow managed to bluff my way through this whole scenario. Perhaps it was the simple fact that I was a female Caucasian. I'd gotten through by the skin of my teeth many other times for the very same reason. Inwardly, I said a prayer of thanks, and we left the station.

Having to return two days later raised the possibility of putting myself at risk or in danger of being arrested and deported. Nonetheless, it was a risk I had to take. It was my priority to get my staff released and safely back to our compound.

Once my mission was accomplished, we would then make the next decision as to how we would proceed. Of course, I knew automatically what my next step would be. It was obvious that I had exposed myself to danger and needed the help of our legal eagles to dig me out. It had been a long night, and although extremely exhausted, I was incredibly emotionally relieved. With the nod of approval from the commander following my word as guarantor, we made our way back to the compound.

Return to Police Headquarters

I now had very little time to waste and knew that it was imperative for me to inform our legal team first thing in the morning about what had happened. That night I barely slept, tossing and turning while thinking about the sequence of events and making a mental note of all the facts I needed to relay to them.

Eventually, I drifted off, only to wake up four short hours later. As soon as I awoke, the return to police headquarters the following day was the first thing I thought of. I wasted no time getting ready and headed straight to the office. I met with a legal adviser who happened to be on his way out that day for vacation. I was relieved to see him before he left, as he was the only guy in theater who had legal qualifications, so I knew his advice would be the best chance I had. He told me that an official letter from the company would be drafted explaining that our company was in the process of resolving the visa issue with the Afghan government. I hoped this would do the trick, along with having a legal representative present just in case the commander had any further questions. (I had already dug myself a shallow grave, so I knew that it would be better for the experts to step in and handle this situation from this point on.)

The arrangement with the commander was for me and my two staff members to return to the station at eleven o'clock in the morning along with the company letter and a legal representative. The legal rep and I had arranged to meet up first thing on Saturday morning to discuss the letter, and since it was a forty-minute journey, we could allow plenty of time for travel. It all seemed cut-and-dried—to the extent that was possible in Afghanistan anyway. What happened next was beyond comprehension.

Once Saturday morning came, I received a phone call from one of the liaison officers informing me that the company letter was ready and they had decided to send the company travel assistant (i.e., the "meet and greet" person) as the company representative. (This assistant was Afghan.) "Give us a call if there are any problems."

I was nonplussed. I didn't know whether to be enraged, disgusted, or scared out of my wits. The mix of conflicting emotions succeeded in making me feel numb. A moment later the numbness gave way to rage, which burned away any fear, but the disgust lingered. "Did they get scared about what could happen and decide to just pull a rabbit out of the hat for a solution?" I muttered, covering the phone so he wouldn't hear me. Out loud, I said, "The representative won't be necessary. Thanks. I'll handle it with my staff."

I preferred to rely on my own abilities than those of a glorified bus driver, thank you very much! In the end I took the letter to police headquarters myself, accompanied by Kareem and my security detail.

The commander was waiting for us as agreed. As had been the case during our first meeting, he was an absolute gentleman.

Kareem presented him with the letter and then went on to explain its contents, even though he had given him Dari and English versions.

The commander continued to appear to be very reasonable, and after a lengthy discussion with Kareem, he requested that we update him as to the resolution of the situation in two weeks' time, as the letter stipulated this as the anticipated date of resolution.

It was as if my guardian angel was protecting me and all my sins were forgiven! We had perhaps earned the commander's trust by honoring the initial agreement, and so he was happy for us to return to the police station once again in the next couple of weeks to inform him of a resolution.

I think we all uttered a sigh of relief that day. Despite the lack of support we received from the company, we were just happy to be free, and we all went back to the compound.

To finish the irony of the story, I was subsequently informed that I should have taken a company representative with me just in case I said something to the Afghan authorities that could have jeopardized the negotiations TerraTota had in process with the government. Of course there was no mention of how the lack of support from the corporate side could easily have jeopardized the safety and well-being of two women who were loyal, hardworking employees. I felt like I had turned my world upside down to expose one corrupt situation only to find myself embroiled in another that was far worse and would be far harder if not impossible to fight. The whole thing made me sick.

And that's not the end of the story. I later learned that one of the reasons why the police commander had been so flexible and accommodating was that his brother had a logistics, supply-chain, and construction company and was interested in doing business with our organization in the future. A few weeks after this incident I found a large presentation folder left on my desk, ready for my perusal. It was a gift from the police commander, who apparently had been desperately trying to contact me through Kareem in order to introduce me to his brother.

Could this whole incident have been carefully orchestrated as a means to fulfill their true purpose? And how involved in it all was Kareem? These questions remained unanswered much to my dismay, as Kareem was someone I had come to trust and rely on. Loyalty in Afghanistan shifted like the desert sands in a windstorm, which was why true loyalty and trust were the most treasured commodities to be found. I prayed that I had not misplaced my trust in anyone else I was close to.

I never did go back to police headquarters to meet with the commander. Nor was there ever a warrant made out for my arrest. The gods or my guardian angel at work again, I suppose. But as much as I hoped that the visa issue would be the last bit of corruption I had to deal with, it wasn't. Not by a long shot. In fact, the export ordeal notwithstanding (and it was the worst challenge I faced personally while in theater), the most horrific situation I had to face in Afghanistan was about to begin.

8

TRUTH AND CONSEQUENCES

Dealing with tying up the loose ends of export seemed a never-ending process. These activities seemed to be the consequences of exposing the truth, and the term *truth and consequences* took on deeper meaning for me. What I had come to think of as fallout management, sort of like damage control but done in reverse, after the fact instead of before. This was more than enough for one person to have to handle on an ongoing basis (usually a daily basis), but more was soon to come. As I said at the end of the previous chapter, the most horrific situation that I would have to face in Afghanistan was about to begin.

This ordeal was not actually mine but one of my employee's. However, extreme harm done to one human being negatively affects us all. This is why violations of human rights are crimes against humanity, the whole of us and not merely the individuals directly abused or impacted. I couldn't help but think that the years of unchecked corruption had led to these human rights violations, as it is all too easy to lose our way along the slippery slope of the downward spiral of wrongdoing.

This was more than just coping with the prevailing drama and intrigue of Afghanistan, and it was more than merely combating corruption born of greed and lust for power. This was a fight against evil in its truest, darkest, direst form—the strong abusing the weak simply because no one will stand up to fight for what is right. I did stand up to fight for what was right as soon as I was aware of the abuses. Of course I did—that is always my gut reaction, and I will follow my intuitive response to it with my dying breath. Tragically, though, my step into the fight came too late.

I relate the story that follows to inspire others to see that our own moral conviction can—and should—power our actions even when we feel it is too late and even when it *is* too late in concrete terms. Our true intentions, whether for good or ill, outlast our physical presence on this earth. We would be wise to remember that. I have faith that the good I have done and the fights I have engaged in to do the right thing—both the battles I won and the ones I lost—will live on.

Aneni

After several long months of intense challenges (the audit, Kurtis's termination, and the visa issue—all on top of fulfilling my duties as GM in Kabul while simultaneously running the KAF project in Kandahar), I decided that now was the time to make a trip home. In addition to wanting to see friends and family, I needed more than just a few days off. This had been my longest stretch in theater, seven months with no more than five days off at a time, and most of my R & R had been in Dubai, which meant that I wasn't technically on vacation. If ever I had earned a holiday, it was now. I was exhausted physically, emotionally, and mentally.

Despite my desperately needing to rest and rejuvenate, the first few days home proved to be a different kind of challenge. My mind was still in overdrive, making me irritable and hyperactive throughout the day and restless at night. I had not really slept during the past several months, and I hoped to break the pattern of insomnia while I was relaxing at home. This did not seem to be happening, and my frustration made the irritability, restlessness, and sleeplessness even worse.

"Letting go of it all is the hardest part, MJ," my dad said quietly in the midst of a vivid deep-pink and vermilion sunset. As usual, he knew exactly what was going on within me, perhaps even better than I did.

All I wanted was to let go of the mental torture I had lived with for the past eighteen months. I told him so.

"We're built to hold on, to fight. That's what makes us good soldiers."

This was the best compliment my dad could pay me or anyone else. It brought tears to my eyes. "Thanks, Dad."

He nodded and gave me a small smile, patted my shoulder, and headed toward the house. At the door he paused, saying over his shoulder, "Don't try so hard to let it go. Just let it happen. Best advice I can give you."

I nodded, turning back toward the flaming ball of the descending sun once the door shut behind my dad. Mentally, I *was* ready. I had worked hard to put the whole export incident behind me, including the audit and all its fallout. The challenge was that *someone* didn't want me to forget so easily. Since flying out of Afghanistan and into Dubai on my way to Australia, I had received numerous persistent phone calls. Of course, every time I answered, the person on the other end of the line would immediately hang up. Sometimes there would just be silence on the other end. These persistent phone calls carried on through the night and continued after I landed in Singapore. (I had decided to spend two days as a stopover in Singapore before I flew to Australia.) I couldn't sleep, and I knew that this was no coincidence. Someone, whoever it was, wanted to drive me to the brink of mental collapse. I was determined not to give in. I had come too far to weaken now, and I was determined to fight back. I *would* find out who was behind this.

I needed some assistance in unraveling this latest mystery, and I had to make sure that I confided in someone I trusted, someone who would not dismiss this as just paranoid behavior. If I could get to the bottom of this latest development, it might provide a clue to solving the larger puzzle (i.e., who the mastermind of the whole export scheme really was) because I knew Kurtis couldn't have done it all alone. The next day I forwarded the number connected with the calls to Nicholas, asking him to get Hasib to call the number and find out who was behind this harassment.

Two days later Nicholas called to tell me that Hasib had contacted the person. "He has no connection to you or the company, Boss. He was told to constantly call your number, and he was paid 400 dirhams for his services." (Dirhams are the currency of Dubai [see glossary], where the calls were made from.)

"Thanks, Nicholas. Let me know if you learn more." We said goodbye and ended the call.

My suspicions were confirmed, and paranoia played no part. I was relieved to know I wasn't losing my mind or my grip on reality, but I was furious that someone sought to perpetuate the nightmare of export. More than ever, I was determined to find out who was behind this. I suspected that it must be someone who felt threatened by the recent scandal in our business, someone who wanted me out of the way and felt that I would crumble if pushed to the limit. I had become the person of interest in more ways than one, and I was not about to also become the victim of anyone's vengeful behavior. The more I thought about it, the more frustrated I became. That frustration quickly ignited into rage.

Fortunately, once I arrived in Australia, Hasib had spoken to the person making the calls, and they ceased. I felt relieved, but as I described, the frustration, irritability, and restlessness did not stop immediately. It was my dad's words at sunset that truly helped me find the peace to let it go. I'd always thought that peace was what we found once we had let go of what we could no longer bear, but now I realized the reverse was true. Peace was the calm center within us that enabled us *to* let go. Dad and my inner compass had done it again! I felt free, and I could now finally take a much-deserved rest.

The next three weeks were spent resting, eating good food, drinking good wine, and just trying to keep all that had happened in the past. I couldn't forget, and I wasn't sure I would ever be able to forgive; however, I could relegate it to history, which was where it belonged. Acceptance was the first step forward, and I kept reminding myself that was so.

My father's intuitive knowing notwithstanding, I couldn't bring myself to discuss the whole scenario with him or any of my family and friends. It was still too fresh, and the wounds were still too raw. It was going to take more than a few weeks to heal those many months of mental anguish and emotional strain. I wanted to use the time to just buffer myself from the past, to recharge my internal battery. When I returned to Afghanistan, I would need all the strength and energy I could muster in order to be at my resilient, focused, and self-reliant best. Plus, I knew that if my parents actually knew all that had happened, they would try to convince me not to go back to Afghanistan. Even if my dad secretly supported my soldiering, my mother's concerns would supersede it, and he would encourage me not to go back for her sake. If presented with such a request, I would give in. I couldn't bear the thought of worrying either of my parents, especially my mum, who had no idea her rosary beads weren't safely ensconced among my most precious belongings at all times. (I still wondered how things would have turned out if I'd had them with me in theater, as there is no underestimating the value of sacred objects of protection. It was water under the bridge, and I'd never get them back; but that didn't cease my wondering.)

All that said, I simply wasn't ready to resign because it would mean that I had given up. I had come too far and gone through too much to throw in the towel now. Besides, I had my loyal staff to consider, as well as my confidant, Niels. Having been through so much together, we had all made a pact to see the next twelve month's journey through as a team. I couldn't let them down, and I couldn't let myself down. Resigning now would mean that those I'd fought so hard to expose would have won. Corruption would have defeated integrity. I simply could not allow that to happen. When I returned from Afghanistan for good, I would tell my family and close friends the truth of all that had happened. For now I had to go on. The battle wasn't quite won, at least not yet.

* * *

I knew there were a lot of loose ends that I still had to tie up, and I also knew that I would continue to have to deal with fallout management and all it entailed, but what I was about to face upon returning to Kabul was far worse than I could possibly have imagined.

A few days prior to flying back to Dubai, I received a call from Grogan, our new HR manager in Kabul.

"One of your staff members, Aneni, has fallen mentally ill," he informed me. "She'll have to be repatriated immediately. She needs to return home in order to seek proper medical treatment, and of course to have the support of her family."

"Yes, of course," I agreed. "Please give Aneni my best regards, and let her know she's in my thoughts. I'm sorry I can't be there to attend to things."

"It's quite all right. This is what we're here for in HR. I'll fill you in when you return."

We ended our call, and I felt saddened; however, it did all make sense, as many staff eventually crumbled under the pressures of being in theater in the long term. I appreciated the notification, as it was more or less a courtesy call. HR could make repatriation decisions without either the approval or the knowledge of employees' managers.

Two days later I flew from Australia via Singapore and back to Dubai. This time it would only be a few hours' stopover time, just enough to do some duty-free shopping. I had planned to spend a couple of days in the office in Dubai prior to flying back into Kabul. It was always a good move to catch up with the headquarters staff, particularly as it pertained to operational support. And of course, I wanted to catch up with Niels as well.

I left Singapore early in the morning, scheduled to land in Dubai in the afternoon. Although I had enjoyed the break from all the mayhem, I now looked forward to getting back into the swing of things, not being one to like staying idle for too long.

As soon as I landed in Dubai, I turned on my cell phone only to discover that I had a series of missed calls. Hoping that it wasn't the recent unknown caller, I quickly scanned the numbers, noticing that they were all from the Kabul office. This was rather strange, as I hadn't received any calls from my staff while I was on vacation, none other than Nicholas's responses to my queries. They all knew how much I needed the rest. It wouldn't be like them to start bombarding me the moment they knew I'd be landing in Dubai. But we did work in a war zone, so it might not have been up to them when to call me. A pit immediately started to form in my stomach, and I started to think the worst. Had someone been injured or killed? Had our KAF site been hit by a rocket attack? (These were all too frequent in Kandahar, as I've mentioned, and we had previously experienced a couple of close calls, often on a daily basis.) It was impossible to guess what it might be in an environment like Afghanistan. There were just too many possibilities to consider.

Rather than wonder and make myself even more stressed-out than was necessary, I decided to just call Nicholas for an update. I was just about to hit his number in my contacts when I received a call from Tucker. He was extremely distressed, and at first it was a little difficult for me to understand everything he was saying. In addition, I was outside the airport by this time, waiting to catch a taxi, and the ambient noise made it almost impossible for me to hear. I undoubtedly missed more than half his words. All I knew for sure was that he was very upset, almost at the brink of tears, which was very unusual. Tucker was very strong and tough, and he rarely stressed about anything. Even during the recent audit investigation, when he had been under substantial scrutiny as warehouse manager, he had shown an amazing amount of fortitude. In fact, he'd helped the rest of us keep on going, myself included. In short, the sudden show of emotions from someone like Tucker was not something to take lightly. I didn't.

"I can barely hear a word you're saying, Tucker. I'll call you as soon as I get to the hotel."

"Okay, Boss. I'm so relieved to talk to you… so glad you're on your way back."

I made that part out clear enough. I felt awful wondering what he'd said that I'd missed hearing, and I was anxious to get to the hotel so I could call him back.

At last, I reached the hotel in Dubai. As soon as I was in my room, I put down my bags and immediately dialed Tucker's number.

"You won't believe what's happened, Boss," he said. "It's Aneni."

The alarm and distress in my warehouse manager's voice came through loud and clear, and with none of the airport's din surrounding me, I was able to hear and understand him perfectly. In a way, I wished I *wasn't* able to. The events he described were nothing less than heinous, the worst kind of brutality and cruelty that one human being can inflict on another.

The long and short of it was that Grogan, our HR manager in Kabul, had treated Aneni, a TCN on my administrative staff, with extreme cruelty and had likely brutalized her as well. Not that I disbelieved Tucker—he'd never been anything other than honest and straight-shooting—but I needed another perspective on the subject from someone I trusted equally before I moved forward with addressing this issue. So I called Nicholas, and he gave me a rundown of what had transpired as well. The details of both their versions were in sync. This had to be addressed immediately, so I prepared to depart for headquarters without delay. Once again I was thrust into a difficult situation completely out of my control and by no fault of my own. This was far more horrific than the corruption related to export, so I felt even more responsible to right the wrong. Immediately was not soon enough.

Knowing many heads would understandably and justifiably roll for this, I nevertheless had to take care with how I proceeded. Accusations with this degree of seriousness had to be made with care. While en route to headquarters, I spoke with each of my key personnel by phone, asking them to describe exactly what they had witnessed or been privy to regarding this incident. This sort of incident would quickly gain the attention of overseas media, other multinational organizations in theater, and highly likely, the military.

I called Nicholas again after speaking with the last employee who had witnessed Aneni's travail. Nicholas was well trained, and he understood the necessity of documenting any incidents that took place in my absence. Given the ordeal of the audit, I'd impressed upon him how essential this was. It was the last thing I told him prior to leaving Kabul for my vacation. Therefore, when he answered my call, I simply said, "You documented everything, didn't you?"

"Of course, Boss. All the details and even a photo."

"I need you to e-mail it all to me, but wait until I phone you from the Dubai office."

I didn't want to risk its traveling through cyberspace until I was ready at the receiving end. Nicholas did as I instructed. Our human rights battle was about to begin.

* * *

Perhaps it was the amount of factual detail given in the incident report. Perhaps it was the photo that literally exemplified the saying, "A picture is worth a thousand words." Perhaps it was a combination of the two. In any case, what my team and I provided to upper management highlighted the absolute mismanagement of a horrific situation. Even worse, it showed that HR had not merely mishandled the situation but had in fact caused it.

Let me back up a bit and fill in all the details. I do not use the words *horrific*, *cruelty*, or *brutality* lightly, but they are appropriate for describing what happened to Aneni. In truth, they are the only words that *are* appropriate. It pains me to write that even now, years later. Aneni was the female employee that Grogan had called me about several days prior, the TCN who had been terminated and was slated for repatriation. However, during the courtesy call Grogan had failed to mention several key events that had transpired. No, he hadn't failed to mention them. He had deliberately excluded them. My horror-fueled rage knew no bounds.

What I learned from Nicholas's incident report was that Grogan had decided to shock Aneni out of her existing state of mind, seemingly mental depression, but this was never clinically diagnosed. Said shock therapy consisted of placing her on the ground outside the warehouse gate. None other than Grogan himself had placed her there! She was utterly defenseless, cruelly left on the dusty ground in the blazing heat of a summer day. She had nothing to shield her from the sun or the heat and no water to drink. As I said, she was utterly defenseless. Barefoot and clad in a minidress and lightweight cardigan, she was essentially dumped into the road along with her suitcase (which contained nothing that would have helped her withstand the elements or protect herself). Left in clear view of all the passing traffic, mostly local Afghan and Pakistani drivers, anything could have happened to her. This was quite likely the worst and most tragic act perpetrated on a human being that I had witnessed during my tenure in Afghanistan (three years in total by the time I left). The worst part for me was that I couldn't help feeling that all this had happened because I wasn't there. It was as if the person responsible had carried out the act believing that in my absence no one would challenge him.

What Grogan didn't realize was that I had a team of individuals who had learned the importance of our bonds. We had become a sort of family, and we supported each other. Nothing was more important in this type of environment. There is no explanation or justification for such an act of brutality, but here is what the HR manager who perpetrated it had to say in his own defense: He claimed to have tried everything to get Aneni to respond, but she was unable to eat, speak, talk, and walk. Indeed, she seemed incapable of any normal voluntary body functions. For some reason her whole body had gone into a state of shock and had seemingly shut down. He never explained precisely what he meant by this. More to the point, instead of using the services to medevac Aneni out of Afghanistan and back to her own country, he chose his own self-devised shock tactic.

Following his depositing Aneni in the dirt like a pile of garbage, the situation deteriorated rapidly. Of course, this was physically, psychologically, and emotionally catastrophic for Aneni, and it was emotionally and psychologically damaging for everyone who witnessed the whole ordeal as well.

One of my admin staff had been on her way to exit our compound when she noticed Aneni lying on the ground. She rushed over, quickly discerning that Aneni appeared to be unconscious. This other staff member immediately went back into the compound in order to alert Tucker. Asking a few of the other guys to accompany him, Tucker raced outside to assess the situation. He immediately went over to the guards stationed not far from where Aneni was lying on the ground with her suitcase, demanding to know how long she had been there and who had put her there. Tucker told the others to carry Aneni inside, as it was clear that she was unconscious and likely dehydrated. It would have been dangerous at best for any of us to remain alone outside our compound. For someone in this state it was potentially fatal, not to mention all the other unspeakable things it was. Though clearly dehydrated, Aneni was unable to open her mouth to receive water and seemed to my staff to be unresponsive. Wondering if she was still suffering from the same mental state as before, they tried several times to ask her what had happened and why she'd been left outside in the dirt. There was no response.

One of the admin staff got a straw, and they began to drip water into Aneni through the side of her mouth, holding up her head and helping her swallow. Apparently, no sooner had they brought Aneni inside and begun attempting to rehydrate her than Grogan burst in, shouting and screaming, demanding to know who had brought her inside. Tucker and Nicholas spoke on behalf of the staff, admitting their involvement and defending their actions. This was the moment when they learned that Grogan himself had dumped Aneni in the dirt!

The incident soon escalated, and there was a serious and heated exchange of dialogue between my staff and Grogan. The whole incident was totally incomprehensible, as I know I've already said. To make matters worse, my guys who had tried to rescue Aneni were now being severely reprimanded by HR, the same person who had put her outside in the first place. Grogan told them in no uncertain terms that the incident was none of their concern and they should not get involved. If they didn't follow his directive as HR manager, they would also face termination. He concluded by informing them that Aneni no longer worked for our organization, and so it was none of their concern. This immediately offended my staff, who felt that anyone as helpless and defenseless as Aneni was at that time should not be treated in this manner. It was barbaric, and they told Grogan so. The situation grew even uglier, severely damaging the relationship between my staff and Grogan, quite likely irreparably so (understandably from my staff's perspective and in my opinion as well). Grogan threatened to terminate my staff if they didn't get back to their duties and leave this situation in his hands. He continually repeated that he was the HR manager and that he would be the one to decide what went on in our compound. My staff was distraught and outraged both by the treatment of Aneni that they had witnessed and by the treatment they themselves had been subjected to by Grogan. They stood their ground with Grogan, and after they exchanged several harsh and heated words, the man tore the ID badge from around the neck of one of my staff, informing him that he had been terminated.

Clearly, this was all designed to terrify my staff into submission, but if anything, it had the exact opposite effect. The entire incident had made them more defiant, determined to stand up to Grogan and to try to defend the clearly helpless Aneni. Aside from feeling that Aneni was family, they also realized that if this could happen to Aneni, it could also happen to any of them. Prickles of fear shuddered along each and every one of their spines, and their anger was all that helped them keep it together.

Despite my despair at not being there to deal with the situation and likely to avert it completely, I was proud to know that my staff had learned to nurture and support each other during times of need. This was something I had worked hard to instill in them, and I was glad to see that my efforts had succeeded. Care and empathy and compassion were not frequent in zones of conflict, and it warmed my heart to see that the harsh environment had not caused them to devolve into greed and apathy or worse, the cruelty exhibited by our so-called human resources representative. I had taught my people to be as tough as they needed to be in order to survive and yet to never let that obscure their ability to care for their fellow human beings. This was the same code I lived by myself, and I would never regret it. I sensed that they wouldn't either.

It was now blatantly obvious that the company's supposed care factor was only a façade, mere lip service. In reality, it came down to protecting business assets, the bottom line, and not our people. I supposed that was the corporate way, and I had just been a bit naive to think otherwise. However, there was a difference between looking the other way because profit was more important than people and wantonly inflicting harm without remorse. It was the latter that I struggled to understand. Why would someone in our organization, whether HR or any other department, feel he had the right to administer his own methodology in an instance where seeking the guidance of a clinically qualified specialist was obviously called for. Psychiatric assessments and subsequent administration of the appropriate treatment was clearly the very least that Aneni needed.

I fought the good fight for what was right, and I stood up for my people. But of course, it was too late in Aneni's case. This tormented me to no end. The eternal question of why persisted, as did the equally eternal absence of an answer. The plain, hard truth is that the most difficult questions rarely, if ever, have answers. We just have to learn to live with what we cannot change or understand.

Postscript: Aneni was a Zimbabwean, and sometime after her repatriation local media in her home country reported that she accused Grogan of rape and other violent acts. Communicating through a relative because her ability to speak never returned, she related all the horrific details. Beyond mere corruption and conflict of interest, this was cruel, horrific brutality of the most barbaric nature. Although the company asserted it would "look into the allegations and proceed accordingly," there seemed to be no urgency to do so, and no actions were taken. Once it was clear that no such actions would ever be forthcoming, my decision not to renew my contract with TerraTota was an easy one.

"Mazar-e-Sharif!"

The Aneni incident on top of the audit and the daily trials of living in theater demotivated my staff dramatically. Understandably, morale was at an all-time low, even worse than during the visa issue. Nothing I tried helped, and even Daisy, Tiger, and our other pets seemed to have little effect on boosting morale. We still had a lot of work to do, and we were expected to get it done. It was clear that termination and repatriation would result if we did not fulfill our duties. Most of my staff, the TCNs particularly, could not afford to lose their jobs or be sent home. Their entire families depended on their income. So despite the heartache we carried, which was hard to let go of and move beyond, we had to carry on. Tucker's "you never know who's who in the zoo" had taken on an even deeper meaning, one that we all acknowledged yet felt disgusted by.

In a way, rolling up our sleeves and getting back to business as usual (Afghan style!) was the best thing for us. For hardworking, dedicated people, work is the best balm there is. And we had plenty of it! Having recently gone through some new operational restructuring following the audit and the recommendations subsequent to it, certain contracts were now in the spotlight.

My new boss, Vaughn, had sent me an e-mail indicating that we had issues with one of our contracts located in the far north of Afghanistan, near Mazar-e-Sharif. This was a site I had previously worked hard to keep, as we had been down this road before, not long after I first arrived. Most of the issues came from an inconsistency within our supply chain, which was one of the many challenges faced by any company operating in a war zone. There were always issues at the Pakistan border, and constant fighting along the pass was one of the main contributors. This particular site was predominantly Swedish, and they regularly consumed large amounts of the moist snus tobacco so adored in that country. Consequently, their demand for the snus was often greater than our supply.

Within an hour of receiving Vaughn's e-mail, I decided that I had to travel to the site myself, as I'd learned that the best way to resolve these issues was to address them in person. I informed my boss that I planned to leave that very day.

The only issue that remained was determining how to get there. There were only two ways to get to Mazar-e-Sharif (Mez, as we called it). Go by mountain road through the Salang Pass or by air. There were only flights twice a week, so the two travel options quickly diminished to one. For me, this wasn't a problem. Hasib and I had made the same journey several times but usually in the summer. I'd only been to the Salang Pass once in the middle of the winter, although I did recall it vividly.

I had only been in Afghanistan for four months, and it was my first visit to Mez, so I'd traveled by air. It was the middle of winter, as I said, and poor weather conditions and snowdrifts forced the closing of the airport prior to my return. As a result, I was literally stuck in Mez for eight days. In a desperate attempt to make my way back to Kabul, I made arrangements to travel back by road, accompanied by two local Afghan guards carrying AK-47s. The guards belonged to a subcontractor doing a lot of work for TerraTota at the time, and they were happy to be of some assistance.

This turned out to be another lengthy driving ordeal. Because of poor visibility and the constant breaking of the chains on the wheels as they went over the icy roads, it took us six and a half hours just to reach the entrance of the Salang Pass. When we arrived, the entrance gates to the pass were closed. We had no choice but to wait for the gates to reopen, so we went to eat lunch in a local restaurant, which meant we were literally in the middle of the mountains in subzero temperatures. Once the guards had scoped the restaurant, making sure we were the only diners, I was escorted into the dining area. I needed to visit the ladies' room first, so once again the guards went on ahead to make sure the coast was clear before they allowed me to enter. I politely asked if there was any chance of toilet paper. One guard grabbed a large plastic jug and proceeded to fill it with icy cold water out of a large trough. Handing the jug to me, he shrugged. It was a case of squat and bare it! I'd endured worse and would endure worse still during my three-year tenure.

The meal itself was quite good—traditional goat stew, vegetable soup, some basic raw vegetables, beef kebab, and freshly baked Afghan bread. It was my first real experience of eating Afghan food. We sat on long cushions placed alongside the wall, and the food was served on a large plastic tablecloth placed on the floor in front of us. They served us strong tea along with the food, and I hoped the combination would sustain us for the next leg of our journey. It was going to be a long haul.

After lunch we made our way back to the vehicle, hoping that the entrance would be open. I could see two snowplows parked next to the entrance to the pass, which meant that they either had already removed excess snow or were about to. We were told to wait at least another hour. The guard responsible for the entrance of the Salang Pass informed one of my guards that there was no chance of the gates reopening that day. Apparently, the pass had experienced a total of sixty-four avalanches that morning, making it impossible for anyone to enter. It was still too dangerous. My chances of traveling back to Kabul by road that day were soon quashed. We had no choice but to start our way back to Mez, which meant another six-and-a-half-hour journey. As it turned out, the airport was cleared before the pass was, so I flew back to Kabul a couple of days later.

Experience had taught me to avoid making the same mistake again. To quote Hasib, "Boss, you have driven *to* the Salang Pass in winter. You have not driven *through* the Salang Pass in winter."

As usual, his wisdom, based on self-evident truth, was irrefutable, so I didn't even attempt to argue. More to the point, I agreed with him.

As it turned out, Hasib had an old friend who had recently been posted to work in the Salang area. He confirmed that the pass was still open. Traveling such a long distance by road meant we would need security. It was impossible to arrange for our existing security company to escort us at such short notice, but Hasib was able to hire two plainclothes CID detectives, Basheer and Omar. Basheer was Hasib's brother-in-law (ex-KGB), and I had met him on many occasions. In fact, he frequently escorted me in and out of KAIA, and we got on quite well. Omar was Basheer's sidekick.

Hasib's friend had reported that there was snowfall in the Salang area, even though the pass was open, and so we expected this trip to be at least an eight-hour journey. I had packed very little, just enough for two days. We did have a full carload of fresh supplies of snus tobacco—a token of goodwill to smooth contract relations. I had planned to meet with the camp commander first thing the following morning. Once I'd accomplished our mission, we would make our way back to Kabul. Of course, this would all depend on the road conditions, as well as the camp commander's availability.

It was a surprise visit, but I hoped that by arriving bearing gifts, my visit would be well received and would produce a favorable outcome.

Before making our way out of Kabul, Hasib collected both Basheer and Omar from the airport. They appeared to be quite excited to be coming with us on our journey, and as they were called at a moment's notice, both of them appeared to be traveling with only the clothes on their backs and their Smith & Wesson handguns.

Our journey began well enough. As we started to make our way toward the Salang Pass, I let my eyes drift shut, wanting to rest a little and knowing that we were about to be on the road for many hours. About three hours later I awoke as our vehicle suddenly stopped. Hasib wanted to rent some chains, which we would need to use on the wheels once we entered the Salang. (Most people rented these just for the journey and returned them on the journey down.)

It was bitterly cold, and Basheer and Omar had the unenviable task of reattaching the chains to the wheels. Initially, these had been attached by the two young boys who rented and sold wheel chains for a living; however, as we began to make our way up the steep mountain gradient, the chains soon loosened and fell off. It was a constant battle to tighten them and keep them attached to the wheels so they could grip the ice. No task for two men in business suits, plainclothes CID or otherwise!

The snowfall was six to nine feet high on either side of the road, covering all of the surrounding earth, vegetation, and most of the houses. Only parts of some of the rooftops poked through the dense carpet of white. As with our first Christmas party, it looked more like a yuletide picture postcard than a war-zone vista. I took several photos with my phone, thinking that this was probably one of the most picturesque views I had seen in a while. Of course, I couldn't help but take a photo of poor Basheer and Omar. They both looked like they were on the verge of frostbite. Every now and then, they would put their hands inside the vehicle, hoping to thaw a bit from the heater's vents. They had to reattach the chains to the tires several times, but they were very good-humored about it all. We all laughed at what a ridiculous experience it was, making our way up that treacherous mountain pass. Now I understood why it was so infamous!

Finally, we saw the entrance to the pass, and the men reattached the chains to the tires for the last time (we hoped). Shaking his head and laughing, Basheer climbed back into the vehicle. "Mazar-e-Sharif!" he shouted, and we all roared with laughter. This had become our catchphrase as we rode along. I couldn't help but smile. Basheer had nothing but adoration for his brother-in-law, Hasib. I felt he loved Hasib like a brother, and so he would do whatever was asked of him just as any good brother would.

Once the chains were securely fastened we continued our journey into the Salang Pass, Hasib carefully maneuvering through the heavy bouts of snow. We weren't the only vehicle making the journey. There were several cars up ahead, including a couple of large coach buses filled with passengers, their luggage secured on top of the roof. (That was typical of long-distance travel in Afghanistan.)

As we traveled deeper into the Salang Pass, the snowfall seemed to get thicker, and the traffic ahead of us started to slow down. We had to travel through several tunnels that had originally been built by the Russians during the 1980s after the invasion. The tunnels were full of trucks, some which had stopped to escape the severe snow conditions.

"It is not wise to stop, Boss," Hasib said.

I nodded my agreement, understanding that we had no choice but to continue forward because we hoped to clear the Salang before darkness set in.

When I looked behind us, I noticed that there was now a long stream of traffic. It was almost like a traffic jam but in the middle of nowhere. As we passed through another tunnel, the traffic had almost come to a grinding halt, and we could see there had been an accident a little farther ahead. A coach bus had somehow traveled off the road in the bad weather and landed on its side in a ditch mixed with frozen mud, ice, and snow. As we drove past, we could see several people were injured and some were dead. Accidents weren't uncommon in the Salang, especially in the wintertime. The accident had halted the traffic not just because of rubbernecking but also because it reminded the drivers of the danger of traveling this treacherous mountain pass in severe weather conditions.

Night began to fall, and it became increasingly difficult to see what was up ahead. Only the lights of the vehicle in front were visible, and the ones that fell behind were a blur. As we continued through the Salang, we passed several road accidents, some of which had clearly ended in tragedy. I was starting to get a little worried for our own safety, and I told Hasib several times to slow down and take extra care. Not that he was driving erratically, but I preferred that we drove as slowly as possible, at least until we had passed through the rough weather.

"Okay, Boss," Hasib said. This was his way of telling me that he was far more capable of ensuring our safe passage through the Salang than I was. Once again he was right, so I just smiled and said nothing further.

We had at least two hours left of passing through the Salang, so I decided to call a colleague whom I would be meeting with once arriving in the camp. This would keep my mind off the treacherous road, and besides, I wanted to give him a heads-up that we were on our way and would be at the camp first thing in the morning. I was about to tell him to keep mum so that I could surprise the commander with the carload of snus when he was the one to surprise me.

"There's no need for this visit, MJ. The decision was made three weeks ago to renew the contract. We appreciate the snus very much, though! You can send it with our next delivery. You ought to turn round and head back to Kabul."

"*What?*" I exploded. I was furious, to say the least. True, they didn't know we were bound for Mez, but support headquarters in Dubai did. Sometimes there were oversights during decision making, but someone in Dubai had clearly forgotten to update our operations on the ground.

Although he did apologize, there was no way we could turn back at that point. We were in the middle of a blizzard, gridlocked in a traffic jam on a mountain pass world-renowned for hazardous driving. It was physically impossible for Hasib to turn our vehicle around.

As I ended the call, I could feel the tears welling inside my eyes. Hasib and the other two men had heard me raise my voice on the phone, and Hasib knew me well enough to know that I was not only angry but also upset. Trying to make light of the situation, I said to Hasib, "Well, do you want the good news or the bad news?"

He knew I was being sarcastic. "Only the good news, Boss! Always."

By this point I began cursing out of sheer frustration, which quickly turned to anger, and with the anger came the tears. I spent the next five minutes shouting and screaming, releasing all my frustration. I hoped this release would allow me to compose myself before we arrived in the camp.

Hasib understood the reason for my anger and outburst, but Basheer and Omar just observed quietly, waiting for the moment when Hasib would be able to explain. At one point a little later on they tried to make me laugh at something they had seen outside. I appreciated their efforts, and I told them so; however, I was having none of it. I was not going to be entertained, amused, or anything else until we arrived safely at our destination.

I continued to stare in silence, watching the black night go past my car window. I let all that had happened constantly replay in my mind. It seemed that the unnecessary challenges were endless. I was able to bear the challenges I'd expected to have to endure, but these unnecessary ones were just impossible to bear. The company knew how much we had to go through in theater, and so their thoughtlessness and lack of regard in these instances seemed to indicate that they simply didn't care. It seemed impossible to draw any other conclusion.

* * *

Our journey through the Salang and into Mez took us almost ten hours. We arrived just short of midnight.

"Mazar-e-Sharif!" we all shouted, and even in my foul mood I couldn't help but give a small chuckle while the three men laughed uproariously. Our catchphrase was uttered as a collective sigh of relief.

That night we managed to stay in Mez's best hotel, a three-star called the Mazar Sharif. Compared to Kabul, Mez was a little less dangerous, so the hotel was our best option for one night. As we had two plainclothes CID, I wasn't worried. The hotel itself reminded me of the 1970s because of its décor. I had one room to myself, and the boys had the two rooms opposite. Although I felt quite safe, I barely slept that night. My mind was still busy going over the day's events and what had transpired.

We woke up quite early the next day so that we could visit the camp first thing. I wanted to return to Kabul earlier than midnight. Both Basheer and Omar, who would have to wait outside the camp, decided to have their breakfast. Hasib and I were escorted by our local Afghan staff into the camp. The news of more snus had soon gotten around the camp, so at least we were able to appease some of our customers. I had my meeting, but not with the camp commander as originally planned. He was busy attending his own security briefing. One of his assistants met with me, and it all went well enough.

We spent about an hour in the camp, and then just as I was about to leave, one of my managers asked me if I could wait a little longer while he prepared a sealed money bag containing quite a large sum that needed to be taken back to Kabul. Hasib was busy assisting with replacing a broken computer monitor and with delivering the snus, but he was within earshot of the conversation. He appeared to be a little anxious and to hover around more than usual. None of this was typical of my driver, but I soon dismissed the thoughts. Hasib was just being Hasib. He was always helpful and could successfully turn his hand at anything, a real jack-of-all-trades.

I told myself that I was just irritable and shouldn't pay too much attention to my mood or thoughts. I was tired, fed up, and cranky. My main objective now was to get back to Kabul as quickly as possible. The last thing on my mind was to add any more time to our journey. Preparing the money would have meant that we wouldn't depart for at least another forty minutes. In the past it had been normal practice for a manager who was visiting a remote location to collect cash, as those sites had no access to a bank. I decided not to follow this practice. If asked, I would say that I had decided not to carry the money because it was a long journey back and I had to travel with three local Afghans. And so it was. We left carrying no more than a few pieces of paperwork and an old monitor that needed to be repaired.

By the time we left the camp both Basheer and Omar were already outside waiting for us. We could now make our journey back to Kabul. All four of us were looking forward to the end of this adventure!

Setting off early would give us a good head start, and hopefully the conditions in the Salang had improved. We had almost a two-hour journey before we even reached the Salang. Between Mez and the Salang, weather conditions were good, meaning that Hasib could do the drive in less time than we had anticipated. In fact, he was wasting very little time, only stopping once at a gas station just outside Poli Khomri (PK for short) to refuel. Originally, we had planned to stop for lunch, but somehow this was forgotten as we carried on through the endless path of narrow winding roads with steep precipices on either side. After I felt a little hungry, I made the suggestion to Hasib that we should stop for him to take a rest and for all of us to have some lunch. We did stop at one stage to buy some nuts and dried fruit in a small village just outside PK, but we managed to soldier on for the rest of the journey. When I made the suggestion again, he replied, "Boss, all our money is finished!" I thought this was a little strange but took his response as an indication that perhaps he was just eager to get back home and could go without lunch.

Once again we entered through the gates of the Salang Pass, wondering if this was to be a repeat of our last experience. Although snow continued to fall, the weather appeared to be not as severe. There seemed to be less traffic, and it was constantly moving. This was encouraging. The chains were at least gripping on the wheels, making it easier for our vehicle to move along the road's icy surface. Those vehicles we had seen overturned alongside the road the day before had since been moved, and their parts were being salvaged by their owners. It was not like back home where a tow truck would be called on. The best they had in this neck of the woods was a small crane and a flatbed if they were lucky or maybe the use of a horse-drawn cart.

We had no sooner gotten through the first tunnel than we faced a convoy of trucks holding up the rest of the traffic. One of them appeared to have broken down and now blocked the entrance to the second tunnel, bringing the entire traffic to a grinding halt.

"We were destined to have another leg of drama in this journey!" I said to the guys.

Basheer said, "Mazar-e-Sharif!"

We all laughed.

In the end it took a crane to remove the container on the back of the truck and several people to push the front of the truck to the side of the road to create room for the traffic to continue. This whole maneuver took about an hour and a half. The time we had gained had soon been lost. By the time we passed through the Salang, it was almost dark, and we still had more than an hour until we would reach the compound.

Hasib was clearly eager to arrive home, traveling at record speed. Several times I asked him to slow down. Usually, he complied, but on a couple of occasions he appeared to ignore me. It was not like him to simply ignore me without so much as an "okay, Boss" or a pithy phrase of wisdom. I wasn't sure if it was the lack of food or if road exhaustion had set in.

After he dropped Omar at his house, Hasib proceeded to drive me back to the compound. Still speeding like a madman, he and Basheer were talking rapidly. I couldn't understand their street dialect but could hear anger in Hasib's voice. On the first leg of the journey his wife had called him several times, and he'd ignored two of her calls. As most wives do, she was just wondering where he was. For some reason he had not told her about our last-minute journey to Mez. Coincidentally, Basheer had not informed his wife either. It wasn't until both wives had called each other at half past eight that night right around the time we were nearing Kabul. They then confronted their husbands via phone, and only then did both men fess up about the journey. It seemed that they were behaving like two schoolboys, and now they were in trouble. Perhaps this was the reason for Hasib's anger. He knew he would have to face the music once he got home to his wife later that evening. I still didn't understand why he hadn't told her to begin with. Having met his wife several times, I knew that if he'd just told her up front, he would have saved himself the present drama. I told myself this was Hasib's personal life and none of my business.

By the time we arrived at the compound, it was just about half past nine—an hour after the wives had called. Hasib wasted no time in driving off after I got out of the vehicle. This was also not like him. I decided that the trip had taken its toll on all of us. It was best to just not think about it further.

* * *

The next day after I told Nicholas all about our wonderful journey, he told me that Hasib's wife had called our IT assistant, looking for her husband, who was not answering any of her calls. She thought perhaps he was having phone problems.

This struck me as even odder than what I'd observed the night before, but I kept my feelings hidden, not even sharing them with Nicholas. For a couple of days I was a little angry with Hasib, although I didn't let my feelings show. His reckless driving had irritated me, especially when he did not slow down as I had requested. I saw another side to his personality that concerned me. He had always been so respectful in the past, following every request I made. He never raised his voice or showed me any form of disrespect. He always treated me with utmost courtesy, even kindness. I felt I had seen this change somehow, even if it would have been imperceptible to anyone else.

Three days later I went on a week's sabbatical, spending three days in Paris and four days in Madrid. New projects were about to commence, so this was my last chance to take a brief rest. After I arrived in Paris, I was still in work mode, as I had been exceedingly busy. But I was now looking forward to unwinding. I had chosen one of the most romantic times of the year to travel to Paris, four weeks before Christmas, but as I was traveling solo, my experience was more likely to be without romance. The rest itself would be welcome enough.

The past year had been another huge rollercoaster of events, so my mind and body kept reliving it all. Sleepless nights were my biggest challenge, even thousands of miles away in a Parisian hotel. I found it exceedingly difficult to breathe at times, and I would often sleep with several pillows to raise my head. I wore heat plasters all over my back, as this relieved the numerous knots in my muscles, helping me to relax my body and my mind.

It was difficult to switch off just like a tap, but I tried.

One particularly restless night I couldn't sleep at all. My mind kept focusing on work. It was almost three o'clock in the morning, and I had left the television on to help me relax. I could feel myself drifting in and out of sleep, and then all of a sudden, I woke up in a panic, drenched in sweat. My mind had slowly started to process some of the events over the past few weeks, and now in the quiet of Paris, it began to reflect, perhaps subconsciously. My panic stemmed from the sudden awareness of what may have been the whole reason behind Hasib's behavior in Mazar-e-Sharif. It was a theory that literally just dawned on me, but there were about eighty thousand reasons why it made sense. Amid all the prevailing drama, I had failed to see beneath the surface and beyond the sequence of events.

What I had realized was that one of the reasons for Hasib's sudden change in behavior could have been the result of his clever plan being foiled. Had he expected me to travel back to Kabul with about US$80,000, giving him motive and opportunity? The more I thought about this theory, the more it made sense. He had come to understand our operations quite well during the time he had been spent in our business. (It was about two and a half years that he'd been my driver plus whatever time he'd spent before that. I wasn't really sure how long.) The US$80,000 was a small fortune to an Afghan, enough to change several families' lives forever.

Strangely enough I received a phone call the following day from Hasib. "Is everything okay, Boss? Are you enjoying your vacation in Paris?"

I assured him I was all right and thanked him for calling. We soon hung up. At first I hesitated in answering his call, but I knew that unless I acted like nothing was wrong, he would become suspicious. And if I was right, alerting him to my suspicions would be a mistake.

I later called Nicholas, and we discussed my theory at great length. He was inclined to agree with me that it was highly possible. The biggest giveaway was the elusiveness with his wife combined with his eagerness to hover around to observe my conversation with my manager. His erratic behavior on the way home just seemed to clinch it. It was a theory that I desperately wanted to be wrong. But it seemed impossible that it was mere coincidence. For two and a half years Hasib had been like a brother to me. Aside from Nicholas and Tucker, I had believed he was the one person I could trust completely. Whether this idea had been carefully premeditated and it was just a question of when he chose to carry it out or a random decision based on sudden opportunity, I would never know for sure. But I did know that Hasib had an uncanny ability to think quickly and to take advantage of opportunities that came his way. All this was true, so it was hard for me to believe that my theory was wrong, much as it pained me. It was my long-held belief that nothing happens without a reason, and my time in theater had proved this true time and time again. I walked a fine and dangerous line, but I'd had no choice about that from the moment I'd set foot in Afghanistan. This was just another situation. It was no worse than any of the others. I just felt worse about it because I had grown to trust Hasib and now I felt personally betrayed. But Afghanistan had taught me that betrayal is in the eyes of the betrayed. The best I could do was focus on what I had learned from dad's advice about letting go. I let myself be still so that peace could fill me, and then centering it in the core of my being, I just let everything else go, let it all disappear into the vast space of life that was beyond my control.

Panjshir and the Mujahedeen

My brief rest in Paris and Madrid came to an end far too quickly, and before I knew it, I was back in Kabul. I forced myself not to think about Hasib, difficult as it was. Eventually, I came to see that worst part of feeling betrayed is that it destroys the warm, pure feelings we have for another person. When we lose someone we love to death, painful as it is, our memories remain, and they help us carry on. Death doesn't change the way we feel about a person; betrayal does. It changes it irrevocably, and there is no going back to the way things were before. We will never feel the same way about that person. When we still have to interact with him or her in the same context as before, this is incredibly hard.

I kept my new true feelings about Hasib in the back of my mind. I had to interact with him throughout each day. I would never feel completely the same way about him, but I couldn't let him know that. And I also realized that no matter how much we trust another person, even if that trust is deserved, we can never completely know another person as well as we know ourselves. (Of course, parents are often able to know their children better than those children know themselves, but that's another story!)

I made the best of it, understanding that in terms of Hasib's beliefs (both Muslim and Communist), he would not see that he had breached my trust. In a way, that helped me move on. Sometimes the only thing we can use to gauge a person's sincerity is his or her intention for good or ill. Hasib had not intended to harm me, only to collect an amount of money that would be a lifetime's fortune for his family. I didn't condone it, of course, but given the prevailing circumstances of life, I could understand and forgive. Perhaps doing so is the only way to heal this world.

Life in theater went on in its usual fashion regardless of mental anguish, moral dilemmas, or anything else. Perhaps because he felt guilty about Mazar-e-Sharif or perhaps because he still just wanted to help me as much as he always had, Hasib accompanied me on my next exciting adventure in Afghanistan.

First here are a few brief tidbits about Afghan geology. Not only does Afghanistan have an endless sea of mountains (as we've seen in previous geography lessons), but it also has a rich abundance of minerals beneath those mountains. Stones of all kinds, including such gems as emeralds, rubies, and spinel were easily found in the Afghan bazaars. The colors were fabulous, even in the raw, uncut stones, and held up to the light, they were breathtakingly dazzling. It often took an expert to know whether the stone was the real McCoy, as well as whether the seller was asking a fair price.

Now here's a brief description of my first experience with Afghan jewels. I decided to purchase three large emeralds from an Afghan jeweler who had sworn on his life that I was getting a good bargain. Several days later I discovered that the US$1,000 I had spent was actually quite a lot of money for 3 carats of Gilson (synthetic emeralds probably worth no more than US$50). I had actually purchased the emeralds based on the recommendation of a colleague who regularly purchased diamonds from the same jeweler. On this particular day he had organized a jewelry show in his office. There were several of us who had been convinced to purchase emeralds. Some who were more adventurous decided to purchase diamonds.

About a week later I was in Dubai, and I decided to take the stones into a jewelry shop in the Gold Souk, where two different jewelers informed me that the stones were synthetic and worth little more than fifty US dollars. Once I made this unfortunate discovery in Dubai about a week later, I wasted no time in informing the jeweler, hoping to get my money back. Since it was a work colleague who had initiated the jewelry show, I also hoped that he would assist me in getting my money back if necessary. When I told him about the emeralds, his immediate response was really quite amusing. He told me that he was sure I would get my money back, as everyone else he knew got their money back. I quietly laughed to myself because it was as if he already knew the stones were possibly synthetic, and having knowledge of this, how could he allow his work colleagues to fall victim to the Afghan's scam? Refusing to let my reaction turn to anger or upset—I'd lost far more than this as a result of my stint in Afghanistan—I kept coaching myself to see the humor and irony in it all.

Upon first making contact with the Afghan jeweler, he appeared to be somewhat busy, as if trying to find excuses for why he could not meet up with me. He made himself look guilty before I even opened the discussion. He was clearly avoiding the obvious. After I made several phone calls, I decided to give him an ultimatum, hoping to sort out this business once and for all. I enlisted Kareem's assistance in this endeavor. (This was long before his odd behavior in Police District 9 during my admin employees' detainment because of the visa issue.)

Reading from the Dari script that Kareem gave me, I told the jeweler, "I just spent a few days in Dubai, and I visited the Gold Souk to get a valuation on my emeralds. I spoke to two different jewelers, both of whom assured me that the stones weren't genuine emeralds. I had purchased Gilson." Of course, there was an instant dead silence on the other end of the phone. Perhaps he had not expected me to make this discovery so quickly, if at all. (As it turned out, a friend who had spent US$900 on emeralds purchased from the same jeweler had also bought Gilson and then had spent an additional US$300 to have it made into a pendant to wear on a necklace.)

From the opposite side of my desk, Kareem gave me a thumbs-up, and I continued to follow his script. Clearly, I was on a roll! I mentioned my friend's story to the jeweler as well and then reminded him that I was well aware that he had a reputable shop in HQ ISAF and that his policy was 100 percent of monies refunded if the stones weren't genuine.

"I often have dealings with several senior members of the military in HQ ISAF, and it would be in your best interest to honor your refund policy," I finished.

There was an initial pause on the other end of the line, which lasted for about twenty seconds. I switched the phone to speaker so that Kareem could hear the jeweler's response. Perhaps after realizing he was about to find himself in a no-win situation, the jeweler quickly began to explain how he had purchased the stones from a different supplier and that he, too, would demand a full refund, which of course he would remit to me and my friend. Kareem scribbled the jeweler's response, so I could know what was going on while the man was still talking. I supposed this was his saving face explanation. He then indicated that he would replace the stones I had purchased with other emeralds, ones he would guarantee as authentic. I politely declined this offer, following Kareem's notes once again, and firmly stated, "Thank you, but a full refund is all that I will require." There was no way I would trust this guy to give me the real thing the next time around, but I needed to remain cordial because I wanted him on my side—at least until I had my full refund.

My powers of careful persuasion had worked, and two days later both my friend and I got our full refunds. Initially, we had been duped by a scam, but we'd managed to beat the crafty Afghan at his own game! We were possibly the few among many who had been duped who were successful in recovering all the money paid. Most had probably made the discovery when it was too late.

Based on this experience, purchasing precious gems in Afghanistan remained out of the question. Many months later, shortly after I returned from the Paris/Madrid trip, I had the opportunity to visit Panjshir, and there, I regained an interest in precious stones, particularly emeralds. This is where Hasib comes back into the story, seeking to offer his assistance. He knew I had been fascinated to learn about one of Afghanistan's most famous heroes, Massoud, who was the former leader of the mujahedeen and who was originally from Panjshir (their home base).

Panjshir was about a three-and-a-half-hour drive from Kabul. It was situated in a valley and surrounded by mountains. Panjshir was quite simply one of the most beautiful places to visit outside Kabul, with its rivers of fresh running water and its tiny orchards and farms where children herded goats along the riverbanks.

In any case, one day Hasib greeted me with a grin when I got into the vehicle. "Great news, Boss!" he exulted, informing me that I had received an invitation from Basheer's superior in the CID. This man was a former general in the mujahedeen, and he had invited me to visit Panjshir, his birthplace and former home.

In spite of all that had transpired, I was touched by the gesture, perhaps more so than I would have been if everything had remained status quo. I readily accepted the invitation, of course, much to the delight of Hasib and by extension Basheer.

The plan was to travel to Panjshir first thing in the morning, leaving at around half past seven. Allowing for traffic, Hasib, Basheer, the general, and I would arrive just before midday and in time for lunch. The general wanted me to join him for lunch at a restaurant situated along the river. We had picked the perfect day to travel to Panjshir. It was about 75 degrees Fahrenheit, with clear blue skies and a gentle breeze blowing.

We ended up arriving just after midday, and we went straight to pay our respects to Massoud's place of rest. It was an incredibly fascinating place to visit. As we drove up to the building, there were remnants of several old Russian tanks that had been lined up and left to rot over the many years since the Russian invasion. This was a part of Afghan history, and it served as a reminder of those who had once invaded and desecrated their land.

The memorial building itself was relatively new, and inside was Massoud's tomb, shrouded in cloth and with a book placed beside it. The book was open to a page containing some of his famous words of wisdom and his photo. Before entering, it was customary to remove one's shoes, and there was a large prayer mat opposite the tomb for those wanting to say a prayer as a form of respect. I stood back and watched as Hasib, Basheer, and the general said their prayers in honor of their late hero. Their reverence was very moving.

The general had bravely fought against the Taliban and the Russians, and he spoke of how difficult it still was for him to deal with the loss of his former leader even after so many years. And so he often came to Massoud's place of rest to pay his respects. (He had been close by when an al-Qaeda-led assassination had ended his leader's life, and he still held on to all those memories.)

Outside Massoud's memorial the Afghans were busy constructing a modern shopping complex made out of stone as if they were anticipating tourism trade in the future. I found this very interesting, as many things would have to change in order for this to happen. Nevertheless, it was inspiring to see that someone had cultivated some faith in the country's future. I had hoped to see a couple of open shops selling emeralds; however, we had been told that the stones were only brought into the village once a month, as they were mined in a remote location more than two hours away. I expressed my disappointment, saying I'd hoped to purchase an emerald as a gift for my mother.

After we visited the memorial, we made our way to the restaurant, which resembled a farmhouse situated along the riverbank. Hasib had asked me to stay inside the vehicle until they had checked to see who was dining inside the restaurant. There were several ANA vehicles parked in the car park, along with two unmarked four-wheel-drive vehicles.

We had to wait for them to leave, and so I sat inside a small room near the entrance of the restaurant, waiting for them to leave. Basheer and Hasib sat outside, guarding both windows to ensure no one knew I was inside. The general, who happened to know one of the ANA commanders, spoke with him. (He knew the commander because some of the ANA in Panjshir had been part of the mujahedeen when they were in operation years ago. It was a small world after all, especially in Afghanistan.)

Waiting for them to leave in their vehicles, we then made our way to a small secluded dining area alongside the river. The area itself was camouflaged by large fruit trees, including a huge mulberry bush, the fruit of which we later sampled. We sat down beside the railings separating us from the banks of the river, sitting cross-legged on the traditional long Afghan cushions. A large plastic tablecloth was placed in front of us, and upon it our modest feast was served. It was absolutely beautiful and tranquil. Only the sounds of the fresh running water and birdsong in the background could be heard. At long last we had found peace in this troubled and tortured land. I was determined to savor every precious minute, and to ensure I would not be disturbed, I switched my phone off. Freedom from all my burdens at last!

It was a delicacy to eat the small fish that had been caught fresh nearby. Lightly fried, they were to be eaten whole except for the tail. I tried a couple of these, and they were quite tasty, although I couldn't bring myself to swallow the eyes. The traditional soup and Afghan bread came next, followed by kebabs with raw vegetables and Palau rice. We washed it all down with chai. The general could see how much I loved being in this environment, and although he spoke no English, through Hasib he made the offer to build me a small house on some land he owned not far away alongside the river, telling me that I could stay there as long as I wanted. I knew that the general already had two wives, and if I may be so bold as to say so, I think was planning on a third—me! Although the offer was quite flattering, I remained as decorous as possible, politely thanking him and telling Hasib to tell him that perhaps one day when the security situation had improved, I would look to spend some time in Panjshir. The general beamed, inviting us to visit the home of his family the next time and to stay as his guests for dinner.

We took our time eating lunch that day, savoring every moment. I thought about how beautiful it would be to actually spend some time living along the riverbanks in Panjshir. After we ate lunch, Hasib, Basheer, and the general took a moment to say a prayer, using a small mat provided for guests after their meal. I used this opportunity to walk down to the water's edge, where I washed my hands in the cold running water. To the side of the bank, I noticed a large metal object shaped like a torpedo. By this time, the men had joined me. Brushing off the grass and brush that had grown over it, we could see Russian letters on one side. It was an old Russian warhead that had dislodged itself along the banks of the river.

On our way back the general decided to take us back to Kabul via a different route. I had fallen asleep in the back of the vehicle, waking up when the tires started bumping over the rocky terrain of a small remote village. Realizing that we had taken a detour and had wound up off the beaten path, I asked Hasib what was happening. When I looked over toward Basheer, who also heard me, he just shrugged his shoulders, opened his eyes wide, and cast his gaze in the direction of the general. It was as if the general had decided to take us on a wild goose chase or perhaps along one of the old mujahedeen horse trails, a trip down memory lane.

* * *

Shortly afterward the general, who remembered that I was interested in purchasing an emerald as a gift for my mother, arranged for me to meet a renowned Afghan jeweler from Panjshir. He had business interests in Kabul, and we were invited to meet him in a guesthouse not far from the Massoud Foundation's official building. Hasib and I arranged to first meet the general and Basheer outside their workplace so that they could then take us to meet the jeweler.

As we entered inside the guesthouse, we were met by an entourage of young Afghans who were extremely hospitable, and after the usual exchange of pleasantries they offered us a seat in their lounge area, which was a huge room decorated with handcrafted Afghan rugs and cushions placed around the walls. As I sat down, I noticed a large framed photo on the wall in front of me. It was the late Massoud together with one of his former leading commanders. It seemed I had entered the safe house of a former mujahedeen! As I was soon to learn, this was not far from the truth.

An elderly man (probably in his seventies) entered the room. He had a long gray beard streaked with white, and he wore the traditional *salwar kameez* attire. As he entered, we all stood up as a sign of acknowledgment, and then one by one, Hasib, Basheer, and the general spoke to him, placing their hands across their hearts as a sign of respect. I followed suit, bowing in acknowledgment and using the same hand gesture. Taking the lead, the man sat down, and one by one, we each sat down cross-legged on the cushions. A young boy came into the room, bearing a large serving tray with tea and dishes of dried fruit and almonds. He appeared to be the elderly man's servant, and he bowed his head as he served us tea. This was followed by a serving of a traditional Afghan dish of yogurt made with goat's milk. (I politely declined, as this wasn't something my stomach was accustomed to eating, and past culinary adventures had resulted in my spending several hours on and over the toilet later on. Dairy was often kept without refrigeration in Afghanistan, so it took a cast-iron Western stomach or a native Afghan one not to react.)

We sat patiently as the elderly man looked over and asked the general if I preferred something else to eat. As he spoke, he looked at me, squinting one of his eyes and speaking quite slowly and softly. He was asking the general who I was and what I was doing in Afghanistan. He appeared to be genuinely interested in why a white female would choose to work and live in a country such as this. The general explained my role to the man, further detailing that I had developed a love for Panjshir. Without giving anything away about his past, the man was surprised that I had visited his home of Panjshir, and he wanted to know why I had chosen to visit there in the first place.

Hasib translated the conversation between the man and the general. I told Hasib to ask the general to explain that I found Massoud rather fascinating, and being interested in history, I had wanted to visit his place of birth and his place of rest. I asked them to explain how beautiful and peaceful I found Panjshir and that

I could well understand why Massoud had fought to defend such a tranquil place.

After he listened to the general's translation of my response (through Hasib), the man smiled, and then he commenced talking to the general about other things—perhaps about the times they had shared together years before—together and with Massoud.

I soon learned through Hasib that two jewelers would be coming with some stones from Panjshir. At first I thought that perhaps the old man himself was the jeweler, but then after I looked again at the photo on the wall in front of me, I soon realized that this was the same man, except he was probably close to twenty years older.

Now I felt a little embarrassed that I had mentioned Massoud, as perhaps the man thought I'd only done so out of association. In order to make my intentions clearer, I turned to Hasib, and as I pointed at the photo, I asked him if this was the same man. Of course, I had been right, and then turning to the elderly man, I remarked that he must have led an amazing life and it must have been wonderful to have known a great man like Massoud. (Hasib and the general provided the necessary translations once again.) I was lucky. The man was still smiling, and he seemed to appreciate my comments and not take offense. One had to be careful. They would always be mujahedeen.

We were soon joined by two men who entered the room accompanied by four others, and I guessed that they must be the jewelers and that they had come with their own security. They resembled any other Afghans in appearance, wearing traditional *salwar kameez*, and both appeared to be in their midforties. Being both educated and businessmen, they immediately spoke to me in English, introducing themselves.

I was relieved to learn that I would be able to communicate with them directly, considering I was now potentially shopping for an item of value. From my previous experience, I wanted to make sure I knew exactly what I was buying. After they introduced themselves, they sat down for several minutes, talking to the elderly man and drinking their tea. This was customary before any business was to take place. I started to wonder what kind of stones they had brought with them since both of them had walked in empty-handed. Perhaps they had to wait for the goods to arrive. Or perhaps their security had them concealed. Not long after, another gentleman, much younger than the first two, appeared; however, he spoke no English. He walked into the room, carrying a small spotlight (like the ones people often use as reading lights on their bedside tables) and a set of large electronic scales. This was beginning to look quite impressive and definitely like the real deal.

Once placing the light and scales in front of me, one of the jewelers began to take out a series of paper envelopes he had concealed under his clothes in a money belt. He then began to open each envelope one by one. Gently shaking the stones onto the carpet in front of us, he moved slightly so that we could see a cluster of emeralds, some raw and uncut, and some cut in all shapes and sizes. It was unbelievable to see. There were at least a hundred stones inside each envelope. He began to explain the difference of each of the emeralds in terms of color and quality. They all looked beautiful to me, but there was a difference in price, which related to the grade of the emeralds and their cut. I began to examine each of the different grades of emeralds, as if I had quickly become an expert. They still all looked gorgeous and perfect to my untrained eye.

Then he presented the *pièce de résistance*—a 76-carat emerald that was almost the size of a playing die but not a perfect cube. It was impressive to say the least. They then explained that if I was interested in larger emeralds, they could show me a 164-carat emerald. I asked them approximately how big that would be in size. Something similar to the size of a golf ball, they said. A little bigger than I had intended to purchase as a pendant for my mother!

After they showed me their collection of emeralds, they had some rather large chunks of raw pink spinel. In total, 317 carats to be precise! (Spinel was a rarer stone, very beautiful and coming in a wide range of colors, with pink and red being the most sought-after. It's quite beloved in Australia because of its association with Queen Elizabeth's crown.) I only wanted to make a modest purchase, a 2-carat emerald if the right deal was struck, and I now wondered if perhaps the general had given them the wrong impression and they had presumed I was some big emerald dealer! They must have presumed that I wanted to purchase a decent amount since the collection they had presented to me was valued at approximately US$2 million at cost.

This would definitely be a shopping trip to remember! I had to appear very interested, and the jeweler told me that we could meet next time to discuss the emeralds in more detail. He had given me a rough idea of what I would pay by buying them in bulk. I told him I would be in touch. The elderly man appeared to be happy and said that this would also be good business for him. It was obvious that any sale generated would give him a cut.

Before we left, I asked the elderly gentleman if he would mind taking a photo with me. It was quite a funny situation, as he was initially caught a little off guard when I went to stand beside him. He then said something to his onlookers, who were now laughing, and stood a little to one side as Hasib took a photo. We also laughed as Hasib and Basheer had their eyes opened wide, taking the photo in disbelief. What I later learned from Hasib was that this was only the fourth time the elderly man had his photo taken in his entire life.

Once we had said good-bye and entered our vehicle, Hasib said to me, "Boss, that's Gada Mohammad, the big general of the mujahedeen!"

I laughed, and trying to downplay the whole situation, I said that it didn't matter. I thought that he was a nice old man who had a good sense of humor.

I had added a new dimension to my shopping experiences, and I knew that this particular experience would be hard to surpass. After all, it wasn't every day that a girl went on a shopping trip organized by the mujahedeen, much less an ex-warlord! I did eventually purchase a magnificent 2-carat emerald for my mother through these same jewelers. How would I ever explain to her exactly how unique the circumstances of its sourcing were?

This was a story I would have to someday confess, for it was one filled with such irony, history, beauty, and splendor that I wouldn't be able to resist. In much the same way that I couldn't resist Afghanistan and its eternal juxtaposition of beauty and harshness, terror and kindness, truth and deceit. A web as intricately wrought and ultimately fragile as humanity itself. Elaborate, magnificent, and utterly impossible to replicate.

EPILOGUE

Many issues that arose in theater had no real resolution. The export ordeal stopped—as did the unknown-caller harassment—but the sense that there was someone else out there responsible, someone with more power than Kurtis and his boss, Adam (whether just 110 or a civilian or military Westerner), never left me. Similarly, I was never able to let go of my feelings of betrayal following Hasib's behavior in Mazar-e-Sharif. He never confessed, and I never confronted him, but the betrayal I felt left a hole between us where once there had been a strong bond. I hated feeling that way. (This was true to a lesser extent regarding my relationship with Kareem, though this was far easier to bear than it was with Hasib.) Worst of all, of course, was the heinous violation of Aneni and all of us by extension. It wasn't any of these things separately but all of them together that eventually eroded my desire to remain as GM.

Quite simply, the longer I remained in Afghanistan, the more tormented I became by the questions that had no answers. I accepted that the most difficult questions rarely, if ever, have answers. We just have to learn to live with what we cannot change or understand. But I also recognized that I didn't want to remain in an environment where I would always be embroiled in drama and intrigue, with corruption and wrongdoing hidden beneath a fragile façade. The countless lame excuses I encountered and the endless reluctance to step up to responsibility and to be accountable made me sick.

At last I decided that it was time for me to end my relationship with TerraTota. Once I could no longer throw myself into my work body and soul, I knew the time had come for me to move on.

End of the Old Road, Start of a New Path

Three years in Afghanistan had made me a veteran in terms of experience. By the time I left TerraTota, I was spending all my energy and effort fighting their way of doing things, a way that I abhorred. Perhaps it had always been this way, and I'd just had tunnel vision, focusing on my team, my work, and my projects and shutting the rest of it out. But once I knew the way it really was and that it would never change, I couldn't continue being a part of it, especially not as a manager. Everything was placed under scrutiny, and nothing was sacred. We had no freedom and no privacy. I would often dispose of any personal documents/information by tearing the paper into tiny pieces and either flushing them down the toilet or incinerating them. Aneni's abuse was far worse than anything the rest of us had to endure, but none of us received treatment that would make us feel valued or appreciated as human beings. Sadly, such an attitude is what enables people to commit atrocities and/or look the other way when others do so. The gray areas of wrongdoing are mere steps apart, and on that treacherous slippery slope, it is all too easy to step from a pardonable error to an unconscionable act. For me, looking the other way was even worse than actually slipping. The least we can ever do is stand up and speak out. Ironically, this is also the most we can do sometimes.

I was not going to sink to the depths of manipulation and corruption, for the next step down the well was unthinkable—unspeakable—and I couldn't guarantee that I might not fall, no matter how much I swore to myself that I wouldn't and no matter how hard I tried not to. I had seen too many people weaken, giving in because they'd lost the will to fight a losing battle. I would never give in. I would be the ruler of my own conscience and beliefs until I drew my last breath, and I would never play the game just for the sake of pleasing others. Money and power are of worth far less than freedom and integrity, and those who fail to see this are missing out on the greatest gifts of being human—other than love, which cannot really exist without freedom and integrity.

* * *

The only hard part was saying good-bye to my team and the friends I had made, even though we all promised to keep in touch. In a place like Afghanistan true friends are worth their weight in gold, as loyalty and trust are the greatest commodities. (Another point I cannot overemphasize!) I now understood how my dad felt about his army mates. Going through hell together forged a bond that nothing could break.

I needed some time and space to process all that had happened, and I wanted to return to Australia in a better, calmer state of mind than I'd displayed during my last visit home. So I returned to Madrid, where I hoped to find the inner peace I sought. (It was there that I actually started writing this book, as the sequence of events had long desired to unleash itself on paper, prodding me quite persistently!) It took almost four weeks to eliminate the past conflict from my mind. But I came to see the struggle as a kind of labor that eventually led to the birth of a new path.

I thought long and hard about the entirety of my experience in theater, with the clarity and perspective that only hindsight can grant us. As I described, on first arriving in Afghanistan, everything is so surreal that it takes every ounce of our energy to just take it all in and try to survive. It takes a while for reality to set in, thereby forcing acknowledgment of the severity of the situation. We know it's a war zone, of course. But it takes some time to actually realize that every expat's existence and prosperity in this war-torn land is the by-product of that entire nation's misfortune. An entire nation that never understands the true meaning of peace never feels it in their mind or spirit. Every day they wake up and go outside about their business, never knowing what will happen or when they will take their last breath. I have heard Afghans express this. They never take life for granted, and because their prayers alone sustain them through this harsh existence, they truly believe that one day they will have a more blessed and brighter future filled with peace and prosperity in the paradise beyond this world.

Who can blame them? Such a belief system offers a special kind of peace, happiness, and hope within. And yet even with all the hope of happiness and peace, this land cannot find its way through the vast, dense clouds of corruption engulfing it. Having as equal a bearing on life as religion does, corruption finds its way into every corner of existence, making the progress of positive change almost impossible to achieve. This corruption is as insidious as it is evil. It is pervasive, all-encompassing, and inexorable. Most mouths are fed from the bowels of corruption, and this seems to multiply exponentially with every day that goes by. The corrupt tangle of export was in fact deliberately and purposely lodged in these same bowels of corruption. All because of boundless greed and lust for power. The greedy few launched this potentially fatal mistake, born of an egregious conflict of interest and destroyed only because the truth came to light and could no longer be denied.

I ask for no applause or even acknowledgment. I did the right thing *because* it was the right thing. That is all there is to it. I only hope that by sharing my story, I will inspire others to do the same. Never sit silent and never look the other way. We each bear equal responsibility for ensuring that truth, justice, honor, and integrity always prevail. It takes resilience to fight the good fight and to speak up for humanity.

May all of us always have the keen intuition, pure intentions, and fine-tuned moral compass required to fight that good fight… and to survive. And may we also always have the loyal friends we need to support and inspire us. It is my sincere wish that this book illuminates the way forward for all who read it.

Glossary

afghani: Currency unit of Afghanistan (approximately 50 afghanis equals US$1.00). [These currency unit values fluctuate constantly. Please check for current exchange rates.]

al-Qaeda: Terrorist organization responsible for the September 11 attacks in the United States, originating in Afghanistan and now operating throughout the Middle East and worldwide.

ANA (Afghan National Army): Main branch of the national military in Afghanistan operating under the Ministry of Defense (MoD) and trained by NATO.

Anno Hegirae (AH): The year according to the Muslim calendar, dating from AD 622, the year of the hegira, Muhammad's flight from Mecca to Medina.

bakshish (a.k.a. baksheesh): Money in exchange for information; any form of bribery or money exchanged in a corrupt or illegal fashion.

bazaar: An open-air market; found throughout the Middle East, Central Asia, and North Africa, typically selling a wide array of items (clothing, carpets, baskets, foodstuffs, spices, etc.); also a main spot for communication and socialization among the local Afghan peoples.

BCPB (Base Camp Planning Board): Group responsible for land approval and building on a military compound.

burqa (or burka): Garment worn by Muslim women, traditionally covering the face and body.

burra bukhi: Expression loosely translated as "you're free to go on your way."

callas: Destroyed; blown up.

CID (Criminal Investigation Division): Special branch of Afghan law enforcement.

Dari: One of the two official languages of Afghanistan (the other is Pashto). Dari is the Afghan Farsi, the Persian language spoken in Iran; Dari generally serves as the common language of Afghanistan, particularly in commercial use (most Afghans are bilingual/multilingual).

dirham: Currency unit of much of the Arab world, including Dubai (approximately 3.67 dirhams equals US$1.00). [These currency unit values fluctuate constantly. Please check for current exchange rates.]

Eid al-Fitr (often referred to simply as Eid): The "Feast of Breaking the Fast"; Muslim celebration of three days of feasting following the end of Ramadan. Traditionally, Eid represents a time for Muslims to embrace the goal of common unity, which often manifests in an escalation of suicide bombings (as described in the book).

Gurkha: Fierce Nepalese mercenaries used by both the British and Indian armies.

HQ: Abbreviation for headquarters, usually used in military or government context.

IED (improvised explosive device): Explosives most commonly used by insurgents.

Inshallah: Expression meaning "God willing" or "with God's help."

in theater: Working in a conflict zone and/or its immediate environs.

ISAF (International Security Assistance Force): Multinational military forces in Afghanistan, led by NATO.

JDOC (Joint Defense Operations Center): Point of control for defense and safety in theater.

Kabul: Province in the eastern part of Afghanistan (a total of thirty-four provinces comprise the country) that includes Kabul City, the nation's capital, referred to simply as Kabul in the West.

KAF (Kandahar Air Field): NATO airbase in Kandahar.

KAIA (Kabul Afghanistan International Airport).

Kandahar: Province in the southern part of Afghanistan, near Pakistan (a total of thirty-four provinces comprise the country); includes the city of Kandahar, which was the capital of the Islamic Emirate of Afghanistan during Taliban rule. (See Taliban.)

Karachi: City in Pakistan.

Mazar-e-Sharif: City in northern Afghanistan; referred to as "Mez" among Afghans and expats in theater.

MoI (Ministry of Interior): Afghan government organization responsible for law enforcement in Afghanistan, including the police force.

MP (military police).

mujahedeen: Islamic guerrilla fighters, literally "holy warriors" (i.e., warriors for the Muslim faith).

MWAC (Morale and Welfare Assistance Committee): A group of military representatives from each of the NATO countries; the MWAC was responsible for approving any new projects on Kandahar Air Field (KAF).

NATO (North Atlantic Treaty Organization): Long-standing alliance of Western nations.

on-selling: In supply-chain industry jargon, the practice of purchasing goods in bulk quantities and at a specially discounted rate, with the express purpose of "selling it on" to another person (or persons) at a profit.

Panjshir: Home base of the mujahedeen during their fight for power (idyllic valley area described in chapter 8).

Pashto: One of the two official languages of Afghanistan (the other is Dari). Pashto is the native tongue of the Pashtuns, the dominant ethnic group in Afghanistan.

Poli Khomri (PK): City in Afghanistan, between Mazar-e-Sharif and Kabul.

PPR (prior permission request): Military jargon for permission requested beforehand.

PX (post exchange): Retail store on a military base.

Ramadan: Muslim holiday involving fasting from dawn until dusk for thirty days.

Salang Pass: Infamous and treacherous mountain pass en route to Mazar-e-Sharif (in the north) from Kabul; this pass is the site of many avalanches, which prompted the Russians to initiate safety procedures there during the occupation of Afghanistan in the 1980s.

salwar kameez: Traditional Afghan attire for men.

soft skin: Slang expression meaning "unarmored vehicles."

souk: Market or exchange (as in the Gold Souk in Dubai).

Taliban: An Islamic fundamentalist political movement in Afghanistan based on strict interpretation of Sharia law, which it enforced while it ruled Afghanistan (Islamic Emirate of Afghanistan, September 1996 to December 2001).

Tarin Kowt (TK): Area of Afghanistan controlled by Dutch and Australian forces within the ISAF.

TCN: Third country national working in theater (refers to Filipinos, Nepalese, Indians, Zimbabweans, etc.).

About the Author

MJ Greene, a native Australian, was born and educated in one of the most isolated cities in the world. However, she was part of the world's minority in that she had lived a sheltered life with a privileged upbringing, something she knew was not to be taken for granted and that would someday be put to better use.

At the age of thirty-seven, MJ had finally come to a crossroad in both her career and her life, and she decided that it was time to seek out a life-changing experience—one that would enable her to fulfill her soul's true mission. She never dreamed she would find such an inner core of strength and resilience, but in Afghanistan that is exactly what she did find; without it, she would not have survived.

Drawing upon her inner resilience and courage, she bravely exposed the corruption and human rights violations that she encountered in her organization. She wrote this book in order to share her experiences and empower other women to muster the courage to reveal the truth whenever it is hidden and to stand up for what is right regardless of the potential personal costs.

CPSIA information can be obtained
at www.ICGtesting.com
Printed in the USA
LVOW08s1151090117
520294LV00001B/100/P

9 781491 709290